Writing Blurbs That Sizzle--And Sell!

3D Fiction Fundamentals Collection, Volume 7

by Karen S. Wiesner

Writers Exchange E-Publishing
http://www.writers-exchange.com

3D Fiction Fundamentals Collection, Volume 7: *Writing Blurbs That Sizzle--And Sell!*
Copyright 2025 Karen S. Wiesner
Writers Exchange E-Publishing
PO Box 372
ATHERTON QLD 4883

First Edition

Cover Art by: GermanCreative

Published by Writers Exchange E-Publishing
http://www.writers-exchange.com

TABLE OF CONTENTS

Author's Note

I'm excited to offer *Writing Blurbs That Sizzle--And Sell!* in this craft writing collection. The one thing all seven volumes have in common is that they're about teaching cohesive three-dimensional writing, whether it's in the pages of a single story, all the series installments, or even just in a book blurb. Here, each one of my writing reference manuals builds on the one that came before, overlapping sometimes because solid three-dimensional writing needs a strong foundation every single time, always offering a new focus of development.

Believe me, writing craft manuals isn't something anyone does for money (though that's nice). It's all about paying it forward, wanting to help other writers navigate their way forward on what can sometimes be a dark and murky path. One reviewer described my craft titles like this: "Karen speaks to you directly, frankly, cheerfully, and writes in a wonderfully entertaining style. She shares all her secrets and lets you look over her shoulder as she does. She never sounds patronizing. Instead, she points out that there is no wrong way to write a book, but that some ways are too ineffective for a writer who wants to write salable books on a regular basis. She doesn't bore you with theories. Karen is like a dance instructor who knows how to make people tango with grace even when they have two left feet." Encouraging you as a writer is what I hope you gain from using my methods.

Happy and productive writing!

Karen S. Wiesner

Collection

by award-winning author Karen S. Wiesner
covers the A to Z's of crafting the highest quality fiction including
how to:

- Brainstorm and work productively to ensure that each stage in the writing process from prewriting to polishing produces masterful results the first time around.
- Create an outline so complete it actually qualifies as the first draft of your book, allowing your first written draft to be final-draft quality.
- Develop realistically three-dimensional and cohesive characters, plots, settings, relationships, and scenes so life-like and memorable your readers will be diehard fans.
- Effectively prepare for a series in advance to prevent painted-in-a-corner scenarios in order to keep fans coming back eagerly for each and every installment.
- Learn innovative techniques to write a complex sequence of stories that require overarching series arcs and immense world- and character-building.
- Craft sizzling back cover, series, and high-concept blurbs for describing, promoting, and selling your books.
- Maximize your potential and momentum for becoming a career author indefinitely.

With step-by-step guidelines, instructions, and tips throughout that are flexible and clearly written, imparting a layman's ease of understanding and can-do motivation, this collection may be the only writing craft books you'll ever need. Each volume has a free bonus companion ebooklet, presented in editable digital format that includes all the aids from the main book you can use in your own writing--and extras! A print edition is also available.

The seven volumes and bonus companion booklets in this collection are:

1. ***First Draft Outline*** formerly published by Writer's Digest Books as *First Draft in 30 Days* {A Novel Writer's System for Building a Complete and Cohesive Manuscript}

2. ***Cohesive Story Building*** formerly published by Writer's Digest Books as *From First Draft to Finished Novel* {A Writer's Guide to Cohesive Story Building}

3. ***Writing the Standalone Series*** formerly published by Writer's Digest Books as *Writing the Fiction Series* {The Complete Guide for Novels and Novellas}

4. ***Writing the Overarching Series*** {or How I Sent a Clumsy Girl into Outer Space}

5. ***Three-Dimensional Fiction Writing*** formerly published by Writer's Digest Books as *Bring Your Fiction to Life* {Crafting Three-Dimensional Stories with Depth and

Complexity}

 6. ***CPR for Dead or Lifeless Fiction*** {A Writer's Guide to Deep and Multifaceted Development and Progression of **C**haracters, **P**lots, and **R**elationships}

 7. ***Writing Blurbs That Sizzle--And Sell!***

3D Fiction Fundamentals Complete Series Collection (7 books in 1 volume)

Find out more here: http://www.writers-exchange.com/3d-fiction-fundamentals-series/

About the Author

In addition to having been a popular writing reference instructor and writer, professional blurbologist and freelance editor, Karen s. Wiesner is the accomplished author of 156 titles published, which have been nominated/won for over a hundred and thirty awards. The books Karen has edited have won multiple awards, and she's judged numerous writing contests.

Her nonfiction has included more than a half-dozen writing reference manuals that teach writers story crafting techniques as well specific facets of the book industry, such as author promotional techniques and the ins-and-outs of electronic publishing.

Karen is the author of sixteen fiction series which cover such genres as women's fiction, romance, mystery/police procedural/cozy, suspense/thriller, paranormal/supernatural, futuristic, fantasy, science fiction, gothic, inspirational/Christian, thriller, horror, chick-lit, and action/adventure. She also writes children's books and poetry. Karen will begin illustrating children's books starting in 2025.

Visit Karen's website and blog at https://karenwiesner.weebly.com/. Check out her Facebook author page here: http://www.facebook.com/KarenWiesnerAuthor. Visit her Writers Exchange E-Publishing author page at http://www.writers-exchange.com/karen-wiesner/.

<u>INTRODUCTION</u>
Judge A Book By Its Back Cover Blurb

"The blurb is the sizzle that sells the sausage." ~KJ Charles from The Art of the Blurb: How to Write Back Cover Copy

In 1939 Nazi Germany, the country is holding its breath. Death has never been busier...and will become busier still.

Liesel Meminger is a foster girl living outside of Munich who scratches out a meager existence for herself by stealing when she encounters something she can't resist--books. With the help of her accordion-playing foster father, she learns to read and shares her stolen books with her neighbors during bombing raids as well as with the Jewish man hidden in her basement. (*The Book Thief* by Markus Zusak)

There are very few people who wouldn't be enticed to read a book with a blurb this compelling.

A blurb is the smell of cookies baking, tormenting us so we eat a half dozen as soon as they're out of the oven and burn our hands carelessly doing so. It's two pairs of eyes meeting across a crowded room and bonds you to one who's no longer a stranger but destiny. It's the flirting before the kiss. It's the thrill of what's to come from finding something that feels like you've waited your whole life for. A blurb is all this and more. Or more precisely, it *should* be all this and more.

But the word "blurb" can be utterly confusing because the usage has become muddled with the passage of time and different functions. For that reason, when people in the book industry talk about blurbs, it's important to be clear on what exactly is being referred to since the evolution of this one word has come to mean many different and, in some ways, disparate things. Even the dictionary and Wikipedia seem unsure which idea to pursue. Depending on which dictionary you use, you'll get versions like this:

"A brief description of something, often intended to make it seem attractive when offered for sale."

"A brief advertisement or announcement, especially a laudatory one."

"A promotional description, as found on the jackets of books."

"A short promotional piece accompanying a creative work."

So what is a blurb? Call it a summary, a synopsis, a story description, body copy or body content, cover, flap or jacket copy, a back ad, or the horrifyingly generalized product description (such as what you'd find at Amazon and other distributor's websites), a teaser or trailer, an endorsement or book review, quote, or "puff" from a fellow author or celebrity--any and all of these are blurbs in one form or another.

Where did all this confusion come from? The word "blurb" (intended as a flamboyant, mocking advertisement) was actually coined by American humorist Gelett Burgess in 1907 when his short book, *Are You a Bromide?*, was presented at an annual trade association dinner. The dust jacket of the work actually showed "Miss Belinda Blurb" in the act of "blurbing". From that point on, the term "blurb" became known for any publisher's contents on a book's back cover. So, in essence, a blurb can be any combination of "pull quotes" directly from the work; reviews; a summary of the plot; an author's biography; or merely claims about the importance of the work either by the publisher or the author. These days, the word "blurb" really means anything that's slapped into a blurb--a combination of all of these willy-nilly. You never know what you're going to get when you're browsing books.

Reviews look good and can be included with any book advertisement, but they're used solely for promotion. They rarely tell the reader what the book is actually about. Research firm Codex Group CEO Peter Hildick-Smith says that, even when a review is given by a reader's favorite author, "such recommendations have only a modest influence on their buying habits". Only about one percent were persuaded to buy a book because of the endorsement--and that percentage equals the number of readers who discovered the last book they read through a search engine. I wouldn't call that truly effectively. Maybe endorsements have value, maybe they don't.

Essentially, review blurbs are separate from story summaries, as is the author's biography. Quotes directly from the work are best used inside the book, on the initial pages or on a blap--the glossy page covered in blurbs that immediately follows the front cover, or around the story summary on the back cover. As for pompous assertions written by the author or the publisher about the work, think about it this way: Saying something is fantastic doesn't make it so. Given that most people assume the author wrote the cover copy, making superlative remarks about your own work will make it sound like you're exaggerating, arrogant or pathetically desperate--producing a childish desire in some readers to want to prove you wrong. Yet the use of these ridiculous assertions is so prevalent, I sometimes wonder if authors think it's necessary to include comments filled with overinflated, self-love in blurbs. I call these "review-slanted" blurbs, and I decry them as the worst form of blurb imaginable...but more on that in Chapter 3.

For the purpose of *Writing Blurbs That Sizzle--And Sell!*, we're going to focus solely on the book blurb throughout this reference, meaning the very short summary of the story plot (essentially what the story is actually about), though I will mention some of the other versions of "blurb" referring to endorsements, excerpts, biographies, or inflated claims later.

Keep in mind a two-fold truth that will guide us throughout this book: a) a blurb shouldn't tell the story; it only tells the potential buyer *about* the story in hopes that he or she will part with hard-earned money to read what's inside, and b) the purpose of a blurb is to sell the book.

Consider the shocking, disheartening facts: In 2016, Bowker reported that more than 700,000 books were self-published in the United States while the number of traditionally published was over 300,000--not including thirteen million previously published books still available. Bookstore sales in 2015 were down 37% with about 2.7 billion books sold in the United States (Statista, www.statista.com). More books are competing for shelf space at physical bookstores as well as those at online distributors than ever before. With oversaturation in every genre, it's becoming more and more difficult to make any one book stand out. Every new publication vies with more than thirteen million other titles available for sale as well as alternative media claiming people's time and monetary resources. As if all that came before wasn't depressing enough, authors are being forced to do more promotion on their own because publishers can only invest a few books in marketing campaigns that are certain to cover all marketing expenses and generate profits. Author promotion is a subject that could and has filled whole books and yet there is no surefire strategy for everyone.

Suffice it to say that all of this leads us to one inescapable conclusion: Our blurbs have to stand out. As KJ Charles puts it so eloquently in her article mentioned at the start of this chapter, "...the blurb should be the most polished passage of writing you do--including the manuscript. Labouring over a [manuscript] and then knocking out a quick blurb is like spending hours creating a marvellous feast of molecular gastronomy and then serving it on paper plates off which your toddler has eaten jelly."

Additionally, remember that the last words most authors write for their books are usually the first that the audience will read. Less has to be more out of necessity. When books were only available in print, a back cover could literally only support around 450 words (and that maximum-amount-you'd-ever-want-to-have might force a small font that's hard to read while also taking up more of the margins). These days, an author has around 75-300 words to "raise a question that can ONLY BE ANSWERED when the reader BUYS and FINISHES the book", according to Michaelbrent Collings.

Now for a little more bad news: While some publishers have in-house blurb writers, for the most part, author themselves are called upon to write their own blurbs--either for an initial submission to get an agent or publisher interested in buying the work or for the actual publication of the book. That's a catch-22 in and of itself. Who's more qualified to write about the book than the author? On the other hand, who's less qualified to market books than most authors?

But, let's really get down to the cold, hard truth here: Authors hate writing blurbs. Want to hear how much? I went eavesdropping around the internet to find out exactly how bad it is and overheard these comments:

"I hate writing blurbs... I cull, switch, tear out my hair."

"I used to hate blurb writing with the heat of a thousand suns. I used to think blurbs were a challenge set by the devil to test my resolve in being a writer."

"For me, writing a blurb is sheer agony. The part I find most frustrating is the word count limit. My publisher requires 150 words or less. Virtually impossible to condense an entire novel to so few words!"

"I dread writing blurbs and put it off for as long as possible."

"I'm forever editing my blurb. You should hear me groan."
"I find writing the blurb more difficult to write than the whole bloody book."

"The only thing more difficult than breaking the entire 400-page book down into 2-3 paragraphs is, perhaps, reviewing the edits of said book!"

"How do you summarize an 80,000-word novel into a 100-

word, must-read-this-book summary? It's like squeezing yourself into a string bikini two sizes too small! How can you pull that off and make it look pretty?"

Apparently, Tolstoy downed a gallon or two of vodka while trying to write the blurb for War and Peace. I doubt there are many authors who could blame him (even as I wonder how he wrote anything so sloshed). There is no better way to test an author's ability to write concisely in a way that engages and entices the reader into wanting more than with a book blurb. The back cover is such a crucial part of the reading experience I don't think it's possible to overemphasize its importance. How many of you have read a story without first knowing the premise? I've never read a book that I haven't read the blurb for first. I'm not alone in that. Most people like to know what they're getting into in advance.

On that note, let's discuss specifically what readers are looking for when shopping for books.

The Purpose of Blurbs

Fact 1: Readers judge books by their back cover blurbs just like they might a cover.

Fact 2: Authors and publishers want them to! To have a reader judge a book by its back cover blurb is *our goal*.

The only problem with this is that we want readers to judge our books to be *worthy* of taking the risk of buying and reading it, not the opposite. For that very reason, an *effectively good* back cover blurb is absolutely crucial to our success.

Let's define our terms before we go any further. Ultimately, it doesn't matter a whit if it's long or short or somewhere in-between. We have a misconception these days that being short by definition makes a blurb good and effective while a long blurb is by default in opposition of that, but both flavor-of the-day trends are illusions that you can't afford to rest on. You can have a thousand word blurb that's so amazing readers devour it and immediately want to read the book just as you might see a short, punchy blurb that's incredibly well-written but doesn't make someone want to read the book. Hence, effectively good means it's both well-written and makes a person want to read the story inside the pages, not just the back--*want to enough to actually pay money to do it.* If a blurb isn't good enough to make someone want to open the book and read, it's not effectively good. An effectively good blurb either is effectively good in making a reader open the book or it's not. That's the bottom line, and all that matters. A blurb can be good and not effective, or effective and not good, but either it's *both* or it won't work. End of story. (That could be literal, you know.)

Beyond this, most authors don't realize that there's a sort of order to the steps a reader goes through in the process of deciding whether or not to purchase and read a book. While the first five steps can go in any order and all degrees of importance are completely individual to the preferences of the reader, the steps are critical for all authors, publishers and distributors to note and address, since overlooking even one can mean the difference between a lot of sales and little or none.

Visualize a reader either in a physical bookstore or a virtual one like a publisher's website or that of a distributor like Amazon. Your reader is perusing a selection of books, interested but not yet motivated to buy. Now imagine that each of the steps below elicits a rating scale in the reader's brain that he might not even be aware has been triggered. Each step can get a rating of anywhere from 1 (drop-it-like-a-hot-potato bad) to 5 (do-not-pass-go Buy This NOW!).

The initial scan of a book will factor in all of the following steps, in any order depending on reader preferences:

Step 1: **Author**. Some readers are loyal and buy anything and everything by certain authors. If they're obsessed with the author, that's all that's needed to prompt a purchase sometimes. If this isn't a must-buy author, then the author in question will play a large, small or anywhere in-between role in whether the rating the reader unconsciously gives is high or low.

Step 2: **Cover**. A lot of people think cover art plays such a huge role in whether or not someone will buy a book that there may be an overcompensation in the industry and thousands of dollars may be spent (needlessly? a moot point) on cover art. The fact is, some readers might be turned off by certain covers, for a variety of reasons that may or may not have anything to do with how attractive or high quality the cover actually is. From my point of view strictly as a reader, while something that catches my eye will be given the full evaluation, a cover that doesn't appeal to me much doesn't automatically put the book out of the running. Regardless of what the cover looks like, if I'm interested in the book for any other reason, like the other steps in this process, I'll give it a closer look. Even if I hate a cover--because it's ugly, doesn't tantalize me, or the design is of poor quality--I may buy a book if the other factors I prize get the thumbs up. But I know cover art does play a larger part in some reader's buying decisions, so it's something I have to be aware of and address as an author.

Step 3. **Genre**. Many readers have only certain categories they're interested in reading in, some only one. I know non-writers who'll read nothing but romance, or another only mystery. That's the go-to category for them. But most of the writers I know read everything, or read in a lot of different categories. But, for many readers, genre does play a factor in whether or not to buy. So genre will play a role, whatever degree, in whether the reader gives this step a high or low rating.

Step 4. **Book size/word count**. I've heard readers say they never read anything shorter than standard-size novel, not even in a collection, mainly because they believe the reader won't or can't create a fully-fleshed out story in the page limitation. Others won't read anything that's too big and intimidates them on size alone because, after all, if you can't say something concisely, then maybe it's not worth saying at all. Most larger books are physically bigger and cost more, and therefore size could be a limitation. That's true of even ebooks, though maybe less so. In this step, extremes in either direction are almost always what tip the balance in favor of or against a buy.

Step 5. **Title**. While there are very few people who would dismiss a book from consideration on the sole basis of the title, or even buy one because of a good one, this is a factor, however small, in a book purchase. Some people would never buy a book if the title was too racy or implied a subject matter they're not interested in or they're flat out against. On the other hand, I have a friend, humorous mystery author Christine DeSmet, who always comes up with these amazing titles: *Misbehavin' in Moonstone, When the Dead People Brought a Dish-to-Pass, Five-Alarm Fudge, All She Wore Was a Bow, Sex with the Man in the Moon*... You get the picture. Her clever titles crack me up and entice me to want to read the stories. Others might have other examples, but titles play their part in making the decision to buy, however slight that part is.

As I said, these five steps can register in a reader's brain in any order and with varying degrees of importance, all based on individual preference. That book can have any conceivable amount of stars, from 0 to 25 at this point, after this first scan is completed. Anything really low will probably be dropped back on the stack (or the page left on a book website) without further ado. Now, imagine, if all five of these factors result in a good amount of stars (the book in question has 25 possible stars that could be awarded at this point--and 25 would practically guarantee the move to the next, most pivotal step...)

The Turning Point...

Step 6: **Reading the back cover blurb**. Like it or not, this is almost always the open-or-oust deciding factor for a reader. Either step 6 gets him to open the book and move into the final step in the process, which is reading an excerpt, or all scanning stars are removed and the book is forgotten, ousted from his thoughts, and he moves on to something else, starting the process all over again. This is the get-off-the-fence point, the denouement, the make-or-break, life or death sentence. If the back cover blurb attracts him, he may read an excerpt and that will seal it for him either way. Some readers will buy then and there if the back cover blurb sufficiently excites them, especially if the book already has 25 stars in the decision-making bank (another reason to do everything right and not neglect but *address* each step successfully).

The sad part is that you can lose a reader completely at any step, at any time, even if he's bought the book but he doesn't enjoy it--that will factor into whether you get another sale from him in the future. Those dollars are the only ones you'll see from that reader. Depending on how vindictive he is, you may find yourself with a bad review posted online for the whole world to see, or he may choose to spread that bad review by word of mouth. Ultimately, it behooves us as writers, publishers and distributors to make sure each step is the best it possibly can be.

THE PURPOSE AND HOW TO USE THIS BOOK

Every author knows what a back cover blurb is, given its high-profile placement on the back cover of every single print copy of a book and now as the accompaniment of electronic copies of the same. At its crux, a back cover blurb strives to be a concise, breathtaking summary of your entire story that includes the major internal and external conflicts and the goals and motivations of the main character(s). All of these things should and have to make the reader want to know more.

Unfortunately crafting an effectively good back cover blurb

is no easy task, and many writers outright dislike writing them, or simply dread the process perhaps because so much is at stake if the blurb fails to engage agents/publishers (for authors submitting) and readers (after you're published). Your back cover blurb can make or break a sale to a publisher as well as to potential readers trying to decide whether or not to fork over the money to purchase your work, given that it's one of the first glimpses of the story and that glimpse had better be utterly intriguing. You may not get a second chance to capture your audience. Many publishers you submit to and certainly readers buy based on a sizzling back cover blurb that convinces them they absolutely have to read the story inside the pages...or they simply set the book down without ever opening it. Additionally, a powerful series blurb can sell not just one book but all of them in that set!

I've been writing my own blurbs from the beginning--hundreds of them now, considering I'm the author of almost 130 books (including 19 series), and I've also helped other authors with theirs for many years, along with writing and/or revising the blurbs for many award-winning anthologies. I'd never done it "professionally", though I have had New York editors tell me I should be writing back cover blurbs for a living. In 2017, on the suggestion of my fiction publisher, I decided to start a small side business. I offered my skills as a blurb writer to other authors and publishers. My first client was that publisher, who had a backlist of well over five hundred blurbs she wanted me to evaluate, revise, worst-case-scenario rewrite from scratch, and also provide series blurbs for all that needed them. Additionally, she wanted me to do the same for all upcoming and future releases. A massive undertaking that took me a few weeks that, hey, I didn't sleep much during, but I was in blurb heaven (have I mentioned how much I love all things blurb?). After that, I started putting on blurb workshops and decided to write this book. It was then that I started looking around to see what other resources were out there about blurb writing. The internet is absolutely flooded with articles written about blurb writing, and I found one 67-page ebook about them at Amazon, but there's not a single other book reference out there that I could locate that definitively discusses everything important to know about blurbs. Talk about a niche crying out for filling!

To that end, the purpose of *Writing Blurbs That Sizzle--And Sell!* is to teach writers and publishers how to craft effectively good blurbs, whether the author is unpublished and submitting to agents and editors or published and writing their own blurbs for books that will go directly to readers, whether the books are large or small, fiction or nonfiction or anything in-between, and whether blurbs need writing from scratch or an existing blurb revised.

This book is broken down into five chapters followed by three appendices.

Chapter One explores the basics of blurb crafting: When to write them, how long a blurb should be, and the three types of blurbs including high-concept, back cover, and series blurbs. Here we'll fill out the High-Concept, Back Cover, and Series Blurb Worksheet that covers all the bases.

Chapter Two will go over how to write a few very specialized types of blurbs including nonfiction, anthology, and children's books that require different techniques than other fiction blurbs.

Chapter Three focuses on a huge selection of tips for crafting blurbs. There are so many pros and cons when writing blurbs a whole chapter is needed to cover them all. Our Blurb Evaluation Checklist is formed from these tips.

Chapter Four offers techniques in sizing blurbs for a variety of applications as well as covers the timely and viable topic of branding with blurbs (and you need various sizes for that).

The final chapter concludes what we've learned about the vital role of crafting effectively good blurbs.

The three appendices contain all the supplemental materials you'll need to work your way through the blurbing process:

- *Appendix A* offers blurbs from published works for you to evaluate with the Blurb Evaluation Checklist in order to hone effectively good blurb writing skills.
- *Appendix B* gives exercises to help develop series, high-

concept, and back cover blurb evaluating, writing, and revising skills--using an All-in-One Worksheet that provides the means to whittle blurbs down to three different sizes.

- *Appendix C* contains the blank worksheets and checklists we've discussed throughout the book that you can use to craft, evaluate, revise and whittle your own blurbs.

Some clarifications about the examples from published novels I've used that you'll find in this book: Fabricating material from published books to fit into sections of my worksheets isn't easy. While I have used examples from other published books, in many cases, I've also used my own books in the examples you'll find in order to rid myself of the discomfort of having to "work backwards" with something not my own too often. Additionally, I use a lot of examples from the works of the authors I've evaluated, crafted and revised blurbs for (through my Blurb Service). Finally, one last note about the examples: Many of them surpass what we'll soon establish as the "maximum word count" for sizing. My critique partner commented on how long most of them were, wondering often if they exceeded the limits I'd set. Remember a few of things when you encounter long blurb examples in this text: 1) Size doesn't matter--effectively good blurbs can come in any size. What I've suggested as ideal isn't in any way set in stone. The sizes are simply goals to shoot for when crafting or revising. 2) Resizing blurbs is mainly a promotional concern, which we'll discuss in-depth later. Again, the sizes I'll suggest as ideal should in no way force an author to conform if effectively good is otherwise at odds with length. 3) These are examples, and I have little or no control over the sizes of them as they come to me. Unless our point is to utilize the blurb as an exercise in resizing, assume the length of any example is beside the point I'm trying to make.

A couple of notes: Throughout this book, for consistency, I'll refer to *characters* in the female point of view. To offer distinction, I'll refer to *readers and writers* in the male POV. Clearly, characters, readers and writers can be of either sex, but, to prevent an erratic jump from one to the other, I've done it this way.

One other thing to take notice of is that a number of the examples used throughout this book are from movies. The reason for this is because that medium is so much more visual and also because the sad fact is that there are more movie-goers than readers these days. 2014 statistics pointed to nearly a quarter of Americans having not read a single book during the year while more than two-thirds of the population went to the cinema at least once during the year and frequent moviegoers attended at least once a month. Safe to say, the fiction in movies may be better known than that in books, although those reading this reference probably read more books than they do watch movies. Ultimately, all the examples are fictional, so I saw no reason not to use some from each medium.

Additionally, I'll note upfront that I believe a series name is part of its branding (see my book *Writing the Standalone Series*). Not only should the series title be included everywhere the name of a book is spoken or written about, but the world "series" or "trilogy" should be *capitalized* in order to further solidify the branding. In other words, I never refer to my series Family Heirlooms as simply that. Always, I refer to it as the "Family Heirlooms Series" because that's the full title and most effective way to brand it to my readers. That's why you'll see every series mentioned within this book with the word "series" or "trilogy" capitalized. We'll talk more about this in Chapter Four.

Note that errors made in any original blurb examples were retained here from wherever the blurb was taken. I didn't correct mistakes anywhere except in my revision example of that original blurb.

One final note of clarification: Keep in mind that you don't have to perform every step in this or any other writing method. Authors are all different, we all think and perform differently, and ultimately it makes no sense to do more work than you need to. The goal for each writer should be to find what works for you personally, as an individual. Most of the time that means finding what doesn't work first. My motto is, utilize what works for you;

discard the rest. The point of worksheets and checklists is to give help in pinpointing problem areas. If you're not having an issue in a certain area, go ahead and skip the in-depth processing. In my writing methods, in particular, my goal is to make sure authors have everything needed to learn to write instinctively. What I mean by that is that through years and endless practice, your brain begins to grasp the basics and even some of the harder concepts of writing, like blurb writing. If you don't feel like some or any of this is instinctive for you, go through the steps as I've set them down, aware that every author's endgame is and should be instinctive writing.

GETTING STARTED

There's no doubt that learning to write effectively good blurbs is critical to your success as an author. There are techniques that can help and may even infuse you with the same enthusiasm I have for writing blurbs. I am wildly, wonderfully *in love* with writing, revising and evaluating book blurbs--for my own books and for the books of other authors, regardless of the genre. Even the most shockingly underwhelming blurbs I've been asked to write or revise have thrilled me with their challenge. My hope is that *Writing Blurbs That Sizzle--And Sell!* will give authors a solid plan of action from start to finish through in-depth discussions, examples and exercises, with leave-no-stone-unturned aids, and a process that will allow you take everything mentioned here into your own blurb writing. Let's get started!

CHAPTER ONE
Crafting Blurb Basics

"You put your protagonist in. You leave the best friend out. You put the problem in. You leave the twist out. You do the Hokey Pokey and leave 'em on a cliffhanger. That's what it's all about." ~Cait Reynolds from The Book Blurb--An Invitation Readers Simply Can't Put Down

It is a truth universally acknowledged that a single author in possession of a good book must be in want of a blurb. But writing blurbs is hard and it's something a lot of authors put off until the last possible minute. Some of the questions that might be circling right now are: What's the best time to write a blurb? How long should a blurb be? Where to start? What to leave out? What to put in? What to avoid like the plague? What's the difference between a high-concept blurb, a back cover blurb and a series blurb, and why are all equally important? What order should you put them in once you've written each? We'll answer all these questions and concerns in this chapter.

First, we should establish that writing blurbs requires an entirely different mindset than writing stories. That might be a good reason for not writing one as soon as you've finished writing the book. Give yourself time away, just enough so you've still got the story firmly in mind, but you've gained sufficient distance to allow yourself to go at blurbing like a fitness coach to make it lean and mean.

Second, yeah, I'm going there: Facts are facts, and the fact is some authors are just not good at writing blurbs...for whatever reason. Too many think that just because a blurb is generally short, it's inconsequential, as evidenced by this quote from Ben Cameron in his *10 Top Tips on How to Write the Best Book Blurb* article: "You've just put your feet up when you get a reminder from the designer that they still need text for the back cover. Another small decision at the end of a long line of decisions, you knock something together in a few minutes and send it off. You may have just doomed your 75,000-word masterpiece..." Did he learn to regret his former blasé attitude about blurbs? Probably.

Others are simply too deeply involved with their own work--therefore, everything is important and must be mentioned. Those authors need to look at the story from a reader's perspective and have a method like the one in this book for getting down to the heart of the story. Some authors can learn to be better or even good at blurb writing with a solid process and practice behind them.

Finally, there are authors who are given literally no say in what makes it on or into their back cover blurbs. The publishing house does that work, and sometimes that's a relief and actually carries rewards. Other times, especially when blurbs are misleading or just downright wrong, that may lead to a lot of embarrassment or even loss of sales. The best case scenario would be for the one who knows the book best (the author) to write the first draft of his own blurb then send it over to a professional blurbologist (that's a real thing!) to revise into something sizzling, and lastly, the blurb goes to a marketing expert to finish it off with whatever a blurb needs promotion-wise. But, let's face it, that situation doesn't happen too often these days. Learning how to do it yourself is probably the way to go for the vast majority.

Let's go over the two most basic questions authors have when it comes to writing blurbs: When to write them and how long they can and should be. Because these questions are usually the ones that are foremost of author's minds, discussing them requires immediate attention and then we'll be allowed to move into the actual process of crafting blurbs.

WHEN TO WRITE YOUR BLURBS

No two authors are the same, and each one has preferences about when to write their blurbs. While I was writing *Three-*

Dimensional Fiction Writing, one of my critique partners was blown away at the prospect of crafting the back cover blurb before a single word of the book had been written. It was inconceivable that this could even be possible, and it seemed backwards to her—writing the story was a prerequisite, in her opinion, since she could only be clear about what needed to go on the back cover after she wrote (and figured out) the story.

After her comments, I can actually see that this makes a lot of sense for most unpublished or newly published authors. However, I'm on the opposite end of this. From my point of view, I can't imagine *not* starting a project with a blurb. Literally, it's the first thing I do once I have the original idea for a story (and/or series) and I've decided on a title. It's really what helps me solidify a story with characters and conflicts that haunt my mind.

I usually write my blurbs years in advance of doing any other kind of writing on a book or series. The blurb finalizes the gist of the story and/or series clearly. Once the blurb is written, I can send it to my fiction publisher, knowing I have a solid story/series concept and I can, without question, write a full story based on it. She accepts the project based on this because she's learned from experience that, based on this blurb, I'll craft a thrilling story/series for her to publish...possibly years down the road from the time she first sees the proposal. Though I sometimes have to tweak the blurb(s) once the book or series are finished, my ideas for the story/series only become clear to me after I've written the (albeit long) blurbs, but I will say that it's a rare thing that any blurb is rewritten extensively after the book or series is finished. I believe it almost goes without saying that my long blurb is money in the bank when written in advance of any other writing on the project, given how it catapults the final story/series development and captures the essence of what will later become hundreds of pages when I begin writing that book or series.

As I said, my initial back cover blurbs do tend to be fairly long, and I strongly prefer to start with the long version so the core of my story is encapsulated in these paragraphs. After the book is written, I'll whittle the long-form blurb (which can be around 450 words in length) down to something shorter that pops. I like to have a 150-word, 100-word, and 75-word blurb for each story so, whatever size is needed for various applications, I have something available. Those three sizes do seem to be what's expected for marketing and distribution purposes. I'm a firm believer that longer blurbs can be more effective than short ones, though my original 450-word ones are usually too long to be final back cover blurbs.

So what's the best time to write a back cover blurb? As a general rule, professional published writers who are allowed to submit story/series proposals that can be accepted by their publishers long in advance of writing the book(s) should learn how to write a blurb before beginning any serious work on a project. For newer writers, the easiest way might be to wait until the story is written *before* attempting any kind of formal blurb, but give it a try beforehand at least once to see where it takes you. Even if you write 2000 words or even more, your story ideas will be much clearer and you can use that to write a more concise, less kitchen-sink blurb.

Bottom line, when you write yours is completely up to you and your particular situation. That said, learning to do it early will immensely benefit you, your story (and series, if you're writing one), as well as your submission/promotion efforts. Additionally note that you can use the techniques in this reference for books you've never blurbed in any capacity before, as well as for books you've already created blurbs for but you want more punch or intrigue in them, or you simply want them to be shorter.

Returning to the axiom in this book, if your blurb doesn't illicit intrigue or the desire to read the books or the series, it's not effectively good. When I begin writing a new blurb (series or single title), I can't imagine a more exciting time for me. Writing your own blurbs should bring forth so much excitement about writing the story/series you'll barely be able to resist jumping into each one immediately. That's another reason for writing them early.

HOW LONG SHOULD A BLURB BE?

There's a huge trend going on these days about short blurbs. I personally believe distributors and a certain high-profile publishing company associated with one of the major book distributors in the world is behind this trend. Many publishers, printers, books packagers, distributors and book promote websites actually do have a limit on how many words can be included as a description. You might have noticed at Amazon, if you want to read any more than the first, say, five sentences, you have to click "read more"--twice, if you can believe that!--to get the full amount that was allowed to be put in by the publisher or author. At Lulu, a printer, you're given a very small amount of space for your blurb and you can't go over that maximum no matter how much you might want to (and you will want to!).

I don't deny that if your blurb is short and punchy, it's practically guaranteed to be intriguingly memorable. But it's a fact that short is not always best. A *too*-short blurb may be less than dazzling. Instead of being memorable, it can lack details to capture true interest in readers. Once, I was revising blurbs for two different authors. One gave me about five total sentences. The other gave me five long paragraphs. Guess which one I enjoyed the most? Yes, I've admitted I prefer long blurbs, but with the short blurb, I couldn't find anything to connect to. Not enough information was given for me to feel any intrigue and desire to read more. The five long paragraphs *weren't enough* to satisfy me for the other book. I loved everything I read and I was just eating it up! But, as a blurbologist, I knew it was far too long for the average reader, so I did suggest cuts. My point is, an effectively good blurb isn't going to fit into any word count minimums or maximums because the point isn't about whether it's long or short. All that really matters when it comes to blurb size is whether it's effectively good.

Genre will play a part in the size of your back cover blurb. Science fiction, fantasy, and historical books (especially if part of a series) may have longer back cover and series blurbs: up to four paragraphs instead of the standard one or two. That's because the blurb may have to make sense of whole worlds, cultures and philosophies, which, in many cases may seem vastly different from what a modern reader is used to. Less weighty genres set in time periods and worlds modern people are accustomed to--such as romance, suspense, general fiction, maybe even speculative stories--rarely have more than two paragraphs that make up the back cover blurb. So, here's a go-to list of our size figures for each blurb type:

A high-concept blurb is rarely more than **a single sentence long but can be up to two sentences** in length. Actual word count is certainly not a factor in this unless your sentences are long enough to be shocking. Most are rarely more than 20 words long.

A back cover blurb can be anywhere from **one to four paragraphs long**. Back in the day when there were only print copies of books, they used to have to fit blurbs solely on the back cover of that physical book (whether it was a mass market paperback, trade or another size). Depending on the size of the paperback, 200-450 words was about the maximum comfortable fit on a back cover. Anything longer and the font would have to be made smaller, or less "blank" space would be available for margins. It is possible to fit about 425 words on a trade size paperback and still have it look attractive and be fairly readable. I've done it with my own. But, as we said, this can be at the expense of a largely readable font size and open space.

A series blurb can also be anywhere **from one to four paragraphs in length--but preferably one** unless it's for a genre that requires a bit more room, as we've already covered.

Between the high-concept, story and series blurbs, you generally have an **absolute maximum of 450 total**

words to use, but **250 or less** *for all three combined* is recommended.

If you don't have any limitations, go with the most effectively good combination of all three blurbs. We'll talk more about whittling blurbs to a variety of sizes for different applications in Chapter Four and actually have some practice exercises to do in Appendix B.

THREE TYPES OF BLURBS

Cait Reynolds makes me laugh whenever I read her Blurb Hokey Pokey included at the beginning of this chapter. Mostly because it's so true! How to write a blurb 101: You put your main character in, you don't need that secondary character. Detail the conflict with just enough to get the questions rising inside the reader's head but not too much that you begin answering those questions or deflating any of the big moments in the book. Hook with a last sentence that drives them panting to open the book and start reading. That's the general idea. But there's a lot more to it because we have to contend with more than just the back cover blurb.

Before we begin that discussion, let's reiterate what we talked about in the introduction. While a blurb can be made up of any combination of "pull quotes" directly from the work; reviews or endorsements from other writers or professionals; a summary of the plot; an author's biography; or merely claims about the importance of the work either by the publisher or the author, the only part of that we're going to deal with in this book is *the summary of the plot*. That's all. Everything else boils down to promotional considerations that have nothing to do with our focus. Whether or not you include them is up to you and your publisher, but I will voice opinions about some of those aspects in later chapters.

How to Write Blurbs

An effectively good blurb has two parts for a single title and three for a series. Surprisingly, this isn't commonly known and so few authors and publishers use and utilize the separate parts--and use them together always, everywhere, every single time! In this chapter, we'll go over all of them, what they are and what they're used for, and, in each case, we'll use the High-Concept, Back Cover, and Series Blurb Worksheet that breaks them down into easy steps and formulas. Finally, we'll talk about the order that each blurb should go in, but I will note upfront here that the order we'll go over each of these doesn't follow the order you should put your finished blurbs in when using them on or in books, for distribution and marketing. I'm presenting the overview discussions in the order I am here--with high-concept first, back cover blurb second, and series blurb last--solely on the basis of the fact that many books are single-titles. Those that are have no need for series blurbs. The discussion on series blurbs is included after the other two that are needed for absolutely every blurb.

Part 1: High-Concept Blurbs

A high-concept blurb is rarely more than a single sentence, possibly two sentences, long. I know, that's going to be a shock for many authors, who only think in terms of shorter-is-better because, currently, it's the flavor of the day advice. That might be true in some or even most cases, but it is possible for an up-to-two-sentences high-concept blurb to be more effective than a single sentence. We'll look at some examples that have both one and two sentences.

The only difference between a back cover blurb and a high-concept blurb is usually length and frequently the high-concept blurb is much more generalized than the back cover blurb. The high-concept blurb precedes the back cover blurb in order of presentation. The blurb doesn't have to be generalized, but it usually is. Almost always, it's a *single* sentence that captures the essence of the story with a solid punch of intrigue straight to the gut. That's the whole point of the high-concept blurb--to be utterly intriguing. We went over the book-shopping process in the introduction. Some readers don't have a lot of patience when shopping for books. They want the punch straight away and *don't bore me with more than a high-concept blurb*! Though few readers actually know it's called that, the high-concept blurb might be all you're given to convince the reader to continue.

As I mentioned earlier, book authors and publishers don't utilize high-concept blurbs nearly enough these days, though all evidence points to the need to do exactly that in promotion and distribution that stimulates the audience to action. The movie industry, in particular, is king of this sort of promotion and that could certainly be the case because they have to be more visualize. Some examples of intriguing high-concept blurbs from movies from a variety of genres--which you should notice as you read are inferred in just a few words without any designation to that fact:

A cryptic message from MI6 spy James Bond's past sends him on a trail to uncover a sinister organisation. *Spectre*

Her life was in their hands. Now her toe is in the mail. *The Big Lebowski*

During the Cold War, a Brooklyn attorney is tasked with negotiating a prisoner exchange between an American pilot who was shot down over the USSR and a Soviet spy serving a 45-year sentence for espionage against the United States. Bridge of Spies

An adventure 65 million years in the making. *Jurassic Park*

Life-changing events cause the relationship of two lifelong friends to be tested as they attempt to deal with the joy and sorrow in their lives. *Miss You Already*

A young Irish immigrant navigates her way through 1950s Brooklyn but soon her new vivacity is disrupted by her past, forcing her to choose between two countries and the lives that exist within. *Brooklyn*

Armies of witch hunters battled their unnatural enemy across the globe for centuries, including Kaulder, now the last, cursed with immortality by the Queen Witch he destroyed and must face again when she's resurrected. An epic battle ensues that will determine the survival of the human race. *The Last Witch Hunter*

Trapped in time. Surrounded by evil. Low on gas. *Army of Darkness*

Earth. It was fun while it lasted. *Armageddon*

One dream. Four Jamaicans. Twenty below zero. *Cool Runnings*

She brought a small town to its feet and a huge corporation to its knees. *Erin Brockovich*

The first casualty of war is innocence. *Platoon*

An American businessman and his family settle into their new home in Southeast Asia only to find themselves in the middle of a violent political uprising. *No Escape*

A gifted gardener and landscaper is chosen to design the landscaping at the palace of Versailles for Louis XIV, a job that brings with it gender and class barriers She must also contend professionally with a controlling royal gardener who begins to fall in love with her. *A Little Chaos*

Fifty million people watching but no one saw a thing. *Quiz Show*

Here are some examples from books (in most cases, refined

slightly, since few books these days have true high-concept blurbs; and you'll notice most of them are mine--nearly all of my books have a high-concept blurb):

The tale of the contestants of a grueling walking competition where there can only be one winner—the one that survives. (*The Long Walk* by Stephen King writing as Richard Bachman)

A missing engagement ring leads to murder. (*On the Rocks*, Book 1: Denim Blues Mysteries by Karen Wiesner)

Six college friends reunite on the coast of Brittany to celebrate one of their own's fortieth birthday with sumptuous food and plenty of wine, setting a table for tricky romantic entanglements, fiery outbursts, and a range of secrets. (*A French Wedding* by Hannah Tunnicliffe)

It began as their dream home...and soon became their worst nightmare. (*In the Dark* by Brandon Massey)

For most of her life, Sibylla Nygard has had horrifying dreams about a house with hidden rooms, shocking secrets...and the vision of her own death. (*Hidden*, Book 6: Bloodmoon Cove Spirits Series by Karen Wiesner)

A secret organisation of powerful individuals welcomes the fulfilment of an ancient prophecy: A leader to usher in an age where they will rule all... (*Nipta* by Omeiza Edwards)

Half boy. Half god. All hero. (Percy Jackson and the Olympians: *The Lightning Thief* by Rick Riordan)

Joined before God and family out of a sense of responsibility? Or love? (*Shadow Boxing*, Book 2: Family Heirlooms Series by Karen Wiesner)

Who would you give up to stay alive? (*What's Left of Me?* by Kat Zhang)

Is murder ever justifiable? (*Tears on Stone*, Book 2: Falcon's Bend Series by Karen Wiesner and Chris Spindler)

Best friends can make the deadliest enemies. (Precious Thing by Colette McBeth)

She has two men, two identities, one choice... (*Restless as Rain* by Karen Wiesner)

A boy with extraordinary powers. An army of deadly monsters. An epic battle for the future of peculiardom. (*Library of Souls*, Book 3: Miss Peregrine's Peculiar Children Series by Ransom Riggs)

Laia is a slave. Elias is a soldier. Neither is free. (*An Ember in the Ashes*, Book 1: An Ember in the Ashes Series by Sabaa Tahir)

An unsuspecting nurse is lured to an ancient family mansion said to hold both ghosts and horrifying secrets in order to care for three orphaned children. (*The Bloodmoon Curse*, Book 2: Bloodmoon Cove Spirits Series by Karen Wiesner)

If you look at all these high-concept blurbs carefully, you'll notice they all have something in common. They all have two components: A *who* and a *what*. That's pretty much all we need here. The who could refer to a protagonist or an antagonist or any general *concept*. In the book world, this is usually the main character but it could also be a group of people, a culture, a planet, whatever--essentially who has the most at risk that the reader is rooting for--the main driving force in the story, whether good or evil

This is a basic formula we can use in the crafting of our high-concept blurbs. For a high-concept blurb, the goal is to come up with one to two sentences (no more than that--but you can start with more and work on it until it's two or less), something utterly intriguing.

Here's the first section of our High-Concept, Back Cover, and Series Blurb Worksheet:

Who:
What:

Let's tag one of the high-concept blurbs from a movie so you can see how it fits into the formula:

A cryptic message from MI6 spy James Bond's past sends him on a trail to uncover a sinister organisation. *Spectre*

Who: MI6 spy James Bond
What: [Receives] A cryptic message from MI6 spy James Bond's past sends him on a trail to uncover a sinister organisation.

Now let's tag one of the high-concept blurbs from a book so you can see how it fits into the formula. I've chosen one of the hardest because literally there isn't a high-concept blurb that can't fit into this two-part-component formula, but it might be difficult to initially figure out what's what for this one. Remember, your "Who" can be a concept, not an actual person or thing:

Is murder ever justifiable? (*Tears on Stone*, Book 2: Falcon's Bend Series by Karen Wiesner and Chris Spindler)

Who: Murder
What: Is it ever justifiable?

Practice Makes Perfect Session:

Try to tag each of the of the fourteen remaining high-concept movie and story blurbs we've used as examples in this section so each fits into the high-concept formula:

High-Concept Blurb

Fill out as completely as possible for the two components that make up this blurb. Remember, the "who" can be a person, a thing, or simply a concept--your main theme.

Who:
What:

Craft Your Own High-Concept Blurb

Using the blurb formula we've talked about in this section, try to craft a high-concept blurb for your own story. Remember, it should ultimately be only one or two sentences, but you can start with something longer at first, to use as your basis. Don't worry if your first few passes aren't brilliant. Keep honing it as we build on this strong beginning.

Part 2: Back Cover Blurbs

At its crux, a back cover blurb strives to be a concise, breathtaking summary of your entire story that includes the major internal and external conflicts and the goals and motivations of the main character(s). A back cover blurb can be anywhere from one to four paragraphs. If the whole package is short and punchy, as we've said, it's practically guaranteed to be intriguingly memorable, but keep in mind that a *too*-short blurb can sometimes be less than dazzling. Instead of being memorable, it can lack details to capture true interest in readers. Throughout this process, you'll be playing with yours to find the right balance. Before we start crafting, let's define the terms that will be on the next section of our High-Concept, Back Cover, and Series Blurb Worksheet:

Internal Conflict

Internal conflicts are emotional problems brought about by *external* conflicts that make a character reluctant to achieve a goal because of her own roadblocks. They keep her from learning a life lesson and making the choice to act. In fiction, external character conflicts are why plot conflicts can't be resolved. Simply put, the character can't reach her goal until she faces the conflict. (Sounds a bit like not getting dessert until the vegetables are eaten, and this is pretty accurate.) The audience must be able to identify with the internal and external conflicts the character faces in order to be involved and to care about the outcome. Character growth throughout the story is key to a satisfactory resolution.

Your first spark of the story in your mind will usually suggest what the character's conflicts are, and many times they're based on someone or something threatening what the character cares about passionately. A loved one is in jeopardy, or something the character wants, needs, or desires above all is at risk of being lost. Questions you might ask yourself to get to the heart of your character's internal conflict: *What are your core principles and values? What will you risk your life for? Why would you put yourself in danger for this?* From these stem internal and external conflicts. It's your job as the writer to give the character incentives (specifically, goals and motivations, which we'll cover soon) not to give up until everyone is safe and the main character has what she was fighting for.

Generally characters have levels of internal conflict starting with the immediate one that's almost always revealed or at least hinted at in the opening scenes. MJ Bush, writing coach, editor and fantasy novelist on the WritingGeekery blog calls the next level the "root desire" and she suggests that you ask your character five times to tell you what her root desire is, digging deeper each time to get to the core. Once you get to it, she advises you to bury it again because, if the reader can see it right away, it'll sound more like you're preaching rather than telling a story. The root goal is something that gets revealed slowly throughout the course of the book. The conflicting desire is, of course, the external one--the obstacle that prevents your character from reaching her root desire or goal in the story.

Internal conflicts need to be sketched for each major character because what's happening in the present will show its origins in the past. Obviously, including the means for the reader to look forward (with hope and/or dread) to what will happen in the future of these internal conflicts is absolutely vital to engaging his interest from start to finish, and we need to see those reflected (concisely and intriguingly) in the back cover blurb.

In S.E. Hinton's classic story *Tex*, the fifteen-year-old loves his horse more than anything in the world. But when his seventeen-year-old brother Mason (who's been standing in as father and caretaker for Tex since their father is almost never around and does nothing to provide for them) sells the horses to pay bills and put food on the table, Tex's world is turned upside down. His horse gave him a sense of purpose, validity, sanity; bottom line: made him happy. Though Tex intellectually understands that his brother had no other choice, he can't accept this. His internal conflict in losing what meant most to him is overwhelmed by the external conflict of his sold horse, and he reacts violently, wanting to get back what he lost. But losing his horse is only his surface internal conflict. The root desire is all about the father who's essentially abandoned them.

Clearly defined conflicts are ones that won't hit your reader over the head or frustrate him. If you don't quite understand the conflicts in your story, your instinct will be to compensate by bombarding the story with unfocused ideas. The reader won't find it any easier to sort through them and identify the true conflict. Loosely defined conflicts usually lead to the reader putting down a book and never picking it up again.

Too many conflicts can easily overwhelm the reader. The same is true if you're unrelenting in driving these conflicts home. I absolutely adore J. Madison Davis's take on this in *Novelist's Essential Guide to Creating Plot*:

"Even the greatest excitement and most spectacular events can become wearying if they are relentless. I remember hearing one disgruntled moviegoer whisper to his wife sometime around the third hour of *Titanic*, 'When is this dang boat gonna sink, fer pity's sake?' The writer who has one unremittingly, relentlessly exciting scene following another can wear the reader out. Too much shouting makes us deaf, and shouting even louder after that will not be heard because of the deafness."

Too many conflicts (especially at the beginning and end of a book) and failing to allow the reader to take a break between action sequences equate to shrill shouting that can deafen your reader. If you want an example of this, try reading Dan Brown's Robert Langdon Series. The action is absolutely relentless. By the halfway mark, I'm usually so exhausted I can barely continue reading. Characters need downtime as much as readers do to prevent overload.

External Conflict

External conflict (plot) is the central tangible or outer problem standing squarely in the character's way that must be faced and solved by that character. The character wants to either restore the stability that was taken from her by or grasp her root desire by thwarting the external conflict, and this produces her desire to act. However, a character's internal conflicts will create an agonizing tug of war with the external plot conflicts. She has to make tough choices that come down to whether or not she should face, act on, and solve the problem. Stephenie Meyer's post-apocalyptic novel, *The Host*, is about a woman, Melanie Stryder, who resists when an alien life force invades our world and forces human beings to become hosts for them by taking over their bodies and eventually the consciousness of each person. Melanie's invader soon realizes that Melanie hasn't relinquished possession of her mind, despite succumbing with her physical body. Though the invader's task is to discover the whereabouts of the remaining human resistance, this soul called Wanderer instead finds itself sharing in Melanie's undiminished longings for the love she lost, that may still be alive and waiting for her. Both Melanie and Wanderer struggle inside one body with their internal and external conflicts of being who and what they are.

Your audience should be able to identify with both the internal and external conflicts a character faces in order to be involved enough to care about the outcome of the story. As we mentioned in the last section, plot conflicts work hand-in-glove with character conflicts. You can't have one without the other, and they become more intense and focused the longer the characters struggle. The stakes are raised, choices are limited, failure and loss are inevitable (these are the future dimensions that create the hope/dread responses in readers). In *Novelist's Essential Guide to Creating Plot*, J. Madison Davis defines plot "like a cone that characters are moving through from the wide end to the narrow. It closes in the farther along they go."

Internal conflicts are different from external, but they're related causally—the best definition of concept I've heard is: "Can't have one without the other." Internal and external conflicts depend on each other, and therefore they need to be cohesive and multi-faceted. Internal conflicts are all about characters, and external conflicts are all about plot. But keep this in mind: Both internal and external plots belong to the main character. After all, if both didn't affect her in some profound way, they wouldn't be conflicts for her and therefore wouldn't even be part of her story. David Corbett says in *The Art of Character: The Five Cornerstones of Dramatic Characterization*, "Characterization requires a constant back-and-forth between the exterior events of the story and the inner life of the character." If your character's internal and external conflicts are at odds, your story will be going in two different directions, which will disengage even the hardiest of readers. In stories that work on a cohesive level, internal and external conflicts travel on parallel tracks, merge and collide in a fiery explosion throughout the course of a book.

Think of the two conflicts this way: Everyone has a passionate hot button. Cruelty to animals, cancer, child abuse. You fill in the blank with yours. But not everyone has the strength of passion for your particular hot button. We're all individuals that way because we usually put our passion into something that has touched us deeply in our lives. If your mother died of cancer, you'll want to see that particular disease cured. It's your hot button. This doesn't mean you don't sympathize and care deeply about other causes, even if you're not quite as passionate about them as you are about the ones that affect you most. What it does mean is that if something critical happens in the area of your passion, you're probably going to step up to the plate and fight for what you believe in.

You're telling a story about your particular characters, and they have hot buttons, too. Since it's their story, their hot buttons will naturally be their conflicts. All of these conflicts must parallel, intersect, and collide for a story to be truly cohesive. So, though the external plot conflicts may stem from an outside force or situation, they nevertheless belong to the main character as much as her internal problems do. Like I said, if she didn't care deeply about the external plot, it wouldn't be her story.

Let's use an example of this from the action/adventure *Die Hard 2: Die Harder*. The rough and gruff main character, John McClane (played by Bruce Willis), is a cop at the airport on Christmas. He's off-duty, but begins to sense trouble is afoot in what seems like the busiest place on earth—and things are looking to get worse before the day is through. The airport cops don't share his uneasiness. They've got their own worries to handle. Though McClane is very reluctant to get involved, his inner integrity won't allow him to stand by. He checks it out, figuring he'll let the airport police handle anything that's amiss.

His gut instinct is dead-on. Terrorists take over the airport. This shouldn't be his problem, but it becomes so because: (1) the airport cops refuse to do their jobs because they're too busy with other tasks; and (2) these terrorists have pushed McClane's hot button. A year before on Christmas, McClane single-handedly took down a band of terrorists at the Nakatomi building, where his wife worked. Terrorists, particularly those who threaten his wife, are undoubtedly McClane's hot button, his external plot conflict.

Enter his cohesive internal character conflict—his wife is

currently on one of the planes circling overhead, a plane that is unable to land and rapidly running out of fuel because of the terrorist attack paralyzing the airport. Not only have these terrorists hit John's hot button, they've made it very personal, and there's no way he can sit back and consider this not his problem. If McClane's wife's plane runs out of fuel, they'll plummet to their deaths. The problem with landing is that the terrorists still have control of the airport, and they've closed down all the runways except the one they need for their own getaway. There are no lighted landing strips, so any landing is dangerous because it'll be done blindly. Without a choice, the pilot in his wife's plane announces to the tower he's making an emergency landing, and, of course, McClane hears it. If he doesn't act this instant, his wife will die and the terrorists will escape. The cone has closed to the point that he has almost no room to maneuver. The suspense is nearly more than the viewer can bear (and he loves it!). All of McClane's goals and motivations (which are so cohesive, we can't talk about internal and external conflicts for this character without including them) come down to stopping the terrorists, and this action, in turn, provides his wife's plane with the lighted strip needed to land. In this example, you can really see the differences between internal and external conflicts, but you see how they relate, connect, and collide.

Let's go over the sometimes-subtle distinction between character (internal) and plot (external) conflicts with some examples from best-selling books.

In all of the *Harry Potter* books, young wizard Harry constantly battles his internal conflict. His parents are dead and he's been forced to live with his detestable and magic-hating aunt, uncle, and cousin. That's a simplification, of course, of a complex situation. The external plot conflict is Harry coming to terms with his inadvertent relationship to Voldemort, who killed his parents, and how his contact with this evil person affects him inside and out. The external plot conflict is evident in every book. You see how the internal and external conflicts differ—one's outside, one's inside—how they parallel, intersect, and collide, and how you can't really have one without the other.

In *Dances with Wolves*, Lieutenant John Dunbar nearly loses his life in the war, and his sense of purpose and self-worth wavers, although his sense of adventure and duty are intact. Feeling like he doesn't belong where he is, he ventures into dangerous Indian country, where he finds his purpose and his self-worth, and he comes to learn that he belongs to and loves the new culture he finds. These encompass his internal and external conflicts. Plot and character conflicts in this story center around the Indians he encounters, which both threaten him physically and heal his soul, showing him both the ugly and honorable sides of his fellow white men.

The reader can't understand why a character reacts to an external conflict until the path of her current internal conflicts is traced all the way back to the roots. External conflicts should provide a tense tug of war between dread for the worst happening and hope for the best to engage readers throughout the evolving story. These need to be highlighted in the back cover blurb paragraphs to produce excitement about reading the story.

Goals and Motivations

In *Creating Characters*, Dwight V. Swain talks about giving the main character drive, which basically entails devising something for her to care about; fitting her with suitable goals, always keeping in mind the direction you want her to go in; threatening that goal; and finally establishing reasons for her to continue fighting against the threat on the road to reaching her goal. Goals are what the character wants, needs, or desires above all else. Motivation is what gives her drive and purpose to achieve those goals. Goals must be urgent and/or monumental enough to motivate the character to go through hardship and self-sacrifice. But the surface inducement that most people will claim--wanting to do the right thing--isn't strong enough in a fictional story. Go deeper. Your character can't simply react to conflict--she must *act* in the face of it. What exactly does she stand to gain if she does something? What will she lose if she doesn't do it? Keep in mind that whatever the external conflict is in your story, it's not simply a container that holds your character, like a potted plant, until she can escape it somehow. The external conflict is the foundation of your story goal/theme, and it's through this "ground" that the roots of her internal conflicts and goals and motivations will branch out and bloom.

Focused on the goal, the character is pushed toward the external conflict by believable, emotional, and compelling motivations that won't let her quit before she reaches the goal. Because she cares deeply about the outcome, her anxiety is doubled. The intensity of her anxiety pressures her to make choices and changes, thereby creating worry and anticipation in the reader. Those are the very things you want to highlight in a powerful, succinct way in a back cover blurb.

In Susan Hill's classic ghost story, *The Woman in Black*, solicitor Arthur Kipps is sent by his firm, leaving his fiancée, to the small town of Crythin Gifford to settle the affairs of the late Alice Drablow. While at the funeral, he sees a woman dressed in black that the children silently watch. Over the next few days, while completely cut off from the mainland at high tide, Kipps goes over the deceased woman's papers at Eel Marsh House. During this time, Kipps discovers the truth about Drablow's sister, the child she bore out of wedlock and was forced to give up to her sister. An attempt to abscond with her son led to him drowning in marshes while his mother looked on helplessly. After her death, she returned to haunt Eel Marsh House and the town of Crythin Gifford. According to local legend, a sighting of the Woman in Black presages the death of a child. Kipps repeatedly sees the malevolent ghost and begins to fear for his fiancée and their future. His goals and motivations evolve constantly around this menacing situation he's found himself in.

Remember, goals and motivations are constantly evolving (*not* changing necessarily, but refining in depth, intensity, and scope) to fit character and plot conflicts. Your character's goals and motivations will certainly adapt throughout the course of a story, since she's modifying or reshaping her actions based on the course the conflicts are dictating.

Let's look, for instance, at Frodo Baggins's evolving goals

and motivations in *The Lord of the Rings*. From the beginning, his goal is to destroy the One Ring of power, passed reluctantly down to him by his Uncle Bilbo. He's fully aware of how the Ring will destroy everything he knows and loves if it falls back into its evil master's hands—this is his motivation for acting against the external conflict. Sauron is amassing an army to destroy Middle-earth, and the Ring is the weapon that will ensure his success. Frodo's goal—to get the Ring to Mount Doom so he can cast it into the fires where it was made and destroy it once and for all—remains firm throughout the plot. In the end, the evil of the Ring makes him seem to change his mind, but readers know that if the Ring hadn't ensnared and poisoned him so deeply, he would never have changed his altruistic course. Along the way, his goals become more focused. He begins his journey in the company of the Fellowship, but after a time he realizes the task belongs to him and he must carry the Ring to Mount Doom on his own, with the aid of his loyal friend Samwise Gamgee. When he becomes aware that he doesn't know how to get inside Sauron's lair (where Mount Doom resides), he accepts the help of the fickle creature Gollum, who's as obsessed with the Ring as Frodo is becoming—pointing toward the fear that Frodo may not finish his quest.

These are all expansions of Frodo's original goals. Same with his motivation: Frodo accepts the mission because of what's at stake—those he loves, Middle-earth, and, most especially, his beloved Shire. His love motivates him to make the choice to do what seems impossible. The depth and scope of his motivation sharpens when he meets his former companion's brother, Faramir, and again recognizes the oppressive weight of all that's at stake if he doesn't succeed. It changes again when he acknowledges that the irreversible damage done to Gollum stems from the evil hold of the Ring and that the Ring is changing him, as long as it's in his possession. It sharpens yet again when he sees the size of the army Sauron is amassing. And when his best friend seemingly betrays him. Again, all of these are offshoots from his original goal and motivation. You can also see that the beginning of the story resonates in the end. No, Frodo doesn't get a happily ever after (Sam gets that instead), yet his story resolution fits perfectly with what we've learned. It's logical, even though it's a twist on what the reader is led to believe is the best-case-scenario ending.

Characters succeed because they rise above their fears, and this requires goals and motivations that are cohesive with the character's personality and the particular skill set you've equipped her with for this task. Also keep in mind that if your conflicts go in a straight line, with no offshoots to complicate them and no failures when the hero makes an effort to solve her problems, your reader will grow bored with the story and less intrigued by the character. You'll rouse more emotion and interest if the intensity of conflicts continues to rise on a causal course. As a story progresses, you'll revisit each main character's internal and external conflicts, as well as the goals and motivations, in order to show the refined growth and development of characters. Just as characters do, goals and motivations change, since the conflicts characters face have an impact and change them in a variety of ways.

Now that we know what a back cover blurb needs to include, we can use a short form to provide the jumping-off point in crafting one of our own. If you start out with something very long--in excess of 450 words--don't worry about it right now. Use whatever you begin with to get down to 2-4 paragraph and about 300 words. This is the next section of our worksheet:

Basic Information: *Fill out as completely as possible, keeping in mind that you may not use all, much or any of this in your final blurb.*
Title of Book:
Genre(s):
Time Period(s):
Main Setting(s):

Basic Character and Plot Information: *Fill out as completely as possible for the major characters in your story (usually no more than two or three main and one villain).*

Main Character Role (specify hero, heroine, villain, etc.):

First and Last Name:

Age and Job:

Description of the character's personality/hobbies/physical appearance/traumas or hang-ups that factor into his or her story conflicts:

Internal Conflict (i.e., character crisis or what's in jeopardy or at stake):

External Conflict (i.e., plot crisis):

Goals and motivations (i.e., what and why character is compelled to act):

Once you've filled out the form above completely, you can inject your story specifics into this formula (note: you would fill this out for each major character):

Who _______________________________
(name of character)
wants to _______________________________
(goal to be achieved)
because _______________________________
(motivation for acting)
but who faces _______________________________
(conflict standing in the way).

Let's do this a little backwards and fill out the forms for *The Woman in Black* by Susan Hill.

Title of Book: *The Woman in Black*
Genre: Ghost story
Time Period: The story isn't specific, though it's presumed to be set during the 1860s (based on details in the story that convey the impression).
Main Setting: Crythin Gifford, a faraway English town in the windswept salt marshes beyond Nine Lives Causeway.

Main Character Role: Hero
First and Last Name: Arthur Kipps
Age: Presumably young, "up-and-coming".
Job: London solicitor
Short description of the character's personality/hobbies/physical appearance/traumas or hang-ups that factor into his or her story conflicts:

Internal Conflict (i.e., character crisis, or what's in jeopardy or at stake): The routine business trip he anticipated quickly takes a horrifying turn when he finds himself haunted by a series of mysterious sounds and images—a rocking chair in a deserted nursery, the eerie sound of a pony and trap, a child's scream in the fog, and, most terrifying of all, a ghostly woman dressed all in black.

External Conflict (i.e., plot crisis that sets the story in motion): A menacing spectre haunting a small English town connected to Eel Marsh House, which stands at the end of the causeway, wreathed in fog and mystery, hiding tragic secrets behind its sheltered windows.

Who (**Arthur Kipps**) name of character
wants (**to conclude what he anticipated would be a routine business trip in his goal of becoming an up-and-coming London solicitor but the job quickly takes a horrifying turn**) goal to be achieved
because (**he finds himself haunted by a series of mysterious sounds and images—a rocking chair in a deserted nursery, the eerie sound of a pony and trap, a child's scream in the fog, and, most terrifying of all, a ghostly woman dressed all in black**) motivation for acting
but who faces (**the menacing spectre haunting a small English town connected to Eel Marsh House, which stands at the end of the causeway, wreathed in fog and mystery, hiding tragic secrets behind its sheltered windows**) conflict standing in the way

Here's the final high-concept blurb and back cover blurb for this book (in the order each blurb should be presented for submissions, distribution and promotion):

A chilling tale about a menacing spectre haunting a small English town.

Arthur Kipps is an up-and-coming London solicitor who is sent to Crythin Gifford—a faraway town in the windswept salt marshes beyond Nine Lives Causeway—to attend the funeral and settle the affairs of a client, Mrs. Alice Drablow of Eel Marsh House. Mrs. Drablow's house stands at the end of the causeway, wreathed in fog and mystery, but Kipps is unaware of the tragic secrets that lie hidden behind its sheltered windows. The routine business trip he anticipated quickly takes a horrifying turn when he finds himself haunted by a series of mysterious sounds and images—a rocking chair in a deserted nursery, the eerie sound of a pony and trap, a child's scream in the fog, and, most terrifying of all, a ghostly woman dressed all in black.

You should have noticed that the formula elements aren't in the same order in the actual blurbs as they're listed on the fill-in-the-blanks form. While the arrangement could end up being in that order, it's rare that the elements will fall neatly into the formula, nor should it necessarily do so. If all blurbs were written exactly the same way, in a formulaic way, they would become boring and lack punch. Your story is original so your blurb needs to be original. The point of the formula is to give you a jumping-off point to honing something intriguing that has powerful impact.

In Chapter Three, we're going talk in-depth about the *should* and *shouldn'ts* in writing back cover blurbs, and there I'll have thirty-five tips to get you thinking about after your basic, original, first pass at the blurb is ready. I'll only say here to remember the axiom we fixed in our minds earlier in this book. If the blurb isn't effectively good, making you want to read the story inside the pages, it won't work. The goal is to get readers to read the book. So keep working on yours until you have that.

Practice Makes Perfect Session:

Try to fill in the form and formula we've talked about in this section on some of your favorite stories as I did with The Woman in Black.

Back Cover Blurb

Basic Story Information: *Fill out as completely as possible, keeping in mind that you may not use all, much or any of this in your final blurb.*
Title of Book:
Genre(s):
Time Period(s):
Main Setting(s):

Basic Character and Plot Information: *Fill out as completely as possible for the major characters in your story (usually no more than two or three main and one villain).*
Main Character Role (specify hero, heroine, villain, etc.):
First and Last Name:
Age and Job:
Description of the character's personality/hobbies/physical appearance/traumas or hang-ups that factor into his or her story conflicts:
Internal Conflict (i.e., character crisis or what's in jeopardy or at stake):
External Conflict (i.e., plot crisis):
Goals and motivations (i.e., what and why character is compelled to act):

Once you've filled out the form above completely, you can inject your story specifics into this formula (note: fill out one for each major character):

Who ___________________________________
(name of character)
wants to ___________________________
(goal to be achieved)
because ___________________________
(motivation for acting)
but who faces ___________________________
(conflict standing in the way).

Craft Your Own Back Cover Blurb

Using the blurb form and formula we've talked about in today's lesson, try to craft a back cover blurb for your own story. Don't worry if your first few passes aren't brilliant and mostly don't worry too much about word count now. Later, we're going to talk about whittling your blurb down to 150, 100 and 75 words. For now, just keep honing it.

Part 3: Series Blurbs

We're making progress! We've already talked about two of the three important blurbs authors have to master writing. Now we're going to talk about seriously under-utilized series blurbs. Some of the same concepts we've covered thus far apply here: At its crux, a series blurb strives to be a concise, breathtaking summary of your entire *series* that includes the major internal and external conflicts and the goals and motivations of the main character(s), perhaps as a group or some other concept (the driving force of the story). A series blurb will be a generalized sentence or paragraph that accurately covers, reflects and describes every single book in the series.

Again, as we've said before, publishers and authors simply don't utilize series blurbs the way they should. Ninety percent of the series you find on Amazon or other distributors and even author and publisher websites have no series blurb connecting all the books--the very information that would tell readers not only why they should read *one* but *all* of them. A series blurb can make or break the sale of an entire set of books to a publisher when submitting as well as to potential readers trying to decide whether to fork over oodles of money to purchase a collection of interconnected stories. Many publishers and certainly readers buy the first book in the series *and every single one after it* based on a sizzling series blurb that convinces them they absolutely have to read not only the first book but all of them in that set!

Writing a series is something that is near and dear to my heart. I've even written two guides to series writing with my books *Writing the Standalone Series* and *Writing the Overarching Series.* With sixteen under my belt or in the works, ranging from three to twelve (currently) books each, writing a standalone story is unusual for me. One book can spawn many more because my characters become so real, I sometimes feel like the secondaries are tugging on my sleeve while I'm immersed in the world they live in, demanding to know when I'm going to write their stories. Series are in hot demand! Ask anyone what the most popular books have been in the last twenty years, and inevitably the answers will lead to books within a series: Game of Thrones, Harry Potter, Twilight, Stephanie Plum, Captain Underpants, Robert Langdon, Star Wars, and basically anything series (okay, and non-series as well) by Nora Roberts. Authors are writing series, publishers are publishing them, and readers are buying them by the truckloads.

Let's first establish that the point of a series is that readers who follow it from one book to the next will get a richer, more complex, and emotional experience than those who only read a single book in the series. Those readers will understand the subtle nuances that one-time browsers won't pick up on. For that reason, the author has to make enough vital connections from one book to the next in their series or readers will lose the purpose in reading that series at all. Therefore, the first step to writing a series blurb is to figure out what ties the books together. This will help us figure out what the "who" aspect is for our series blurb form.

Types of Series Ties

If each book in a series doesn't somehow tie together or have a touchstone that helps the reader figure out how they're connected, you could hardly call these books a series. I like how Mary Jean Kelso, author of the romantic historical Homesteader Series, puts it: "There needs to always be a firm stake to tie the story to. You can wander off into other places and introduce new characters but, in some way, the main element will always be in the back of the reader's mind. For instance, even though my characters go to other places and get involved in different scenarios, they always come back to the homestead. It is that drive to return 'home' that seems to hold the series together." When you're considering what the touchstone of your series is, ask yourself what "home" you'll be returning to in each story.

For the purpose of this section, we'll go over the four distinct types of series ties, but always keep in mind that authors frequently combine one or more of these in a single series. There are so many different combinations you can use to make your series stand out as unique in a sea of competition.

Recurring Character

In a recurring character series, a single character (sometimes called a continuity, or continuing, character) is the touchstone of the series and comes back in each story. Sometimes a recurring character story actually has two characters that make appearances in each book and are both the main characters of the series. For instance, Tommy and Tuppence Beresford are a sleuthing duo created by Agatha Christie. For the most part, both make appearances in every book, and the stories shift between their individual points of view.

The reader follows the recurring character from one journey—something that must be personal and emotional and provide growth for the character—to the next. Almost always in a series of this type, there's a large cast of secondary characters and these are brought forward or dropped back, depending on the particular book. Ongoing casts of this type keep the recurring character fresh for the reader. This type of series is very popular in mystery/suspense stories, as well in the fantasy, science fiction, and paranormal genres.

For example, Agatha Christie had her popular Hercule Poirot and Jane Marple series. Bella Swan was the primary character in Stephenie Meyer's Twilight Saga. James Bond chases espionage and action and adventure everywhere he goes, from one book to another. Ben Holiday was the main character in Terry Brooks' unforgettable Magic Kingdom For Sale – Sold! Series, set in the magical kingdom of Landover. Brooks did a spin-off of the five-book series in 2009 with the High Lord of Landover's daughter, Mistaya, which takes place five years after the events in *Witch's Brew*. Dan Brown has sent his recurring character, Robert Langdon, through fast-paced treasure hunts in several Robert Langdon novels. Diana Gabaldon's mega popular Outlander Series defies categorization but currently includes many huge novels that center around a time-traveling nurse in the 20th-century and her 18th-century Scottish husband. The Lord John Series was a branch off of the original series, including a secondary character that was part of the main series.

Central Group of Characters

The central group of characters type of series has a core set of characters with either a loose or specific connection that ties them together, and one or two of these are featured in each subsequent book. Generally, the first book in the series sets up the central characters and their ties to one another. These stories are usually standalone books that have roots in the first story. Rowena Cherry illuminates, "Instead of everyone having one adventure all at the same time, they take turns." Popular groups for this type are family/relatives, friends, co-workers, or members of an organization. Generally, romance, women's fiction, paranormal, science fiction, and fantasy are popular candidates for this type of series.

Justine Davis' Redstone, Incorporated was romantic suspense that featured a group of people employed by Redstone, Incorporated. Kate Jacobs' The Friday Night Knitting Club Series, as you would expect, focused on a group of knitters. Debbie Macomber had something similar in her Blossom Street Series. Terry Brooks' long-running fantasy series, Shannara, includes members of the Ohmsford clan throughout numerous generations (and series off-shoots). Terry also has another series, Word and the Void, in which he portrays an urban, post-apocalyptic world where an invisible war is waged in contemporary America and all over the world while Knights of the Word battle the Void's demons. In a seriously cool move, Terry combined his Shannara and Word and the Void series' in his Genesis of Shannara Series.

In nearly all series with a core group, all the characters are introduced in the first book in smaller and larger degrees and will continue to make cameos throughout the rest of the books in the series. You, the author, will need to connect these characters in a way that you can bring them back together naturally in later book. Additionally, in real life we tend to hang around with people who like us, but in fiction, stories must have a variety of contrasting characters—some who are likable, and others who aren't. It's your job as a series author to create a believable connection between these very different characters.

Premise/Plot Series

While characters are nearly always the most important part of any story, many series use a premise or plot as the basic theme that connects each of the books. This could cover just about anything: a shared theme, object, or even timeline. We're going to talk more about arcs--which are in large part about premise and plot--later in this section. A premise-/plot-based series is one you almost always see in action/adventures, suspense and thriller, inspirational, and paranormal, horror, science fiction, and fantasy genres.

Inspirational romantic suspense author Hannah Alexander's Hideaway Series focuses on medical mysteries. The long-running Rogue Angel Series, written by many authors, features archaeologist and heir to Joan of Arc's mystic sword, Annja Creed.

In each novel, an adventure based on history, mythology, or heavy fantasy has Annja looking for lost cities, mysterious codes, and puzzles. Christy Poff writes a torrid romance series called Internet Bonds in which all the stories have a connection to the internet. In my Family Heirloom Series, each story passes down a nugget (or heirloom) of faith, including accepting God's will (book 1), building love (book 2), healing (book 3), forgiving (book 4), learning trust (book 5), and persevering in adversity (book 6).

The premise of each of Tom Clancy's Net Force Series is a special division of the FBI that is set up to combat internet crime. Linda Varner Palmer's Silhouette romance series, Home for the Holidays, revolves around the holidays. In Janet Elaine Smith's Women of the Week Series, the common thread is that each of the main women of the books are named for the day of the week they were born (the first one is *Monday Knight*) and their entire lives revolve around the line for their day from the old poem, "Monday's child is fair of face..." Carl Brookins crime series, Sailing, is about a couple who sail in and out of venues of murderous trouble.

Charlotte Boyett-Compo is best known for her signature Reaper creations. "They appear in each and every one of my series. Hybrid were/vamp shapeshifters, they have dark hair, amber eyes, wear all black, and are very strong Alpha males with tragic pasts. Readers love that conception. The first Reaper came out in 1998 in *BloodWind* and that book has sold more than any of my other eighty novels. It is being turned into a screenplay as well. The Reapers have earned me many fans over the years and the latest series, The Western Wind Series, has been gaining me new readers consistently for the last several years. I have readers tell me they love the Reapers."

In the first four books in Jane Toombs' Dangerous Darkness Series, the heroes were once in a Special Ops group together, but the paranormal element in each book is different. In the last four books in the series, all the heroines and the one hero are in the same witch family and what each faces is a different paranormal element. Incidentally, this would also make this series a Central Group of Characters type.

Setting Series

The setting series is almost as popular as the character series, although, of course, if you don't have wonderful characters to fill these settings, your stories won't be as magical. With setting serving as the tie-in for each book in the series, you're free to create a colorful world that your readers will enjoy visiting time and time again. Setting series can have characters that change, but the place is always the same or a recurring character will return to the series setting. For instance, Harry Potter goes to Hogwarts in each book in the series. Nearly every genre of series uses this kind of touchstone.

In my contemporary romance Cowboy Fever Series, I created the fictional place of Fever, Texas, where all the neighboring ranches in the series are set and visited during the course of the series. My police procedural Falcon's Bend Series, written with Chris Spindler, is set in our fictional town of Falcon's Bend, and my paranormal/horror romances set in the magical horror children's story place of Woodcutter's Grim is a setting readers enjoy returning to with each new installment in the series. I've also created a spooky little town called Bloodmoon Cove for my Bloodmoon Cove Spirits Series. Additionally, I created the small town of Peaceful, Wisconsin for my Family Heirlooms Series, but it carried over into the spin-off series, the Friendship Heirlooms Series, and even in two non-series books, Home and Destiny which are part of my Peaceful Pilgrim story set.

Mystery author Marilyn Meredith's Deputy Tempe Crabtree Series is set in a small mountain community near an Indian reservation. In most of these books, an Indian legend or mystical aspect is a major component. There is also quite a bit of conflict going on with Tempe and her preacher husband when she dabbles in the supernatural.

In Vijaya Schartz's sci-fi/fantasy romance series Chronicles of Kassouk, a human science spaceship named Noah's Ark crash-lands on an unknown frozen planet renamed New Earth. The survivors, while fighting the elements, eventually lose their technology, but the animals are released and many species survive. Civilization starts from scratch on a small scale. When the series picks up again several centuries later, they have achieved a thriving medieval civilization, until space-faring races intervene. Sometimes the series stories are many years apart. The society struggles, grows, and matures from crisis to crisis and learns from various outside influences, not all beneficial.

Janet Elaine Smith's cozy mystery series, Patrick and Grace Mysteries, has odd number books set in New York City, where Patrick and Grace live. The even number books travel all over the country. The author hears from readers all the time, asking her, "When are Patrick and Grace coming to my town?"

What ties your series together is extremely important, since it's what will bring readers back for more. While there will probably always be some overlap in your ties, being able to define your series ties will help you establish the pattern from one book to the next, making your tie(s) strong throughout each story in the series. The series ties will also, as we said, help us figure out what the "who" aspect is of our series when filling out the next section of the High-Concept, Back Cover, and Series Blurb Worksheet-- coming soon.

Finding the Focus of a Series

Though I believe planning is crucial to the success of a series, I've discovered in my experience that there are few set-in-stone rules. Should each story in a series have an overall series arc that runs through each book and ties up only in the final one? Or is it adequate if each story has a loose connection to the others and each individual book has its own story arc that ties up fairly neatly at the end? For every dozen books you can find that do one or more of these things, you can find just as many that don't. Although we're going to try to answer these questions, be aware that there are few rules for this process except the ones you make for yourself—or the ones your publisher requires you to abide by.

Story Arcs

In its simplest form, the story arc is an extended or continued storyline. That's fairly easy to grasp, right? But when it comes to what this definition actually entails and how it serves its purpose in the course of a story...well, that's where things get murkier. In a story, an arc is supposed to move the character or situation from one place to another. Essentially, we're talking about change here--the quest, the causality of narrative, domino-effect transformations. In a story, this follows a pattern that can be described as ordinary life in balance: The character is brought to a low point and the structures he or she has depended on are removed. Therefore the character is motivated and/or forced to find new strength or situations without these structures, and he faces his demons and triumphs. Resolution ensues, restoring balance. All this happens in every story, between the front and back cover. Without out, there can be no reader satisfaction. The story arc is packed into one book. In a series story, a story arc is short-term because it will be neatly tied-up in a single book within the series. That might sound strange, but this will make more sense when you realize that the series arc is the long-term thread running its course through *every book* until the series concludes.

Series Arcs

Every story has to have a story arc and we've gotten a basic understanding of what this entails. Most series will have an overall *series* arc along with the individual story arcs specific to a single book. A series arc is the overarching plot that is divided between several interconnected stories.

An overall series arc is introduced in the first book in the series, is alluded to in some way in every single subsequent book, but is only fully resolved in the final book in the series. The series arc is usually separate from the individual story arcs, but both are crucial and must fit together seamlessly. The individual story arcs are, as we've shown in the last section, short-term. They're introduced, developed, and concluded in each individual book. The series arcs are long-term and are introduced in the first book, developed over the course of the middle series books, and resolved in the final book in the series. As an example, in *Harry Potter and the Chamber of Secrets*, the story arc is the chamber of secrets plotline. The overall series arc, in the most simplified terms, is good (Harry) overcomes evil (Voldemort)—and that's true for every book in that series. The series arc runs beneath the individual story arcs in each book.

There is an exception to every rule, and that's the case here: Certain types of series don't really need series arcs because they're open-ended. No clear end is in sight, and therefore there is less need for a tightly delineated series arc that must resolve in the final book. In an open-ended series (such as some sleuth mysteries with a single recurring character—i.e., Hercule Poirot and the like), each book in the series is a standalone. There's little need to come up with a series arc since the author isn't planning to have a plot thread running through the entire series that will conclude in the final story. Though the "Hercule Poirot Series" eventually did end, a series arc didn't run through each of the stories. Even Poirot's final case was a standalone (though this case connected to details of the very first mystery he solved). In an open-ended series with an infinite number of books, the resolution the author has promised and the reader expects won't come in a final series book but at the end of *each book* in the series. Those resolutions are the ones that fans are looking for and must be given in order to feel satisfied. In any case, keep this disclaimer in mind if you're writing an open-ended series: While you're not required to have a series arc in this one instance, it wouldn't hurt to have one. You can include one even in an open-ended series. If you choose not to, you'll work with story arcs for each standalone book in your series. In a series book with a clearly-defined series arc, each book in the series will contain scenes and subplots that advance the series arc. These are interspersed with individual story arcs, and, most of the time, the writer switches back and forth between series and story arcs throughout the course of each. In the final book in the series,

series and story arcs will merge in the way you've lead your readers to expect. All of this is essential to gaining reader favor and satisfaction.

The easiest way to discover your overall series arc is to know the type of series tie that will connect all the books. Your series tie almost always indicates what your series arc should be. While in suspenseful books, this might be earth-shattering in the final book in the series, that's not necessary for all series. Sometimes the resolution of the series arc is subtle and joyfully tearful. An emotionally satisfying final scene will be exactly what readers are looking for.

Establishing the basics for each book in the series can give you the author insight for further-reaching possibilities as you write each new book in untold ways, but can also give you an edge when trying to sell the series. The first step in figuring out where you're going with a series is to blurb the series. The series blurb should tell readers how all the books in that series are connected. If the series blurb is done well enough, those sentences will accurately reflect what every book in the series is about in a concise, intriguing summary. Remember, you're not focusing on individual stories at this point—you're looking at the series as a whole, attempting to give readers the gist of what the *series* is about. Having a series blurb that includes the series arc and is paired with every single book in the series (everywhere without exception!) frees the author to concentrate on the *story arc* each individual book in the series covers with her back cover blurbs.

Be aware that, if you have a central group of characters, you generally *won't* name each main character specifically in the series blurb, though you might end up doing that. Instead, you'll usually sum up the overall premise of the series and how it affects the group as a whole. At this stage, it's fine to have something as simple as "Cast of Characters will find soul mates," or "College professor follows the trail to an ancient artifact that could save the world or destroy it". You'll build on this jumping-off point as we go along, fleshing it out as much as possible.

As for how long it should be, most series blurbs range from

one to four sentences, but keep in mind that certain genres (or series) may need longer ones--possibly even longer than four sentences. As we said before, genre can play a part in the size of your series blurb. Science fiction, fantasy, and historical books in a series may well require longer series blurbs, possibly in excess of four paragraphs. That's because the series blurb has to make sense of whole worlds, cultures and philosophies, which, in many cases may seem vastly different from those a modern reader is used to. If readers don't understand the premise of your series in the blurb, they may not bother try reading the first book.

Now that we know what a series blurb needs to include, we can use a short form to provide the jumping-off point in crafting one of our own. This is the next section of the High-Concept, Back Cover, and Series Blurb Worksheet:

Basic Series Information: Fill *out as completely as possible, keeping in mind that you may not use all, much or any of this in your final blurb.*
Series Title:
Genre(s):
[Who] Series Tie(s):
    Recurring or Cast of Characters Series
    Premise/Plot Series
    Setting Series

Basic Series Arcs:
[What] Conflict or crisis that sets the series in motion:
[Why] What's the worst case resolution scenario to the crisis situation?

We're going to use a modified variation of our "formula" for the series blurb:

Who ______________________
(Series Tie)
What ______________________
(Conflict or Crisis)

Why ______________________
(Worst Case Resolution Scenario)

Note that resolutions are not usually needed in the series blurb, since you don't want to defuse the intrigue or tension, but sometimes a resolution will work well in the overall series blurb. Play with it to see all the alternatives.

Let's fill out the form and formula, this time with The Expanse Series. The books don't technically have a series blurb-- not a definitive one anyway--the way the TV series does, but I've put together a slightly hybridized version below.

Series Title: The Expanse
Genre(s): Science Fiction
[Who] Series Tie(s): Premise/Plot Series (though it could fit in other categories as well), in this case a futuristic galaxy that humans have developed and colonized. I.e.: Hundreds of years in the future, humans have colonized the solar system.

Series Arcs:
[What] Conflict or Crisis that Sets the Series in Motion: The U.N. controls Earth. Mars is an independent military power. The planets rely on the resources of the Asteroid Belt, where air and water are more precious than gold. For decades, tensions have been rising between these three places.
[Why] What's the worst case resolution scenario to the crisis situation? A police detective in the asteroid belt, the first officer of an interplanetary ice freighter and an earth-bound United Nations executive slowly discover a vast conspiracy that threatens the Earth's rebellious colony on the asteroid belt. Earth, Mars and the Belt are now on the brink of war. And all it will take is a single spark.

We're going to use a slightly modified variation of our blurb "formula":

Who (**Hundreds of years in the future, humans have**

colonized the solar system. The U.N. controls Earth. Mars is an independent military power. The planets rely on the resources of the Asteroid Belt, where air and water are more precious than gold. For decades, tensions have been rising between these three places.) Series Tie

What (**A police detective in the asteroid belt, the first officer of an interplanetary ice freighter and an earth-bound United Nations executive slowly discover a vast conspiracy that threatens the Earth's rebellious colony on the asteroid belt.**) Conflict or Crisis

Why (**Earth, Mars and the Belt are now on the brink of war. And all it will take is a single spark.**) Worst Case Resolution Scenario

Here's the blurb for The Expanse Series:

Hundreds of years in the future, humans have colonized the solar system. The U.N. controls Earth. Mars is an independent military power. The planets rely on the resources of the Asteroid Belt, where air and water are more precious than gold. For decades, tensions have been rising between these three places. A police detective in the asteroid belt, the first officer of an interplanetary ice freighter and an earth-bound United Nations executive slowly discover a vast conspiracy that threatens the Earth's rebellious colony on the asteroid belt. Earth, Mars and the Belt are now on the brink of war. And all it will take is a single spark.

Practice Makes Perfect Session:

Try to fill in the form and formula we've talked about in this section on some of your favorite series as I did with The Expanse Series.

Series Blurb

Basic Series Information: *Fill out as completely as possible, keeping in mind that you may not use all, much or any of this in your final blurb.*
Series Title:
Genre(s):
[Who] Series Tie(s):
  Recurring or Cast of Characters Series
  Premise/Plot Series
  Setting Series

Basic Series Arcs:
[What] Conflict or crisis that sets the series in motion:
[Why] What's the worst case resolution scenario to the crisis situation?

Once you've filled out the form above completely, you can inject your series specifics into this formula:

Who ________________________
(Series Tie)
What _______________________
(Conflict or Crisis)
Why _______________________
(Worst Case Resolution Scenario)

Craft Your Own Series Blurb

Using the blurb form and formula we've talked about in this section, try to craft a series blurb for your own series. Don't worry if your first few passes aren't brilliant and mostly don't worry at all about word count now. In Chapter Four, we're going to talk about whittling your blurb down to 150, 100 and 75 words. For now, just keep honing it.

Blurb Order

There is an order in which finished blurbs should be

presented either in or on books, for distribution and marketing. When utilizing your blurbs (and they should be used together whenever possible), they should be listed in this order: 1) Series blurb, 2) high-concept blurb, and 3) back cover blurb. In almost every case, the series includes the generalized concept of what every single book in the series is about so it needs to come first. Plus, because the series blurb talks about the series arcs and you can include all those there, you're free to use the story blurbs to focus entirely on the individual stories and their particular story arcs. The high-concept blurb is a lure--it's where you drop your line in the reader's water. It should be so compelling it can't be ignored. Once you've lured readers in, the back cover blurb follows--and that must end on a high note, a hook that snags reader interest firmly.

But let's go it one further. Authors and publishers need to use and utilize the separate parts of every blurb, including series, high-concept, and back cover blurb together always, everywhere, every single time!

***

When to write blurbs depends on the author but writing them as soon as possible will benefit you, your story/series in crazy-good ways. While size shouldn't be a factor in writing effectively good blurbs, unfortunately it is these days. There are maximums so strongly encouraged they've become the norm. However, armed with the knowledge of what we're ideally shooting for in terms of length, we moved into the exciting process of how to write all three kinds of blurbs with a simple worksheet (you'll find the blank version of it in Appendix C). An effectively good blurb "package" for a single title has a high-concept and a back cover blurb, presented in that order. For a series book, those two are paired with the series blurb, which is listed first. They should always be used together--the individual pieces of a whole. In the next chapter, we're going to talk about three specialized types of blurbs, for nonfiction titles, anthologies or collections, and children's books.

CHAPTER TWO
Specialized Blurb Writing

"The trick with writing a great blurb is to give away enough of what's inside the book without giving any plot spoilers or going so in-depth the reader doesn't want to read on. You want to catch the reader's attention, give them the content, and then give them a reason to care. What you leave out is as important as what you put in--the point is to entice, not to inform." ~Ian Chandler from 3 Steps to Writing a Back Cover Blurb That Sells

Not all types of blurbs are the same. Several are so specialized that I felt a separate chapter was needed to adequately cover them. How do you write a blurb for something that's really about setting yourself up as some kind of expert in something--which is what most nonfiction books attempt to do? How do you write a blurb for something that has three to thirty stories and long blurbs for all of them definitely aren't going to fit on the back cover? What about children's books, where two creative talents (an author and an illustrator) deserve equal billing? Let's discuss each of these and potential ways to avoid the pitfalls of writing these kinds of blurbs.

NONFICTION BLURBS

One of the most notable ways authors and publishers use to handle nonfiction blurbs is to stuff them full of puffed-up claims (either written by the publisher or the author, which is the height of narcissism, in my opinion). While including reviews for professionals, authors or others in the field that's being covered in the book are great, they aren't and shouldn't be part of the summary of what the book is about because, even if these are from credible sources, what does it tell the reader about the book or why they should read it?

Additionally, the author is not the focus of a blurb. Credentials or experience that allows the author to handle this particular subject could be vital to include and, while most experts do recommend putting information about that into the back cover blurb, again, this must be *separate from the book summary*. Both reviews and credentials are promotional considerations. They have nothing to do with what the book is actually about, so those should be included separately, not as part of the summary.

In her article *Compelling Back Cover Copy: Not Too Little and Not too Much*, Jane Friedman recommends asking yourself two questions: 1) Why and how will the reader benefit from the book and 2) how the book addresses the problems and how they can be overcome or managed successfully. The book's content isn't as important as how it can help, inform or entertain the reader. Readers should be the focus--the audience. The suggested format for writing nonfiction back cover blurbs is:

Step 1: High-concept blurb--the key selling point of the book--that's usually written in the form of a question.

Step 2: A 100-200 word summary that expands on step one and adequately demonstrates the true value of the book.

Step 3: A bullet list of features or benefits that readers will be provided in reading the book. The recommended number of bullet points should be no less than three and generally no more than five. Strangely, an odd number has been shown by marketing experts to be most effective amount of bullet points. Also note that all bullets need to have the same style, such as "Feed, Train, Develop" or "Feeding, Training, Developing" when presenting.

Step 4: A final sentence that includes a promise to the reader and closes the topic with a hook.

Because I believe example is the best teacher, here are some nonfiction blurbs I've revised. I'll include the original blurb followed by my revision (and explanation for the changes) of it:

Cool Off The Hot Seat! Tips for 'Acing' Your Job Interview
by Rebecca Rothman McCoy
Self-Help/How-To

Original blurb:

You're sitting across the desk from an interviewer and the butterflies in your stomach feel like hummingbirds. Your palms are sweating, your heart is racing. You want this job. You need this job! You wonder if the interviewer notices your discomfort. And what can you say to set you apart from all the others?

Yes, you're certainly in the hot seat now, but careful preparation can help you stay cool, calm, and collected. Is there some hidden magical secret which will help you to land this job? Not really, but if you are unsure of what to say or do and don't know the tricks that can set you apart from your competition, then this book is for you!

Written by a staffing industry professional with more than twelve years of interviewing experience, *Cool Off the Hot Seat!* answers all your questions about job interviewing, from obtaining the interview to the follow-up afterwards. Here are just a few topics you will read about:
* Tips on how to research companies you are interested in
* Making a great first impression
* Appropriate clothing and accessories
* Answers for those tough questions
* What the interviewer is looking for
* The most effective ways to do assertive follow-ups
* Working with recruiters
In addition, there is a special bonus section on how to do media interviews like a pro!

This guerrilla guide to interviewing gives you all of the substance you need, with none of the fluff you don't. You won't be bored with theory or have to wade through obscure statistics in this book. Everything is designed to get you up and running as fast as possible, while covering all the important areas you'll need for a successful job interview. You can read the book start to finish, or use it as a reference book, flipping to the chapter dealing with your particular situation. Either way, you're bound to find many helpful hints that you can use immediately to boost your interviewing confidence and presence!

This was really well done, needing just a little bit more refinement. What I liked about the first paragraph was the indication of being right there in the hot seat, but I thought it could be even more "hot". I think it makes a promise that this book can help someone be rid of such a horrible chain-reaction in an interview altogether.

Your interviewer is staring you down from across his desk and the butterflies in your stomach are more active than Hitchcock's Birds. Your palms are sweating, your heart is racing, and the worst-case scenario is all you can envision in your future. You want this job. You need this job. You have to have it...! Has he noticed my discomfort? you wonder as you stutter when asked what sets you apart from all the others that have been interviewed before you.

No doubt about it. You're firmly in the hot seat. But careful preparation can help you stay cool, calm, and collected. If you've ever wondered if there was some hidden magical secret that would help you land the job of your dreams, the bad news is, no, not really. But if you're unsure of what to say or do during a job interview and don't know any tricks to set you apart from your competition, then this book is for you!

Written by a staffing industry professional with more than twelve years of interviewing experience, *Cool Off the*

Hot Seat! answers all your questions about job interviewing from obtaining the interview to the follow-up afterwards. Here are just a few topics you'll read about:
* Tips on how to research companies you're interested in
* Making a great first impression
* Appropriate clothing and accessories
* Answers for the toughest questions
* What an interviewer is looking for
* The most effective ways to do assertive follow-ups
* Working with recruiters
* Handling media interviews like a pro

This guerrilla guide to interviewing technique has substance without fluff, theory or obscure statistics to wade through. The layout of the book is designed to get you up and running as fast as possible while covering all the important areas you'll need to know in order to nail a successful job interview with all the poise and confidence you need and none of the butterflies!

Laugh Out Louds For Moms
by Robin Helene Vogel
Humor

Original blurb:

LAUGH-OUT-LOUDS FOR MOMS, a funny, lyrical, wondrously-illustrated book dedicated to mothers everywhere, is guaranteed to make you laugh out loud as you read familiar little poems and brief anecdotes about the pitfalls, pratfalls, joys and horror stories of mothering. From pregnancy cravings to projectile vomiting to post-birth, permanent weight gain to pediatrician's visits to despising your kid's choice of mate, this book will make you realize that you're not alone in the insane asylum that is motherhood, and there are others who are sitting in playpens in fetal positions, sucking their thumbs, just as you are!

Filled with whimsical illustrations by Caroline Christian, LAUGH-OUT-LOUDS FOR MOMS will lead mothers, new or old, on a familiar journey that will stir up memories ad laughter for many years to come.

I took the "you" point-of-view out of this to remove the author interjection style with my revision:

Dedicated to mothers everywhere, readers will laugh out loud as they read familiar little poems and brief anecdotes about the pitfalls, pratfalls, joys and horror stories associated with being a mother. Pregnancy cravings, projectile vomiting, post-birth and permanent weight gain, pediatrician's visits, despising your kid's choice of mate--all the predicaments are included to amusingly affirm to readers they're not alone in the insane asylum motherhood can so often be. Rest assured that others are also sitting in playpens in fetal positions sucking their thumbs!

Five Key Skills
by Alan Strickland
Self-Help

Original blurb:

The human race is made up of all sorts of people. Some are naturally outgoing and seem to get on well with everyone they meet. Others are quieter, keep themself to themselves and are fairly passive in their social interactions.

A few lucky individuals can speak confidently to a hall full of people or in a one to one discussion. Others have trouble in stringing a few words together in a conversation and their worst nightmare would be to stand up and address a large gathering.

Some people seem to be really organised. Their lives run like clockwork, they finish everything they embark on, they decide what they want to do then just do it. The rest of us suffer from occasional bouts of indecision, lack of motivation, inability to set priorities and a tendency to start a new task before completing the first.

This book explains in easily understandable and practical terms, how you can improve five key personal skills and lead a more fulfilled and balanced life.

That first paragraph was a killer--literally. The rest of the paragraphs were organized in a way that wasn't logical. I fixed the problems in this way:

Are you someone who has trouble stringing together a few words in nearly every conversation and your idea of an absolute nightmare is standing in the front of a room and addressing a large gathering? Do you suffer from occasional or frequent bouts of indecision, lack of motivation, the inability to set priorities and a tendency to start new tasks before completing others?

Few are lucky enough to be able to speak easily and confidently, taking command of a hall full of people in various degrees of alertness, or simply finessing a one-on-one discussion into a memorably lively chat. The organized few run their lives like clockwork, finishing everything they embark on. When they decide what they do, they do it and beautiful memories are made.

In easily understandable and practical terms, this book endeavors to improve five key personal skills that may lead to a more fulfilled and balanced life for anyone who suffers from common maladies like social awkwardness and disorganization.

ANTHOLOGY BLURBS

Anthologies or collections of stories, whether by the same author or a wide variety of authors usually follow a theme, and that theme is the key to writing the blurbs since you can't fit more than a handful of actual book blurbs onto a back cover. Focus the first paragraph on the theme without falling into author or publisher conceit.

For the second section of an anthology blurb, take three or four of the strongest stories and include a one-sentence "high-concept" blurb for each one, since those stories might do a more compelling job of selling the collection than even an overall blurb of theme may. Readers want to know what they're going to get in advance.

The final sentence(s) in the anthology blurb may include the purpose of the collection (maybe it's a writer's group anthology or a selection of genre-specific stories that a high-profile author or editor is compiling). It should also include a hook. It's here in the last paragraph that I've noticed that most authors/publishers of anthologies fall into self-praise or overblown promises with words like ("exciting", "suspenseful", etc.). Actual reviews given by others or author biographies should be included separate from the blurb summary.

Here are some revisions of I've done of anthology blurbs:

Four in the Park - Four One Act Plays
by S. B. Sturdevant
Play Collection

Original blurb:

Mourning the Marigolds is the story of eccentric, sixty-ish Bessie Levinson, as she sits on a park bench in Russell Square Park in London and tells her story to Charlie Hampton, a stranger.

It is also about Father Frank McAllister, an Irish priest, also in his sixties, who happens to be strolling through the same park with his niece, Julie. As they rest a moment on another bench, he tells his very similar story.

Through several Memory Scenes, we see Frank's and Bessie's love affair as it unfolds and then ends. We are witness to the bitter good-bye she faced when leaving her

Jewish home in New York and defying her strict and domineering father. We are also witness to the struggle Frank must go through in order to come to his final conclusion. We become part of the pain that accompanies their lost love, and witness the difficult choices that come with true devotion. And finally, we learn of the broken hearts that have been with them both for the past forty years.

On this particular, chilly autumn afternoon, however, with Bessie's beloved Marigolds about to gasp their last - there is a chance meeting of the two old lovers...

A DAY in the LIFE of ELEANOR DUNCAN: Eleanor Duncan is a 72 year old, homeless woman living on a park bench in Central Park. She believes her bench to be her "home", which is wonderfully located so that she can overlook the skaters and the lovers. She has been on the streets for 24 years and wouldn't have it any other way.
On this Christmas Eve, Eleanor welcomes a string of visitors - from Joey, a 10- year-old boy, to her elderly sister Ruby and a few interesting guest in between. She regales them all with stories from her past, which reveal much insight into the character of Eleanor Duncan. As she enjoys her Christmas Eve dinner, a gift from her sister, she is surprised by her final visitor of the day - the last visitor of her life.

WEDNESDAY is a short one-act about an aging woman who chances to meet her long-time housekeeper in the park after thirty years. The time has been kind to one and not so kind to the other, and as the two elderly woman sit in the chill of a late November afternoon they discover that their differences are not nearly as great as they once thought.

THURSDAY tells about two sisters in their seventies - one with Alzheimer's, the other her caregiver. It is about coping and unconditional love.

These stories sound charming and nostalgic. I did a bit of polishing to bring out the most concise heart of each in my revision:

Four one-act plays in one volume.

Mourning the Marigolds: Eccentric, sixtyish Bessie Levinson she sits on a park bench in Russell Square Park in London and tells her life story to Charlie Hampton, a stranger. Elsewhere in the park is Father Frank McAllister, an Irish priest, also in his sixties, strolling with his niece. He's telling Julie a very similar story... Frank's and Bessie's love affair unfolded and ended. However, on this particular chilly autumn afternoon, with Bessie's beloved marigolds about to gasp their last, there's a chance meeting between two old lovers...

A Day in the Life of Eleanor Duncan: Eleanor Duncan is a 72-year-old homeless woman living on a park bench in Central Park. She believes her bench to be her "home", which is wonderfully located so she can overlook skaters and lovers. She has been on the streets for twenty-four years and wouldn't have it any other way. On this Christmas Eve, Eleanor welcomes a string of visitors and regales them all with stories from her past. As she enjoys Christmas Eve dinner, she's surprised by her final visitor of the day...the last visitor of her life.

Wednesday: An aging woman chances to meet her long-time housekeeper in the park after thirty years. The time has been kind to one and not so kind to the other. As the two elderly women sit in the chill of a late November afternoon, they discover their differences may not be as great as they always thought.

Thursday: Two sisters in their seventies--one with Alzheimer's, the other her caregiver--have taught each other about coping and unconditional love.

The Stregoni Sequence, Book 3: Wish Granter and Other Enchanted Tales
by Christine E. Schulze
Christian Young Adult/Fantasy Short Story Collection

Original blurb:

In *Wind Whisperer*, Aurora is cursed with eternal invisibility--until David discovers her. David is the only person in the world besides Aurora's captor who can see her. An old Stregoni Benefici, he understands a thing or two about dark spells. But the breaking of Aurora's spell will summon an ancient enemy, throwing the two of them into a dangerous love triangle.

In *Truth Gazer*, Sarah travels to Lisallight for the first time. She finds herself involved in a deadly mystery and must quickly learn that looks are not always what they seem. Can she use her gift to decipher friend from foe, real beauty from false, before more lives are lost?

Finally, in *Wish Granter*, Grace is given a very special gift--a gamelan, a musical instrument which, when played correctly, unleashes a genie. A genie whose origins are tied to dark secrets--and to a secret saboteur within the very castle walls. Grace must make her three wishes count if she hopes to save both the genie and her friends from a terrible fate.

These exciting stories filled with mystery and magic conclude Schulze's trilogy, The Stregoni Sequence. Sit back, prepare for adventure, and grab your magic books--there are a few last spells to be broken before the end.

I took out the review slant and polished up the rest of the blurb below:

Three tales of mystery, magic, and a few last spells to be broken before the end.

In *Wind Whisperer*, Aurora is cursed with eternal invisibility until David discovers her. David is the only person in the world besides Aurora's captor who can see her. An old Stregoni Benefici, he understands a thing or two about dark spells. But the breaking of Aurora's spell summons an ancient enemy, throwing the two of them into a dangerous love triangle.

In *Truth Gazer*, Sarah travels to Lisallight for the first

time. She finds herself involved in a deadly mystery and must quickly learn that looks are not always what they seem. Can she use her gift to decipher friend from foe, real beauty from false, before more lives are lost?

Finally, in *Wish Granter*, Grace is given a very special gift--a musical instrument which, when played correctly, unleashes a genie...a genie whose origins are tied to dark secrets and to a hidden saboteur within the very castle walls. Grace must make her three wishes count if she hopes to save both the genie and her friends from a terrible fate.

The Adventures of Mycroft Holmes

by Sam Bonnamy

Mystery (Historical) Short Story Collection

Mycroft Holmes is not so unlike his younger brother Sherlock. Mystery-solving and clever solutions set in the eighteen-eighties are afoot in a collection of tales featuring "The Other Mr. Holmes". Tearing through London in hansom cabs and knee-deep in the twists and turns in pursuit of adventure alongside Mycroft is his plucky, crack-shot mistress Anna.

Volume 1: The Other Mr. Holmes

Original blurb:

Queen Victoria's personal diary goes missing, and an equerry is murdered. The murderer must be found, and the Queen's comments on some of her ministers must never reach the Continental press. Mycroft Holmes, Sherlock's elder brother, is the man to find the murderer and save Her Majesty's reputation. His mistress Anna, herself a crack shot, joins Mycroft in an attempt to keep the damning volume out of the hands of dastardly foreign agents.

"The Adventure of the Royal Revelations" is the first of three stories in "The Other Mr Holmes". In the second, Mycroft and Anna set out to save the reputation of a leading actress and keep the unique gemstone, the Flame of Natal, from the grasp of audacious thieves, while in the last story they cross swords with one of the deadliest enemies of Mycroft's brother--Colonel Sebastian Moran.

I felt the title of each story was necessary to keep the "review-slanted" angle out of the back cover blurb. When the series blurb is put together with each back cover blurb on these volumes, I think the consistent manner of presenting each volume works well below:

"The Adventure of the Royal Revelations": Queen Victoria's personal diary goes missing, and an equerry is murdered. Certainly the murderer must be found; however, the Queen's comments on some of her ministers must never reach the Continental press. Mycroft is just the man to find the murderer and save Her Majesty's reputation. Mycroft and Anna attempt to keep the damning volume out of the hands of dastardly foreign agents.

"The Adventure of the Flame of the Natal Retrospect": Mycroft and Anna set out to save the reputation of a leading actress and keep the unique gemstone, the Flame of Natal, from the grasp of audacious thieves

"The Adventure of the Reuters' Agent Summer": Mycroft and Anna cross swords with one of the deadliest enemies of Mycroft's brother--Colonel Sebastian Moran.

Volume 2: Mycroft Up Against It

Original blurb:

Once again Anna and Mycroft Holmes tear through London in hansom cabs as they pursue three further adventures set in the eighteen-eighties. Mycroft puffs and pants his way through his cases, applying not only his keen mind but also, in one case, the precepts of the Kama Sutra, while Anna hobnobs with Buffalo Bill, Henry Irving and Oscar Wilde.

In "The Deadwood Stage" an anarchist threatens mayhem at Buffalo Bill's Wild West Show and Anna finds herself having to impersonate Miss Annie Oakley before the Prince of Wales.

Anna is accused of committing murder during a performance at the Lyceum Theatre. Henry Irving and Ellen Terry believe in her innocence, but will Inspector Athelney Jones? The answer lies in "Murder At The Lyceum".

"The Green-painted Door" is the site of a hideous slaying in Wimbledon. Oscar Wilde may exercise his scornful wit, but Mycroft Holmes is roused to action again. His privately-printed copy of the Kama Sutra (translated by Sir Richard Burton) stimulates another kind of action as Anna has every reason to know.

For consistency, the blurbs follow what was started with the revision of the first blurb.

"The Deadwood Stage": When an anarchist threatens mayhem at Buffalo Bill's Wild West Show, Anna finds herself having to impersonate Miss Annie Oakley and hobnobbing with Bill himself before the Prince of Wales. Mycroft puffs and pants his way through another case, applying his keen mind.

"Murder At The Lyceum": Anna is accused of committing murder during a performance at the Lyceum Theatre. Fellow actors Henry Irving and Ellen Terry believe in her innocence, but will Inspector Athelney Jones? Mycroft must find the truth before it's too late.

"The Green-painted Door": At the site of a hideous slaying in Wimbledon, Oscar Wilde exercises his scornful wit, but Mycroft Holmes is roused to action yet again. His privately-printed copy of the Kama Sutra (translated by Sir Richard Burton) stimulates another kind of action, as Anna has every reason to know.

CHILDREN'S BOOKS

I believe children's books (whether picture books or midgrade readers or young adult) may be some of the hardest books to write blurbs for. As we said about nonfiction, one of the most common way the authors and publishers handle these blurbs is by cramming them with praise (usually self-praise of the story and/or the illustrations). Getting away from that is extremely hard. But remember that while including reviews for professionals, authors or others in the field are wonderful, they aren't and shouldn't be part of the summary of what the book is about. Rave reviews are fantastic, but they don't always tell the reader about the book or why they should read it. The summary must be separate from the reviews and over-inflated claims.

Beyond that, one thing I've really noticed is that so many of children's books don't seem to have a real plot--not the way we think of them for fiction that's written for young adults or adults. I think that's because children's books must be, by necessity, extremely simple without complicated themes. Again, that's why the books themselves and the blurbs are so tricky to write. Additionally, you don't want a lot of suspense or scariness in a children's book. Anything that could really jazz these up has to be toned down so no one has nightmares or simply can't connect with the story.

I've revised many books in this genre, and, as much as possible, I try to take the review slant and conceit out. Since these are very short and the most complicated of all genres to blurb, I've included twice as many examples of them than the others. As you'll see in these revisions, sometimes I was left with very little to work with for an actual summary of the story:

My Mommy Is Insane
by Koni Coward
Children's Picture Book

Original blurb:

"My Mommy Is Insane" is an adorable Children's Picture book, written originally by Koni Coward as a poem. This humorous look at Mommy's frazzled nerves is illustrated by gorgeous artwork by Mary Lacro-Mauritz.

Every mother of small children will identify with this book, as will the children who love to drive their mother's crazy!

This was a review-slanted blurb almost entirely, but it wasn't a back cover blurb the way it was originally written:

Mommy's frazzled nerves are humorously illustrated in this original poem. Mothers of small children can identify with this book just as children who love to drive their mothers crazy will want to linger on every single page of mischief.

Imp-Probable Journeys
by Aleksandra Zajackowski
Midgrade Reader/Fantasy

Original blurb:

An oddly paired duo, Pete, a computer "junkie" and class nerd, and Lilly find themselves trapped in a time warp. As they travel through time and space they have to solve numerous mysteries of the past or rescue some unusual characters they meet along the way.

Their missions are as exciting as they are dangerous, but the children are helped by a mischievous clay imp and his magical powers.

However, they soon realize that the wacky little mascot offers more than the simple thrill of adventure and breaking away from his dominance will become their greatest challenge.

I made an assumption in my revision based on the original blurb, which offered the "oddly paired duo" reference that only showed one side of the odd duo. Upon learning more about the story, I revised the blurb in this way:

A smarty-pants duo, Pete is a computer junkie and the class nerd; Lilly a skinny, awkward girl spouting factoids she learned from countless books--including the dictionary she reads with as much enjoyment as a novel. When Pete and Lilly find themselves trapped in a time warp both dangerous and exciting, they travel through space and time to solve mysteries of the past. Along the way, they rescue unusual characters including a mischievous clay imp with magical powers. It isn't long before Pete and Lilly realize their wacky little mascot may not intend to offer them friendship and loyalty. Breaking away from his dominance may become their greatest challenge to getting home again.

Dani Pepper and the Spelling Bee
by Cathan
Midgrade Reader

Original blurb:

The State Spelling Bee Championship. Wow!

Dani Pepper, self-proclaimed and second-best speller at Fisher Pitt Junior School takes us on the journey to the finals of the state championship. With her best friend Danny and her nemesis--the stuckup Mary Ellen--they get ready for the big day.

The whole class takes a bus trip to the library to work on essays and learn new words. Meanwhile, the word 'catastrophe' causes a great kerfuffle between Dani and Mary Ellen. Sometimes words can be so confusing.

The big day is almost here. Dani is excited because she's going to wear her wonderful MTV- inspired outfit: a yellow jumper, red- and green-striped stockings, and green ponytail scrunchies. Mary Ellen says that outfit isn't lady-like.

Who will win the coveted championship trophy?

There was a lot of unnecessary information in this blurb that stole the tension, so my revision addressed that:

Dani Pepper is the second-best speller at Fisher Pitt Junior School. When she's chosen for the State Spelling Bee Championship finals, she's thrilled. She and her nemesis--the stuck-up, first-best-speller Mary Ellen--prepare for the tournament. The whole class takes a bus trip to the library to work on essays and learn new words. In the spirit of competition, Dani and Mary Ellen are caught in a kerfuffle over the word 'catastrophe'. Finally, the big day is upon them. Who will win the coveted spelling championship trophy?

<h3 style="text-align:center">Where Does Bubblegum Come From?</h3>
by Rosalind Goly
Children's Picture Book

Original blurb:

"Where Does Bubblegum Come From?" tells a real story of how bubblegum was created, and how a mistake isn't always a mistake. The WOB books are a learning tool and are interactive with http://www.thewob.com website.

A W.O.B. is actually an acronym for "World of Babies" and it is in this world that children's imagination and love of learning is sparked. The WOB character is designed to capture the child's attention, while teaching basic reading, spelling and grammar. All children are curious and the WOB is just the character children can relate to.

W.O.B. was a mouthful. I tried to make the revised blurb read with more flow:

In this real story of how bubblegum was created, a mistake is sometimes the start of something new and wonderful.

This W.O.B. book is a learning tool interactive with the

http://www.thewob.com website. W.O.B. is an acronym for "World of Babies". In this world, a child's imagination, natural curiosity, and love of learning are sparked. W.O.B. characters are designed to capture attention while teaching basic reading, spelling and grammar.

George and His Magic Mirror
by Debra M. Scatasti
Mid-grade Reader/Young Adult

Original blurb:

George is a smart, nice boy in the sixth grade, with two siblings and a loving home. His life is about to change dramatically with the death of his Grandfather.

He has been left a Mirror in his Grandfather's Will. This is not just any mirror, it is an extraordinary mirror which will take George on trips into fantasy lands and lead to many great adventures. These all happen without any time passing on earth.

So now George has a double life: the intrepid explorer, never knowing what land awaits on the other side of the mirror and the school boy growing up into adulthood.

I attempted to liven the blurb up and introduce tension and conflict, which were wholly lacking in the original version with my revision:

George is a smart, nice boy in the sixth grade with two siblings and loving parents. When his grandfather dies, his life is dramatically changed. Unexpectedly, George has inherited a mirror--and not just any mirror. This extraordinary looking glass takes George on trips into fantasy lands he's only dreamed of, where he can have his own adventures. When he returns to his regular life, nothing has changed and no time has passed there. George becomes a boy with a double life: An ordinary school boy who will grow up into adulthood...and the intrepid explorer who never knows what awaits him on the other side of the mirror.

Being Kind to George
by Jo Dunningham
Children's Picture Book

Original blurb:

'Being Kind to George' is based on a true story and real life characters. Set in a beautiful Country Park nestling in the heart of Wiltshire, England, it tells the tale of how man can affect the wildlife around him.

The story tries to show how even in kindness, man can damage not only the delicate balance of the environment in which animals live, but by befriending a wild animal they can remove the instincts that help it to survive.

The original blurb had very little flow and necessitated revision:

Based on a true story, real-life characters and set in a beautiful country park nestled in the heart of Wiltshire, England, one man learns how easy it can be to damage not only the delicate balance of the environment animals live in but how befriending a wild animal removes instincts that help it survive.

Writing blurbs for nonfiction, story collections, and children's books are particularly hard, but hopefully I've offered some method to the madness in writing these specialized blurbs.

***

Certain genres are complicated to blurb and require a deft hand to prevent author conceit, inflated claims, and too little detail about the actual stories included to generate true interest. In the next chapter, we'll go over a mass listing of blurb tips for any genre.

CHAPTER THREE
Blurb Do's (But Mostly Don'ts)

"Don't give it all away on the first date... Have some class. You want your potential reader to buy your book, don't you? Try not to give away too much of the plot. It's finding that fine line between revealing enough for your reader to want to know more and maintaining an air of mystery." ~Frances Reid Rowland from The 5 Core Elements of a Book Blurb (And Why You Should Know Them)

As I've probably stated before in my writing reference titles, articles and workshops, I'm not a big believer in hard-and-fast rules, and even the ones stated in this chapter can be legitimately broken. I break them all the time myself--if you take a look at the blurb examples on my Blurb Service website. The list in this chapter includes the things that are best to do or not to do and there's good reason for treading carefully when defying any of them. That said, if something works, it just works and who cares about rules when it does? But be careful in any case. On the basis of this chapter, I've also created a Blurb Evaluation Checklist that includes all of these things that you can use when evaluating your own blurbs as well practicing with others.

Let's go over thirty-five tips to think about when it comes to crafting and revising blurbs.

Should My Character Be Invited to the Party?

If a character is a main character, that's a strong reason to include her in the blurb; however, I don't think it's necessary in every case, especially if the blurb reads better and is more compelling with the inclusion of only one character. Most secondary characters won't be included because there usually isn't room or necessity. Don't overload a blurb with too many characters. One or two protagonists, one antagonist should be sufficient for any one blurb. Too many people mentioned in a blurb will make the entire summary feel impersonal and things get muddled, maybe prompting the reader to wonder who the heck's story this is anyway. An emotional connection can't be made when there are too many directions to focus on in a few short paragraphs.

A Rose By Any Other Name

A *main* character's name (first, not always surname) is considered important in a blurb almost always, especially if more than one main character is brought up in the back cover blurb (naming names avoids confusion). While a series or high-concept blurb can be generalized, the back cover blurb isn't and should never be. Name your main character(s) in your back cover blurb. Don't call them the unspecified "a driven cop" or a "distressed mother" for two paragraphs. Think "ingenuous Harvard symbologist Robert Langdon", "fearless wizard Harry Potter", "plucky, boldly curious amateur sleuth Nancy Drew". Allow readers a glimpse into the world of the character that's distinctly personalized.

As a kind of humorously exaggerated example, let's read the back cover blurb for *Harry Potter and the Sorcerer's Stone* entirely devoid of his name, with just unspecified generalizations instead:

An [eleven-year-old boy] has no idea how famous he is. That's because he's being raised by his miserable aunt and uncle who are terrified [the kid] will learn that he's really a wizard, just as his parents were. But everything changes when [this guy] is summoned to attend an infamous school for wizards, and he begins to discover some clues about his illustrious birthright. From the surprising way he is greeted by a lovable giant, to the unique curriculum and colorful faculty at his unusual school, [the little dude] finds himself drawn deep inside a mystical world he never knew existed and closer to his own noble destiny.

We're all laughing here, but I've read so many back cover blurbs where it almost seems like the author went out of his way to avoid naming his character, like the name is attached to a curse or something (yes, another Harry Potter reference). When unspecified characters are referred to in this way all through a few paragraphs of blurb, the result can be a feat of hilariously-written acrobatics.

Descriptor Punches

Brief reference to who a character is, her age, what she does for a living or as a hobby can add short, punchy, and efficient descriptions that give solid information (characterization!) without taking up a lot of space. Imagine you're trying to fix your best friend up with another friend you think would be perfect for her. Essentially you have a few, very carefully chosen word choices to sell your best friend on this blind date. You would choose those words with utmost attention to detail. In the same way, when characterizing those mentioned in our blurbs, we have to use the most powerful descriptor punches.

Look at this one for *The Last Apprentice* by Joseph Delaney. There's a whole lot of characterization (and plot) given in a few short sentences:

Twelve-year-old Tom Ward is the seventh son of a seventh son who has been apprenticed to The Spook, whose job it is to ward off witches, boggarts, and ghosts from his domain in the English countryside. Twenty-nine other apprentices have gone before Tom. Will he be able to succeed because he is able to see things, or because he is left-handed, or because his Mam has taught him Greek?

Right Place, Right Time

The main time period(s) and setting(s) are also worth including, especially if they're a focus of the story. Most modern stories don't require specific references to either in the back cover blurb. But do try to include this information in the same way we described in the last paragraph--in a setting descriptor punch, so you can have the most impact with very few words used. You can even combine them, such as "Manhattan socialite". Let's look at an example of a setting descriptor punch from Stephen King's *It*:

> Welcome to Derry, Maine, a small city as hauntingly familiar as your own hometown...only in Derry the haunting is real.

The time-period can usually be drawn from the blurb without the need for overt declarations, as you can see they were in most of the high-concept blurbs we looked at for movies and books in Chapter Two, and in this example from *The Scandalous Flirt* by Olivia Drake:

> Aurora Paxton was once the belle of the ball, the most sought-after debutante of the season—until a scandalous mistake ruined her. Shunned by her family, Rory was banished to the country to live in disgrace.

Bring the Past to the Present

Present tense is the common means of writing a back cover blurb and for good reason--present tense allows for more zing and tension. I really like how Ava Jae defends present tense usage (although she's talking about writing a book--but the principle is the same) in her article, *Why Use Present Tense?*: "You see, when written in present tense, the reader is experiencing the events of the book at the same time as the narrator, and it's this feeling of going through the plot together (immediacy) that tends to create an instantly closer relationship. ...written in past tense can create the same sort of relationship...but the effect of the narrator recounting the story (...past tense) is a half-step farther than the narrator experiencing the novel with the reader. The immediacy of present tense works particularly well in fast-paced, action-packed novels...adds an extra edge—the characters are going through their battles with the reader. The protagonist hasn't experienced this already—and thus isn't telling us about a battle three years ago that they very clearly survived from or else they wouldn't be around to tell the story—so there's an added sense of vulnerability. ...the sense that things are happening now can give the added feel that anything could happen—even, possibly...the death of the protagonist."

Keep it in Perspective

Third person is almost always the only satisfying point-of-view for a back cover blurb--and that's even if your book is written in first person. While writing a book in first-person is popular, since it allows "the narrating character to directly address the reader by funneling the entire story through his head...[to] pull readers directly into the story and create an unprecedented amount of intimacy between them and the character" (from K.M. Weiland's article *Don't Even Think About Using First-Person Unless...*), this perspective in a back cover blurb is even more perilous than in a story. First person is one of the trickiest viewpoints to utilize because the narrative voice has to be so amazing, there's simply no qualification for good or okay. If it's not absolutely dazzling, it'll fail to draw the reader and will instead repel him.

This example from *The One Man* by Andrew Gross, a WWII thriller, is of course simply taking a blurb and writing it in first-person POV without any dazzling changes, but I think it gets across the message how awkward back cover blurbs can be written in first-person (but some may be persuaded the opposite if they have an affinity for first-person POV):

I'm an American Intelligence lieutenant and I routinely decode messages from occupied Poland. Having escaped the Krakow ghetto as a teenager, I long to do more for my new country in the war. But never did I expect the proposal I receive: to sneak into the most guarded place on Earth—the notorious Nazi concentration camp at Auschwitz—to find and escape with renowned physicist Alfred Mendl, the one man whom the Allies believe can help them win the war.

Establish the Genre Through Mood

There's a trend to include a paragraph within the blurb that focuses entirely on what the genre of the book is. Go to Amazon and check out bestsellers or new books, and you'll be hit over the head with genre inflations, like this one in the back cover blurb summary:

> From the mind of *Wall Street Journal* bestselling author Christopher Greyson comes a story with twists and turns that take the reader to the edge of madness. *The Girl Who Lived* should come with a warning label: Once you start reading, you won't be able to stop. Not since *Girl on the Train* and *Gone Girl* has a psychological thriller kept readers so addicted—and guessing right until the last page.

I truly hope the author didn't write this. I suspect the publisher or whoever inputs publisher information for a publishing company did it.

Incidentally, genres are even listed within the title now on Amazon. I haven't checked other distributor websites. Look at the example I've included next. The "blurb genre summation" above the author's name is from this book, which is how it's listed at Amazon:

The Girl Who Lived: A Thrilling Suspense Novel
by Christopher Greyson

Here's another one:

The Marriage Lie: A bestselling psychological thriller
by Kimberly Belle

There are so many now, it's rare to find a title without a genre over-inflation. I can't get on-board with this practice. To me, it's a lazy man's way of conveying information.

A clever writer will make the genre(s) specific to his story apparent in the back cover blurb without allotted a paragraph to tell the reader pointblank, though I do believe this something a publisher usually does and the author has no control of it. If you have any say, instead of actually ascribing genre in a paragraph of the blurb, convey the category without the designation. Can you guess the genre of these books below based solely on the blurbs (I'm not including authors or titles, since either could give away the answer and we only want to look at the blurbs themselves to figure out genre)?

> Naomi Bowes lost her innocence the night she followed her father into the woods. In freeing the girl trapped in the root cellar, Naomi revealed the horrible extent of her father's crimes and made him infamous. No matter how close she gets to happiness, she can't outrun the sins of Thomas David Bowes.
>
> Now a successful photographer living under the name Naomi Carson, she has found a place that calls to her, a rambling old house in need of repair, thousands of miles away from everything she's ever known. Naomi wants to embrace the solitude, but the kindly residents of Sunrise Cove keep forcing her to open up—especially the determined Xander Keaton.
>
> Naomi can feel her defenses failing, and knows that the connection her new life offers is something she's always secretly craved. But the sins of her father can become an obsession, and, as she's learned time and again, her past is never more than a nightmare away.

Genre(s):

~*~

Jon Bennett and Erin McCoy are two of the shrewdest strategists on Wall Street and close friends of the president of the United States. Their secret project: a billion-dollar oil deal off the coast of Tel Aviv and Gaza that could form the basis of a historic peace treaty and bring enormous wealth to every Israeli and Palestinian. But nothing has prepared Jon or Erin for the terror that lies ahead.

Genre(s):

~*~

Soldier. Summoner. Saint. Orphaned and expendable, Alina Starkov is a soldier who knows she may not survive her first trek across the Shadow Fold—a swath of unnatural darkness crawling with monsters. But when her regiment is attacked, Alina unleashes dormant magic not even she knew she possessed.

Now Alina will enter a lavish world of royalty and intrigue as she trains with the Grisha, her country's magical military elite—and falls under the spell of their notorious leader, the Darkling. He believes Alina can summon a force capable of destroying the Shadow Fold and reuniting their war-ravaged country, but only if she can master her untamed gift.

As the threat to the kingdom mounts and Alina unlocks the secrets of her past, she will make a dangerous discovery that could threaten all she loves and the very future of a nation.

Welcome to Ravka...a world of science and superstition where nothing is what it seems.

Genre(s):

~*~

Fresh from the convent, Beryl Seaton accepts a position as governess for the Brooks family. When she arrives at the family's remote house, however, she discovers that a terrible secret is waiting for her in the nursery. Desperate to help her employers in their hour of need, she nevertheless struggles to look after their son. What happened to Stephen, to leave him the way he is? What happened to the previous governess at Grangehurst? And what causes the sobbing sound that seem to drift through an empty room? By the time she uncovers the awful truth about the family, and about little Stephen, it might be too late for Beryl to ever leave.

Genre(s):

~*~

Threatened by a stalker, she turns to the only man who can help her--the man who walked out of her life ten years ago.

Artist Victoria Whitlock escapes the clutches of a stalker only to stumble into the arms of the man she never wants to see again, bad boy prosecutor Garrett Reynolds. To protect Victoria, Garrett whisks her away to an isolated lodge. Major problem for Victoria—how does she help Garrett capture the stalker while guarding her heart against the man who broke it once before?

Garret thought his heart had healed when Victoria left him ten years ago. Garrett's bigger problem—capture the stalker determined to imprison Victoria. Keeping Victoria safe is no easy task for Garrett, but getting her to trust him is an entirely different challenge. He puts his life on the line to guard the woman who is more deserving of love than any woman he's known.

But love takes a back seat to the Whitloch-Reynolds feud. At the center is the Crystal Creek Ranch. The Whitlochs own the ranch. The Reynolds are the rightful heirs.

Genre(s):

For your own blurbs, connect the genre(s) of your story in your mind and evaluate whether each genre is effectively portrayed. If you have a romantic paranormal, both the romance and paranormal aspects should be obvious in the blurb, even if it's just in the manner of what's conveyed. If it's a paranormal, your blurb should feel eerie, maybe even a little scary. Suspense in any form should induce tightness in your chest as you read the blurb. Looking at the high-concept blurbs we discussed in Chapter One and Two, I bet you could see the genre in the short sentences of the stories.

Watch Your Language

The actual language you use does relate to genre since the category of a book does tend to suggest a certain tone or vibe. Robert Lee Beers writes a noir mystery fantasy series with a "trope", hardboiled private detective like Sam Spade with his Tony Mandolin Mysteries. His blurbs reflected the niche genre, but, in revising his blurbs, I suggested going whole hog in that regard. The original and revised blurbs were hilarious. They instantly make you want to read the entire series in one sitting.

Some authors believe voice in writing is the be-all, end-all of everything. I'm not totally convinced about that, and that could be because I don't have one definitive voice. For every genre, and sometimes every book, my voice changes to suit the characters, the genre, the plot. But I think voice does play a part of back cover blurbing because the voice of a blurb and the language used does give the reader something to look forward to when the voice in a blurb matches the voice of the story, as all Christine DeSmet do, such as this one from *First-Degree Fudge*, Book 1: A Fudge Shop Mystery:

New candy store owner Ava Oosterling specializes in making heavenly homemade fudge and fresh starts. But she's just found out that her newest flavor is to die for...

Between getting her store up and running and uneasily settling back into her charming Lake Michigan hometown, Ava Oosterling has her plate full. She hopes using local fresh dairy and her own flavorful imagination to cook up one-of-a-kind fudge will also create a brand-new start for her. And if she can tempt wealthy ex–film star Rainetta Johnson to try her newest creation, Cinderella Pink, at a local fund-raiser, maybe her road to big-time success will be short and sweet.

But when Rainetta chokes to death on a stolen diamond hidden in the fudge's fluffy depths, Ava is pegged as the prime suspect. Now saving her business and reputation means investigating a batch of townspeople who had numerous reasons to hate disdainful, hard-bargaining Rainetta. With Ava's best friend and her former flame in the suspect mix, she must figure out who the real culprit is fast or face a very bitter end...

Shame on You

A blurb should never be misleading. The blurb should sell the book that you wrote--not the book you wish you'd written, the one you feel you should have written, and it should never mislead the readers about what the story inside the pages is about or like (i.e., if the book itself is a depressing war account, the blurb shouldn't be written from the POV of a soldier giving a rip-roaring comedy act).

If you want to hear a haunting example of a blurb misrepresenting a story: Apparently once upon a time the *TV Guide* including this blurb in a listing (maybe they were trying to see if we were awake?): "Transported to a surreal landscape, a young girl kills the first person she meets, and then teams up with three strangers to kill again." I bet you can guess what story this is describing...but doing so in the most misleading, shocking way possible about a beloved, classic story that transports most people somewhere over the rainbow.

Be In Control of Your Hyperbole

Embellishment, overkill--it's the stuff of blurbs and that's not a bad thing, though you don't want to tip right over the edge into pure melodrama. If the stakes aren't high enough, then you risk not having an irresistible lure, as you see in these:

"A terrible virus has spread across the planet and turned the human race into bloodthirsty monsters. Mankind's only hope for survival is scientist Robert Neville, the one person left unaffected by the epidemic." (*I Am Legend*, Richard Matheson)

"Langdon is instantly plunged into a clandestine world of Masonic secrets, hidden history, and never-before-seen locations--all of which seem to be dragging him toward a single, inconceivable truth." (*The Lost Symbol*, Dan Brown)

"En route to London from New York, Flight 305 suddenly loses power and crash-lands in the English countryside, plunging a group of strangers into a mysterious adventure that will have repercussions for all of humankind." (*Departure*, A.G. Riddle)

The right hyperbole, controlled and decisive, can have incredible impact. Don't neglect the oh-so-subtle art of hyperbole in describing your story.

A Good Title is To Be Chosen Rather Than Riches

Link your title with your blurb. While you don't have to go overboard in this regard, I always appreciate it when the back cover blurb shows me why a book has the title it does. It creates a connection that compels my interest to see how it gets worked into the book itself. However, it isn't something you want to hit the reader over the head with. In general, mention it once, mildly refer to it throughout the book, and use it once more near the end so the sentiment attacked to your title might become trite, annoying or silly if it's overused. This is just the high-concept blurb of a young adult science fiction book, *All Rights Reserved* by Gregory Scott Katsoulis:

In a world where every word and gesture is copyrighted, patented or trademarked, one girl elects to remain silent rather than pay to speak, and her defiant and unexpected silence threatens to unravel the very fabric of society.

The reason the author chose his title is obvious, isn't it? *The Program* by Suzanne Young (with just the first two lines) makes the reason for the title clear as well:

> Sloane knows better than to cry in front of anyone. With suicide now an international epidemic, one outburst could land her in The Program, the only proven course of treatment.

Make a Mountain Out of a Molehill

A blurb isn't the place to ascribe importance to unimportant details. Dropping tantalizing phrases into a blurb like "he has a past that no President should have" will place importance and intrigue on something that may have no place in the book. Beyond that, these details in a blurb can be vague, making the reader wonder the purpose in including it. In this example, *Mirror, Mirror* by Dalziel Laing, a lot of information is introduced (note that this is the version I received, complete with errors):

> "Mirror, Mirror" is a mystery story with two parallel tales. One tale covers a century. It is the history of the Tremble's, Roger's family. It gives a graphic insight into the psyche of 'Roger' the serial killer. The other tale covers the timeframe of a week. It follows Inspector Georgina Borg's pursuit of a serial killer. She has been unable to crack the killer's identity. The murders have been over a period of ten years. She has followed the trail from Sydney to Melbourne. All of the victims have been loners or with distant family and without husband and especially kids. Cate, the last victim, however has a different profile entirely. Borg knows it is the same killer, but why this change of modus operandi? She feels that this will be the killer's downfall.
>
> Borg is convinced that latest victim may complete and solve the serial killers puzzle and reveal his identity. In the meantime Borg's life is an emotional mess. She is unable to commit herself to a permanent relationship with Professor

Richard Thompson, but is madly in love with him. During her investigations into the latest killing, Richard becomes a prime suspect!

The two stories reflect upon each other and finally, in a macabre twist, come together. Georgina is then faced with a race against time to try and stop her now 'revealed' killer from leaving her precinct, and perhaps eluding the clutches of the law forever.

As it was originally written, I didn't believe this blurb made any sense. For a long time, I read and reread it trying to figure out how to fix it and I finally decided that these two parallel plotlines spoken of were confusing everything, especially the "century" one. I saw no choice but to take that one out and work with what was left. The reader could easily find that out once he started reading the book. My revision made for a zippy, internal and external conflict driven blurb:

Inspector Georgina Borg's life is an emotional rollercoaster. She's deeply in love with Professor Richard Thompson yet can't get herself to commit to a permanent relationship--a puzzle even she can't explain adequately. At work, she's in charge of a case pursuing a serial killer who's remained a mystery for ten long years. She's followed his distinctive but maddeningly elusive trail from Sydney to Melbourne. Now suddenly the killer targets a victim with an entirely new profile. Despite the change in modus operandi, Borg is certain it's the same killer. Just when she thinks she's close to solving the puzzle and revealing his identity at last, her should-be, would-be fiancé becomes the prime suspect!

If you've introduced something into your blurb that sounds big and important, but ultimately isn't, or if it's something that shouldn't be revealed anywhere but on the pages of the book itself, leave it out.

Should I Resist Asking Provocative Questions?

Journalist Barbara Walters used to make her living asking provocative questions, but in a blurb it's best to avoid them. While everyone has done this because this can turn up the suspense in a hurry, consider these questions and what they all have in common:

Can our intrepid heroine navigate the murky waters of betrayal before it's too late?
Can they survive to face another day?
Will Most Wonderful Hero of All Time get what he deserves?
Will Evil, Nasty Hero get what's coming to him?

The answer to all these provocative questions is almost always yes. And that's why asking is almost silly, a cop-out, an easy way to ratchet up the tension. If the answer is yes and everyone knows the answer is yes--you, your publisher, the reader, the person standing next to the reader, and her grandmother--then why ask the question? That said, I'm guilty of doing it and most authors are because sometimes it's the only thing that works. But, as a general rule, avoid it.

Enough With the Questions Already

Don't flood your back cover blurb with questions. One or two in just the right place can be effective, but remember the reader doesn't know anything about this book. If you're asking questions, one after the other, relentlessly, he'll be forced to freak out and scream, "How in the heck am I supposed to know? Stop badgering me!" Goodbye, dear reader. Let's exaggerate again a bit to get the point across, using Landfall by Jerry Aubin. Below, I've replaced most of the original, second paragraph of the blurb with a string of relentless questions:

Launched as the last gasp of humanity, the Ship set out to preserve the species by seeding the universe with one billion colonists. Generations of Crew, trained to be either Flight or Marines, have spent 5,000 years protecting the Ship and its civilian cargo from the constant threat of alien violence.

Fifteen-year-old Zax has always had trouble fitting in with the other cadets, but is he finally on the cusp of attaining his dream and gaining entrance to the Pilot Academy? Will catching the eye of the Flight Boss and winning him as a mentor guarantee Zax a top spot? Will the shocking discovery he makes along the way destroy not only his career, but also the Ship itself?

The focus and suspense in this story is entirely lost in the onslaught of badgering questions.

Quick, Tell Me in One Sentence...

Here's another problem I see so often, I guess it's become industry standard or it's just been done so often, authors think it's how it's supposed to be done. Generally the first sentence of the blurb is worded in such a way that the reader is immediately in the mindset that an interviewer has said to the author (who's sitting in the hot seat): "What's your story about? Tell me in a single sentence." In other words, the first sentence (or the last) of the blurb has something like this:

"MY STORY is about a rapist hunting his prey in the big city."

Most authors know what I'm talking about when I say, in being put on the spot about coming up with some brilliant one-liner that's supposed to convince someone to buy and read...we croak! Stutter! Fail! And a sentence in a back cover blurb that has the author trying to puke out what their story is about in one sentence has the same result: Croak, stutter and fail. Avoid it unless your goal is to kill your blurb in one sentence.

Pardon My French, But Blurbs Need to Use Strong, Visual Language

Use words that evoke vivid images in your blurb--strong, direct, sharp, intriguing, compelling, powerfully impacting, proactive words that will resonate with readers. But also keep in mind that a blurb is the wrong place to have long sentences. Short and to the point will motivate a reader better than long, complicated sentences. Take look at this example of fairly short sentences and extremely vivid word usage from *The Gender Game* by Bella Forrest:

A toxic river divides nineteen-year-old Violet Bates's world by gender. Women rule the East. Men rule the West. Welcome to the lands of Matrus and Patrus. Ever since the disappearance of her beloved younger brother, Violet's life has been consumed by an anger she struggles to control. Already a prisoner to her own nation, now she has been sentenced to death for her crimes. But one decision could save her life. To enter the kingdom of Patrus, where men rule and women submit.

Everything about the patriarchy is dangerous for a rebellious girl like Violet. She cannot break the rules if she wishes to stay alive. But abiding by rules has never been her strong suit, and when she is thrust into more danger than she could have ever predicted, Violet is forced to sacrifice many things in the forbidden kingdom ... including forbidden love.

In a world divided by gender, only the strongest survive...

Also keep in mind that short words can become "keywords"--literally. Relevant keywords are ones that search engines can index. Your blurbs could be indexed with keywords, and that's good promotion.

"Stop!" she said.

Never use dialogue or dialogue tags in a back cover blurb without very good reason. Second thought, forget this 'good reason' stuff.

There's not good enough reason 99.9% of the time. So don't do it. Here are some examples of blurbs I've revised that contained dialogue, starting with the original and following with my revision of the blurbs:

Mary Anne
by Daphne Saxby Taylor
Historical/Australian Fiction

Original blurb:

"Sold!" wept Mary Anne on her deathbed. "Sold for a bottle of rum!"

"Love him," her mother had said. "Loving is not always easy. It will mean caring for him, cooking and cleaning for him--and bearing his children. But it is a hard man indeed, who can resist consistent love for ever."

It had all begun in peaceful Hertfordshire. But boredom, recklessness, his swashbuckling life in the army of the East India Company--had changed all that. Then had befallen a chance encounter in far away New South Wales--an enslavement to rum--and an overseer's words "The establishment looks more favourably on married men. More chance of a pardon. And possibly of a grant of land."

Gentle Mary Anne becomes an unwitting player in this heart gripping story of life as it was in the penal colony of New South Wales in the mid-nineteenth century.

MARY ANNE, a compelling story with an imperative that drives the reader to the last page.

This blurb may make sense to someone who knows the history behind the story, but from the standpoint of one who doesn't, this blurb was nearly incoherent and the use of dialogue and dialogue tags was the first I'd ever encountered. The review-slant at the end with the author deciding for the reader that she's written a compelling story that can't be put down and that readers will find heart-rending also put me off. The revision I suggested to fix the biggest problems left me with little story summary to offer but I do think it was enough to be compelling:

> In peaceful Hertfordshire of New South Wales in the mid-nineteenth century, a bored and reckless man who leads a swashbuckling life in the army of the East Indian Company is told by the overseer that a married man has more chance of gaining a pardon from the penal colony and being granted land.
>
> Gentle Mary Anne becomes the unwitting wife of such a man, sold for a bottle of rum. With no other prospects, she takes her mother's advice to love and care for her husband and his children in hopes that loving a hard man consistently will bring about the happily-ever-after she longs for.

In this example, once I revised the blurb, I found a lot to be intrigued by and I don't have a single doubt that the book the blurb described was fabulous and well-written. It received a 5 star review on Amazon. The blurb just needed to reflect that.

I find dialogue and the corresponding tags in a blurb so awkward, they tend to embarrass me more than the time a friend of mine came out of the bathroom trailing a long line of toilet paper that may have been still connected to the roll on the bottom of her shoe.

Keep the Peek in the Pages

Here's another tip that I almost feel should go without saying, and yet I'm going to say it because I've actually seen it done. Don't use excerpts (or pull quotes) directly in your book on the back cover. Save those for the excerpt page after the cover. I once revised the blurb of an author who basically took what I'm convinced was a 75-word excerpt from the book and put it on the back cover. There was absolutely no setup to what was going on. There was dialogue, introspection, an action of exploding from a chair in anger...in the back cover blurb. There were a few short paragraphs before and after this excerpt which were made more confusing because of the excerpt instead of explaining anything.

From my point-of-view, the excerpt seemed random, without purpose, without setup, without the slightest bit of enlightenment about who these people were, what they were doing, or why they were doing it.

Just as an example of how jarring this can be, let's look at a truly random, just over 200-word excerpt from J.T. Ellison's *So Close the Hand of Death*:

Once he hit sixty, he followed her path to the door. He pushed his finger into the white button, heard the shrill bell ringing. A woman's voice, tinny and thin, said, "Yes?"

"Delivery for June Earhart."

She buzzed him in without saying anything else. The door unlocked with a snap and he pulled it wide, allowing enough room for the handcart to fit in, adjusting his cap lower on his head. He didn't want his face to be seen. There were cameras in the foyer, he knew from earlier reconnaissance.

He thought about his target. He loved the way June looked. Brown hair, brown eyes, five foot six, somewhat lumpy, but that was just because she enjoyed her food and didn't exercise. Not lazy, never lazy. Just...padded.

He'd watched her take lunch all this week: Monday was McDonald's, Tuesday Subway, Wednesday a couple of iced crullers and a sugary juice smoothie from Dunkin' Donuts. Thursday she'd stayed in, but this afternoon she'd gone for a grinder, thick with salami and ham and cheese, with a side of potato chips. He wondered if she would smell like onions or if she'd been considerate enough to chew some gum, or suck on a Tic-Tac.

I don't deny there could be some intrigue in this, but there's also a lot of confusion. Who are these people? What in the world are they doing? What's motivating them? Imagine this as a back cover of a book. It could do nothing but elicit confusion in every reader, who's expecting a summary of the story, not an actual scene from it.

Good Fiction: Character, Plot, and Setting. Always.

You better believe that characters need to have characterization even in a short back cover blurb and their internal and external conflicts need to be as evident as their goals and motivations in that place. What is a back cover blurb if a summary of the character, the plot, conflict, the reason to read? What are the stakes? If there aren't any, then your blurb (and book) isn't strong enough. Give the reader someone and something to root for. Setting doesn't need a lot but a hint always enhances. Just like with a character, you can personalize a setting within a blurb in just a few words. All three elements of good fiction need to be included in a blurb. Always. Concisely. Intriguingly, with tension.

Here are some examples taken from bestsellers with all the review-slanted and overinflated comments removed. Pay special attention to how each has strongly described characters, plot and setting in a small amount of space (you might also want to try to guess the genre based on the tone of each):

The Winter Sea
by Susanna Kearsley

History has all but forgotten...
In the spring of 1708, an invading Jacobite fleet of French and Scottish soldiers nearly succeeded in landing the exiled James Stewart in Scotland to reclaim his crown.

Now, Carrie McClelland hopes to turn that story into her next bestselling novel. Settling herself in the shadow of Slains Castle, she creates a heroine named for one of her own ancestors and starts to write.

But when she discovers her novel is more fact than fiction, Carrie wonders if she might be dealing with ancestral memory, making her the only living person who knows the truth—the ultimate betrayal—that happened all those years ago, and that knowledge comes very close to destroying her...

Way Station
by Clifford D. Simak

An ageless hermit runs a secret way station for alien visitors in the Wisconsin woods. Enoch Wallace is not like other humans. Living a secluded life in the backwoods of Wisconsin, he carries a nineteenth-century rifle and never seems to age-a fact that has recently caught the attention of prying government eyes. The truth is, Enoch is the last surviving veteran of the American Civil War and, for close to a century, he has operated a secret way station for aliens passing through on journeys to other stars. But the gifts of knowledge and immortality that his intergalactic guests have bestowed upon him are proving to be a nightmarish burden, for they have opened Enoch's eyes to humanity's impending destruction. Still, one final hope remains for the human race...though the cure could ultimately prove more terrible than the disease.

Camino Island
by John Grisham

A gang of thieves stage a daring heist from a secure vault deep below Princeton University's Firestone Library. Their loot is priceless, but Princeton has insured it for twenty-five million dollars.

Bruce Cable owns a popular bookstore in the sleepy resort town of Santa Rosa on Camino Island in Florida. He makes his real money, though, as a prominent dealer in rare books. Very few people know that he occasionally dabbles in the black market of stolen books and manuscripts.

Mercer Mann is a young novelist with a severe case of writer's block who has recently been laid off from her teaching position. She is approached by an elegant, mysterious woman working for an even more mysterious company. A generous offer of money convinces Mercer to go undercover and infiltrate Bruce Cable's circle of literary friends, ideally getting close enough to him to learn his secrets.

But eventually Mercer learns far too much, and there's trouble in paradise...

The Mirror of Blurb and Book

If you want to get down to the core of your story (just as we talked about in the last point with character, plot and setting), then write a back cover blurb for it. All three of the elements need to be evident in the blurb for it to be effective, as we said, in greater or lesser degrees, but if conflict or characterization are lacking in your story, you'll almost always see what's missing nakedly in your back cover blurb. The blurb will mirror the book. It has to! Any struggle at all in trying to figure out exactly what your story conflicts are may be a strong indicator that these same things are lacking in the book. This is another reason to write your story blurbs first, before doing any work on the book itself. Writing a blurb forces you to think deeply about the core elements of good fiction before you commit yourself to hundreds of pages and only then figure out that something crucial is missing.

Without *character*, there is no story; without character, there is no blurb.

Without *conflict*, there is no story; without conflict, there is no blurb.

Without *setting*, there is no story; without setting, there is no blurb.

Your story may be the origin of the problem if you're trying to write about an invisible or poorly constructed conflict in the story and your mind goes blank.

Information Overload!

Don't overload your blurbs with too much information or complicated concepts. Maybe your character Zelsa

Abdoeiaelkleadk Shultamoaton lives in Oaidahfaohg and rides a Qpdfoapagjoargj to work where Zelsa Abdoeiaelkleadk Shultamoaton is the YuPu Mointan. Within your book, you have space and the creative means to describe what these are in terms readers can understand. But in a back cover blurb, Zelsa lives in the desert and rides a horse-like creature to the temple where Zelsa is the High Priest.

Additionally, in a back cover blurb, we don't need to know every detail of your characters' lives and we certainly don't need to know what they do from one chapter to the next outlined in the blurb. We need the focused, most important details of character, plot and setting and tension.

Here's an example of a series of story blurbs I revised that started with such insanely complicated visions, I had trouble seeing the forest for the trees at first:

The Islands of the Sixteen Gods Series, Book 2: Beloved of the River Goddess
by Stephen Symons
Fantasy

Original blurb:

After a year of torment and pursuit halfway across northwest Kalion, Edrun and Jina have finally found themselves both safe and well-funded. They decide to take a long, leisurely and much-deserved holiday in the fascinating Temple-City of Hazek, while they decide on their future.

Their happy idyll does not last for long. While enjoying a lazy lunch outside a tavern, Edrun, to his horror, finds himself publically hailed as a Lord of the Gathering. The warrior aristocracy of the Islands of the Sixteen Gods are very protective of their status and privileges, and are swift to inflict punishments both brutal and bloody upon those who would usurp their position. Moments later Edrun and Jina discover that their former nemesis Halgar Rassvorea is in Hazek, and has in mind a sadistic revenge against them for the trouble that they caused him in the past.

Immediately any thoughts of a peaceful and prosperous life ahead are shattered as they realise that Hazek is no longer safe for them. They decide to make for Amronulu, the citadel of the Lords of the Kalalutorm whom Edrun befriended after he had defeated them at the battle of Garinesigas. Their plans are soon cast into disarray as, barely having left Hazek, they rescue the fiery Adeta, the daughter of a wealthy merchant, from brigands who are attacking her. Adeta is fleeing an arranged marriage and Ordron insists return her to her betrothed, the arrogant and sadistic Lord Ordron Mailaranarad. But Lord Ordron is anything but grateful, and soon Edrun finds that he must once more fight for his life and that of Jina.

The back cover blurbs for all the individual stories in this series needed revision, due in large part by all the unnecessary details that the simple summaries that were most exciting were mired in. I "freed" those by whittling each one down to get to the heart of the story, as you'll see in this revision:

After a year of torment and pursuit halfway across northwest Kalion, Edrun and Jina have finally found themselves both safe and well-funded. They decide to take a much-deserved holiday in the fascinating Temple-City of Hazek while they decide on their future.

While enjoying a lazy lunch outside a tavern, to his horror, Edrun finds himself publically hailed as a Lord of the Gathering. The warrior aristocracy of the Islands of the Sixteen Gods are very protective of their status and privileges and are swift to inflict punishments upon those who would usurp their position. Moments later, Edrun and Jina discover a former nemesis is also in Hazek and has in mind a sadistic revenge against them for the trouble they caused him in the past.

Making for a citadel that was once a safe haven for them, their plans are soon cast into disarray when they're forced to rescue the fiery daughter of a wealthy merchant from attacking brigands. Once more Edrun and Jina find themselves in a fight for their lives.

Keep in mind that if your back cover blurb has complicated concepts that only someone who's actually read the book could really understand, you've done this backwards. In other words, if you have to read the *story* in order to understand the *blurb*, you've missed the point of a blurb. The blurb should make the story understandable and intriguing.

Information Under-whelm

Too little information is just as bad as too much. I revised a blurb once that basically had something like this:

A death. A concealment. A pledge.
When Mike's aunt gives him a map marked with two Xs, it leads not to buried treasure but to secrets.

There was so little to work with, I requested that the author flesh out characters, conflicts and goals and motivations. Even the high-concept blurb felt sparse to me. Someone's dead, okay, but who, how long ago, what were the circumstances? Something's hidden, great, but what kind of concealment? A pledge, all right, but what about it? What did it matter? Everything about this blurb made me want to know more. While the blurb as I revised it held some intrigue, it still wasn't enough to actually pull readers in, to get them to pick up the book and figure out what it's actually about by reading it. Yes, short is good, but too short can totally fail to garner interest and intrigue.

Say What?

Does your blurb make sense? Is there anything confusing in it? I revised a blurb once that had me scratching my head until I made sense out of it:

Embrace of Memory
by Vicki McElfresh
Fantasy

Original blurb:

> The past stalks Cree Lin in dreams of fire, pain and power he cannot control, but he doesn't remember the events that left him scarred and shamed. He knows his out of control magic left a village in ruins. He knows people died, but he remembers nothing except fire and pain. He's forsworn all magic, except his gift with animals. He returns to the village he destroyed, hoping to recover the memories he's lost and somehow make restitution for his sins.
>
> In the village he meets Benjamin, a blacksmith who should hate him, but who seems determined to help him make peace with his past. Benjamin convinces him to seek out Mirayla, the healer who had treated his wounds years earlier. Finding Mirayla means facing his past, including the dark memories he's shared with no one, memories that hold the key to unlocking his untapped potential.

Some of the original blurb confused me and seemed contradictory (i.e., if he can't remember, he can't have memories, dark or otherwise...) so I tried to remove that where I saw it and work around the suggested premise. I did delve into a few assumptions near the end of this revision because it seemed to need a greater punch there. Also, I took out the mention of his magic with animals only because what form that took was necessary to including it--can he talk to animals? heal them? something else? As is, it was confusing to include that. I think my revision turned something that originally had a lot of potential (and I'm sure the novel itself is wonderful) into something clear and exciting:

> Cree Lin is being stalked by his past in dreams of fire, pain and power he's unable to control. Upon waking, he can't

remember fully the events that have left him scarred and ashamed, but he does know that his reckless magic use brought ruin to an entire village. Innocent people died, and he's to blame. For that reason, he's sworn off all magic. Desperate for closure, he returns to the village he destroyed, hoping to recover what he's lost and somehow make restitution for his sins.

In the village he meets a blacksmith who should hate him, but instead Benjamin seems determined to help him make peace with his past. At the blacksmith's urging, Cree sets out to find the village healer. Locating Mirayla means forcing himself to delve into the dark recesses of his mind...places he fears hold the key to unlocking his potential for unequalled power--and even greater destruction.

Needless to say, the very last circumstance you want to confuse a reader is with the blurb because that book will be dropped faster than a hot potato. Make sense of your story in plain English.

Your Synopsis is Showing, Dear

Does your blurb read more like a synopsis than a brief summary? Too much plot, too many details, too wordy? I was given this "blurb" to revise for *Hit and Run* by Bob Rich:

HIT AND RUN is inspirational fiction, designed to induce culture change: away from hate, prejudice, aggression, selfishness, toward compassion, decency cooperation. It is also speculative fiction, in that a paranormal device is used to connect the narrator, 84 year old Sylvia, to the protagonist, Charlie, 14, who commits a horrific multiple murder at the start of the book. Word count is 99,800. The theme of the story is the power of unconditional Love, the Love in the bible, although the book is not at all religious, and will appeal even to an atheist. It also demonstrates well-researched psychological processes showing how people from the worst backgrounds can become decent, upright people. The most important requirement is deciding to copy one or more suitable role models.

Old Sylvia barely escapes death when a teenage driver slaughters six children and the crossing supervisor. Being an artist, she draws his portrait. That night, he appears to her through a process neither understands, cursing and abusing her. At the victims' memorial service, someone wishes for vengeance. Sylvia responds, "Hate begets hate, vengeance only leads to vengeance, violence feeds on itself. Only love can stop the endless cycle. Only love can turn hate into love." Charlie gradually accepts her support when she cares for his little brother, Tommy, taking him to visit Charlie in prison. He decides to model his behaviour on her. Meanwhile, a gang attacks Charlie, who kills their leader, adding manslaughter to charges of murder. Sylvia's speech has inspired the local community, resulting in a team to support Charlie and Tommy, including bereaved parents. Charlie keeps growing in decency and wisdom through several other crises. He accepts his jail term. Sylvia knows that her final task is over. After her final contact with Charlie, her son finds her dead, with a smile on her face, and the record of the remarkable nine months completed. This book is that record.

Trying to craft this isn't a back cover blurb wasn't easy, but here's what I came up with:

Eighty-four-year-old Sylvia barely escapes death when a teenage driver plows down six children and their crossing guard, never looking back. Shaken, Sylvia finds herself drawing his portrait, creating a disconcerting connection with this fourteen-year-old boy that allows the police to locate and arrest the culprit of the heinous hit-and-run. That night, Charlie appears to her, through a supernatural process neither understands, cursing and abusing her.

At the victims' memorial service, the outcry for justice and vengeance is almost as violent as the original crime committed. Sylvia's words of wisdom that hate begets hate, violence feeds on itself, and only love can create love is all that keeps a retaliating crusade from ensuing.

Driven by the brief supernatural connection they'd shared, Sylvia visits Charlie in prison, seeking to understand the troubled boy and offering to bring his little brother for visits. Gradually, Sylvia's gentle sagacity makes inroads in winning Charlie's support but long-held habits are hard to break and it isn't long before Charlie finds trouble even in jail. Can one woman's tenacity and belief in the power of love make a difference in an entire community...and in the life of one boy who wants to believe and change?

Whittling and honing in on the gist of the story and characters is the best way to avoid a synopsis which reveals all instead of a summary that captures only the heart.

Colloquialism and Cliché

Avoid both of those tongue-twisting C's if at all possible. What makes sense in one country might not make any sense at all with another. Books are distributed all around the world these days, so it makes a lot of sense to avoid non-typical phrases in favor of general usage. I had an incident in revising a back cover blurb with an Australian author who used the phrase "at the tip" when describing a place where a murder had taken place. (The blurb in question is actually in Appendix A: Wendy Laing's Joe Doe Mystery Book 2, if you want to read it.) I'd never heard this phrase before. I assumed she meant something like "at the coastline". I asked her point-black what "at the tip" meant since it was important to her to keep it in. Long story short, I finally found out that "at the tip" meant "at the rubbish dump", or in very general language, at a garbage dump. She had no idea that this wasn't a common phrase everywhere. While I'm sure some people would have realized what this meant, you can't assume everyone will, so it's best to avoid colloquialisms in blurbs altogether.

In the same vein, don't assume every single person on the planet knows everything you do. Maybe you're a war buff and a genius to boot. You wrote a book about a war; it's obvious you know what you're talking about. But don't assume everyone who reads your book (or wants to) has the same level of understanding for your subject. Forgive your reader for being a moronic simpleton. Perhaps the fact that he's looking at your book as a potential purchase allows him leniency. Plain language, especially for a complicated subject, is always best in a blurb. And acronyms--blurbs are absolutely not the place for that black hole of potential confusion. Finally, clichés will steal precious words that you could use for powerful, impacting words that draw a reader in. Avoid them as you would a semi barreling down on you.

Save Your Bullets

Bullet lists, that is. In a blurb, it's never permissible to include a bullet list of events that happen in the story in place of actual fiction summaries (though they are effective in nonfiction blurbs, as we talked about in Chapter Two). If the book blurb isn't fleshed out enough, readers won't be drawn in--and they certainly won't be lured by itemized lists of plot-points. For instance:

> In *The Most Amazing Story Ever*, the mystery of the kid with the panpipe is finally unraveled, the true power behind Blah-Blah's Legacy is revealed, the jaw-dropping fate of the barefoot girl is unveiled. This and many other discoveries await the reader within this mind-blowing tale of suspense.

I've seen this so often in blurbs, it isn't funny. Imagine if we actually put in a bullet list, as this blurb implies:

In *The Most Amazing Story Ever*:

-the mystery of the kid with the panpipe is finally unraveled

-the true power behind Blah-Blah's Legacy is revealed

-the jaw-dropping fate of the barefoot girl is unveiled
This and many other discoveries await the reader within this mind-blowing tale of suspense.

Have we actually learned anything about the characters, the plot, the setting from this bullet list or what's before and after it? A fiction reader doesn't want a shopping list of things he's going to pick up only by reading the book itself instead of a proper summary.

The I'm-Without-Equal Author Review Slant

We're not talking about actual reviews or endorsements from other authors or professionals--those are legitimate but they're not part of a back cover summary (even if they may be put wrongly with the blurb). Never, ever for any reason include a "review slant" to your back cover blurb. What do I mean by that? Here's an example that's not from an actual blurb but a kind of consolidation of what I've seen predominately, usually tacked needlessly on the end of the blurb:

"In this gripping tale of heartbreaking betrayal and whipsaw action, readers will fall in love with these intriguing characters and their lives will never be the same as they're compelled to reach the last page."

I have the feeling a lot of authors will laugh and claim they haven't done this in writing their own blurbs, but such a huge number of back cover blurbs out there have something like this. As we said, this is not an actual review from a credible reviewer. This is the author imposing the rose-colored view of his own book on his readers, not only lauding his work in bold word pictures but proclaiming it something that it may not even actually be. Review slants in a blurb reek of desperation and arrogance. On principle alone, some readers will blow you a raspberry and say, "Pass." Or, worse, they'll try to prove you wrong by blasting the book to the stratosphere everywhere they can.

But publishers are also guilty of these kinds of review-slanted blurbs. Instead of a summary of what's in the story, you'll find paragraphs talking about how great the author is, with or without reviews from credible reviewers, nothing that actually summarizes the story. It's okay if the reviews are there *in addition to the story summary*; it's not okay if they're used *in place* of the summary.

When I first went to Amazon to find out about The Twilight Saga books at that time when it was all the craze and I still hadn't read it, I couldn't find a single page that gave me a summary of what to expect in each title. Instead, the virtues of the author were extolled (again, with or without actual reviews). At that point, I didn't know the author, hadn't read anything of hers, but I wanted to read this series--preferably starting by figuring out what in the world the series was about in the first place. But it didn't happen! I had to read the books to figure it out. If they weren't so popular, I might not have bothered with the series without the back cover blurbs to guide me. Ironically, the back cover blurb for *Twilight* is fabulous and sells the book without all the inflated blurbs:

> "About three things I was absolutely positive:
> First, Edward was a vampire.
> Second, there was a part of him--and I didn't know how dominant that part might be--that thirsted for my blood.
> Third, I was unconditionally and irrevocably in love with him."

If It Can't Stand Alone, It Can't Stand. Period.

Here's the hardest part of series blurb writing: You have to write every blurb as if this is the first and only book in the series. If you don't or can't, you really will lose new readers. Even those who are fans might be lost, given that they may read books years apart. The back cover blurb of a series book can't be written as if everyone will understand it...unless you don't care whether new readers ever start the series after Book 2. If a back cover blurb is overwhelmed with the kind of complicated information that makes no sense unless you've read the book (or previous ones), it will seem as if the story has no rhyme or reason. Where to begin? There's nothing user-friendly about complicated series books. If a reader hasn't committed from the beginning, there's a sense of, *What's the point? I'll be lost by those new to the series.*

Find a way to write your series back cover blurbs so they're accessible instead of terrifyingly intimidating and off-putting. Imagine someone picking up a series book for the first time and tailor the back cover blurb in a way that will welcome new readers, regardless of where they're starting from. From that point, write your series back cover blurbs as if each book is a stand-alone title. Introduce characters, settings, and plots as if they're brand new.

Don't Give It All Away on the First Date

Just like a reviewer shouldn't in a review, the author must *never, ever, ever* give away a twist or the end of the story in the blurb. I'm using *A Christmas Carol* so you can see an example of a blurb that gives away the ending. True, who hasn't read, heard of, or seen a movie version of this story? But when writing your own back cover blurbs never give away the ending of the story. Note that the high-concept sentence included is condensed from the 2009 Disney animated movie of the book, since the book itself didn't have one:

Ghosts of Past, Present, and Future take miserly Ebenezer Scrooge on a journey in the hope of transforming his bitterness.

On Christmas Eve, Scrooge is haunted by the ghost of his former business partner Jacob Marley, who warns him that he will be visited by three spirits. During the night, the ghosts of Christmas Past, Christmas Present, and Christmas Yet to Come show Scrooge the scenes of his youth, the poverty-stricken Christmas currently being endured by his loyal clerk Bob Cratchit and his crippled son Tiny Tim—and the lonely future that awaits him if he continues in his grasping ways. He awakens on Christmas morning chastened by his nocturnal experiences and resolves to be a better man.

In another example, I was asked to revise the back cover blurb of a children's book called *The Magic Kite* (originally titled *Su Ling's Kite*) by Joann Rohrbach that was going to be reissued.

Original blurb:

Su Ling's Kite is a delightful story based on facts. Su Ling, the little Chinese princess, saves her honorable kingdom from falling into the hands of enemy soldiers. With the help of an astrologer, some kites, and the people in the kingdom, Su Ling masterminds a plan to save her kingdom in a peaceful way that benefits everyone. Building kites is an interesting and fun hobby

This delightful folk tale will warm the hearts of all kids, young and old. It captures the mystery and magic of Chinese culture along with their expertise in kite building and flying.

Since kites never seem to go out of style, you might decide to try it. At the end of the story, you will find some helpful kiting tips. With a little time, patience, and decent weather, you too can have a beautiful kite soaring high in the sky.

I found a lot of repetition in this "review-slanted" blurb. In my revision, I simplified it greatly, took out the repetitiousness and the review-slant as much as possible:

Can a small princess save the people in her honorable kingdom from falling into the hands of enemy soldiers in this magical, fact-based Chinese folk tale? With the help astrologers and kites, Su Ling masterminds a plan to win peace that benefits everyone. Learn the timeless, ancient art of building and flying kites that will soar high in the sky while discovering the fate of Su Ling and those in her kingdom.

After this was presented to the author, she wasn't happy with it (though we ended up using that version for the high-concept blurb). She preferred her original, longer version, but I had very definite issues with simply bulking up a blurb by falling into a review slant or repetitiousness and--worst of all, in opinion-- telling the whole story within the blurb as it's so easy to do that with a children's book, which is short to begin with. I decided to try something different. I researched kites and decided to use the most fascinating aspects of that research within the blurb. I think it added intrigue without falling into all the pitfalls. At the time of this writing, I haven't heard the author's opinion on this revision.

Can a small princess save the people in her honorable kingdom with kites?

5th-century BC Chinese philosophers are credited with the invention of the kite using the plentiful silk and bamboo that are native to the continent and ideal for kite building and flying. By 549 AD, these versatile and colorful winged, tethered heavier-than-air crafts were being used to measure distances, test the wind, lift men, signal, facilitate rescues, as well as communicate and send messages for military operations. But beloved kites are best known for the fun they provide those of every age!

Su Ling and her father, the Emperor, watch the nobles in their honorable land flying their kites and he explains that they're carrying a warning of the soldier camps surrounding the kingdom. How can they prevent their people from falling into enemy hands?

Long years before, the Emperor reluctantly placed a ban on kite-flying to protect crops. In this magical, fact-based Chinese folk tale, Su Ling's cheerful spirit refuses to be dampened as she enlists the aid of the children in the kingdom and astrologers to mastermind a plan using kites and the enemies' own superstitious natures in order to win peace. Learn the timeless, ancient art of building and flying kites that will soar high in the sky while discovering the fate of Su Ling and those in her kingdom.

Don't deflate the big moments or surprises in the book by detailing them in your blurbs. A common guideline is to stick to only information that can be found *in the first three chapters* of your book.

Beyond that, all you want to include are vague hints about the complications to come.

The High Note

End your blurb on a high note, the highest of all. That last sentence needs to sizzle, not fizzle. You've already dropped your line throughout the blurb, but the last sentence is hopefully where you reel the reader in. That hook had better do its work. If your last sentence is weak, you could lose the catch. Sometimes making the last sentence in a blurb a question or an exclamation can add intrigue. Adding ellipses can also make the reader eager for more.

As a "blurbologist", I see this so often it isn't funny: Instead of a cliffhanger at the end of the blurb, it's like the author threw up his hands and said, "I don't know!" with the last sentence. I can't tell you how many times I've been deflated instead of energized by the final sentence. As an example from an absolutely fabulous author I've read and is a good friend of mine, here's one I've revised that originally had a deflating final sentence:

Dangerous Waters Series, Book 3: Unquiet Spirits
by Dee Lloyd
Paranormal Romance

Original blurb:

Headstrong Kit Schofield, convinced that the hit-and-run that almost killed her was a random act of violence, heads north to her family resort at Spirit Lake. Not-so-convinced lifelong buddy Bart Thornton joins her as self-appointed bodyguard, much to Kit's chagrin—at first.

Disturbing old secrets and equally unsettling ghosts lurk in the lodge and the calm waters of the deceptively peaceful resort...and a deadly, elusive killer strikes again.

But all this fades into the background when one kiss unleashes unexpected, unwelcome and totally distracting passion.

Two lusty ghosts who drop clues about old murders and insist Kit and Bart are soul mates further confuse their lives.

My revision:

Headstrong Kit Schofield heads north to her family resort at Spirit Lake, convinced the hit-and-run that almost killed her was a random act of violence. Not-so-convinced, lifelong buddy Bart Thornton joins her as a self-appointed bodyguard, much to Kit's chagrin--at first.

Two lusty ghosts drop clues about old murders and insist that Kit and Bart are soul mates. One kiss proves it, unleashing unexpected, unwelcome and totally distracting passion between them.

Disturbing old secrets and equally unsettling ghosts lurk in the lodge as well as in the calm waters of the deceptively peaceful resort. In the calm, a deadly, elusive killer strikes again...

Remember what we've already said: The blurb is frequently the first thing that's read about a book. Don't let the last sentence be the *last* someone would want to read. Make that hook the very best part of the blurb, sending readers scrambling for more.

I'm Embarrassed to Have to Say This...

Mostly because I shouldn't have to but...I have to. *Revise your blurb* just like you do every other single piece of writing you produce. As Michaelbrent Collings says, "Blurbs ARE hard! That's the point, partly: like so much in the world of writing, people think, 'I can do that!' with little thought about the skill and practice that goes into it. It's more than jotting down whatever word-vomit a person barfs up. Practice, practice, practice. My first good blurb was two sentences, and it took almost a week to figure it out." A book blurb isn't simply a one-off. *Finished the book, now I'll churn out a summary in thirty seconds.* It shouldn't be word-vomit. It's an evolution. You start with the big picture (and it might be wordy); you whittle it down; you refine and hone it and make it shine like a diamond. You keep doing that until it's breathtaking. In Appendix B, we're going to do some exercises to practice this, and, in every one of them, you're going to revise the blurbs multiple times.

You've Gotta See the Baby

Just like you'd send your book out to critique partners or beta-readers, send out your blurbs. Show them off, especially if you have various sizing. See which has gets the most favorable responses. If you don't have anyone to give you feedback, you can start your own blurb exchange club with other writers online. Test the waters before the book is published with one certain blurb.

A Blurb is For the Reader

Obvious, huh? But most authors seem to think the blurb is for someone else--themselves, a publisher, the characters. But the reader is your audience. The blurb is your sales pitch, a love letter, a means to tell the reader what to expect, a promise that you make that this is just a taste of something even better. You're not explaining something or informing the reader of anything (that's boring); you're enticing them to come in and join you for adventure. You give away *enough* without giving away *everything*. The blurb is where you ask questions (though usually not in the form of question), where you raise questions in the minds of readers...but you don't answer them in the blurb--you answer them in the book. To raise those questions without actually asking questions is a phenomenally clever feat that all authors should learn to master.

With a blurb, you set a scene so compelling, it's like the door that leads the reader into your world. Either the door gets opened or it doesn't. The purpose of the blurb is a-three-fold C for a reader: *capture*, (to provide) *content*, (to give a reason to) *care*.

Above all, realize that every single word matters in a blurb. Picture readers in a bookstore browsing books or online at a computer they can be called away from at any second. You have about ten seconds (the "10 Second Elevator Pitch" you may have heard about!) to get them hooked. Arguably, these 250 or so words may be the most important you write because they're the ones that either make or break you.

Please, Sir, I Want Some More

A blurb is a summary of the story that's rife with suspense, intrigue, a reason--every reason--to want to keep reading! If the reader isn't left with the desire to read more, the blurb isn't effectively good and it's time to start over.

Practice Makes Perfect Session:

Using the Blurb Evaluation Checklist included here (and Appendix C), use it in your evaluation of the blurbs included in Appendixes A and B as well as the blurbs of other published novels.

Blurb Evaluation Checklist

Pros

On the "Pro" Blurb Evaluation Checklist, we only want to see checks in the

"Yes" column. Any checks in the "No" column should send you back to the blurb to fix the problem pinpointed.

Pro	Yes	No	Comments
Are the main characters actually named in the back cover blurb?			
Are there short, concise "descriptor punches" included in the blurb for the main characters?			
Is there a simple, descriptive inference of time and place in the blurb?			
Is the blurb written in present tense?			
Is the blurb written in third-person POV?			
Is the genre evident in the blurb (preferably without actually saying what it is)?			
Does the blurb capture the mood/tone/language inside the book?			
Are the stakes made clear with just enough hyperbole to induce excitement?			
Is the reason for the title of the book evident or inferred in the blurb?			
Are strong, compelling, impacting words and short sentences used in the blurb?			
Does the blurb make sense?			
Are hints of three elements of good fiction--character, plot (internal and external) and setting--included in a blurb?			
Are the characters goals and motivations clear and concise in the blurb?			

Does the blurb give just enough information/intrigue to make the reader want to continue the journey by reading the book?			
Is a series installment blurb written as if it's the only book in the series? Can it stand alone and make sense of the story inside separate from the other books in the series?			
If the book is part of a series, are all story arcs kept within the individual back cover blurbs while the series arc is clearly defined in the series blurb?			
Is the back cover blurb of a series book written so that book and the series itself are accessible and *welcome* new readers, regardless of where they're starting from?			
Has the blurb been revised multiple times so it's as tight and impacting as possible? Is it available in a variety of sizes, preferably 150, 100, and 75 words?			
If the book is part of a series, does it have a series blurb, a high-concept blurb, and a back cover blurb that are used in every promotion, at every distributor's website?			
If the book is a single-title, does it have a high-concept blurb and a back cover blurb that are used in every promotion, at every distributor's website?			
Has the blurb gotten feedback from critique partners, readers			

	Yes	No	Comments
or beta-testers?			
Has the blurb raised intriguing questions in reader's mind that can only be answered by reading the book?			
Is the blurb effectively good (i.e., not just well-written but capable of convincing readers to part with hard-earned dollars to read)?			

Cons

On the "Con" Blurb Evaluation Checklist, we only want to see checks in the "No" column. Any checks in the "Yes" column should send you back to the blurb to fix the problem pinpointed.

Con	Yes	No	Comments
Are there more than 3 characters mentioned in the back cover blurb?			
Is the blurb in any way misleading?			
Are there any unimportant, unexplained, overblown details mentioned needlessly in the blurb?			
Are there provocative questions asked in the blurb that you already know the answer to?			
Are there more than two questions in a row in the blurb?			
Do any of the sentences in the blurb read as if the author was asked: "What is your story about? Tell me in a single sentence."			
Are there long, hard-to-digest			

sentences used in the blurb?			
Is dialogue (or dialogue tags) used in the blurb?			
Is the blurb, in whole or part, actually an excerpt from the book?			
Are you struggling to find the conflict in the blurb because maybe it's a mirror of what's lacking in the story?			
Is the blurb overburdened by too much information or complicated concepts? Is there an assumption that everyone knows what something in the blurb means when they might not? Would you have to read the *book* to understand the *blurb*?			
Is the blurb so lean on details, it fails to draw interest?			
Is there anything in the blurb that could be confusing?			
Does the blurb read more like a synopsis than a brief summary?			
Does the blurb include colloquialisms or clichés?			
If the blurb isn't for a nonfiction title, does it contain a bullet list of events in place of actual summary?			
Does the blurb contain any author review-slanted phrases (basically reviews of the work written by the author of it himself)?			
Is the back cover blurb of a series book written so that book and the series itself are			

terrifyingly intimidating and off-putting--not at all welcoming to a new reader?			
Does the back cover blurb give away or deflate a twist, the ending, a surprise inside the pages?			
Does the last sentence of the blurb fizzle instead of sizzle? Is there a hook that has the reader champing at the bit to read the story?			

Evaluate Your Own Blurbs

Using the Blurb Evaluation Checklist included here (and Appendix C), evaluate your own blurbs.

***

Writing blurbs isn't easy. There are so many pitfalls, so many things not to do, the process becomes a little terrifying. This chapter full of tips along with The Blurb Evaluation Checklist and exercises in the back of this book should help take the fear out of learning this tricky art. In the next chapter, we'll talk about blurb sizing for a variety of applications as well as branding with blurbs.

CHAPTER FOUR
Blurb Sizing and Branding

"I used to tell people 'Start small--write your epic and work your way UP to short stories.' There's something incredibly difficult about writing careful, short pieces. [Additionally,] the outside of your book--the cover design, the spine, the lettering, EVERYTHING-- is for one purpose: To separate readers from their money. Your blurb is part of that." ~Michaelbrent Collings from Blurbs That Bore, Blurbs That Blare

In the first chapter, we talked about how long (or short) blurbs should ideally be. Frankly, longer blurbs tend to get the short end of the stick when it comes to publisher, distributor and promotional websites and, in part, because readers may not have the time or inclination to read something long. Bottom line, the only reason for shortening a blurb that's already effectively good is because we're forced to because of publishing and marketing considerations and limitations.

Like it or not, authors do have to think about branding as well. These days, writers are the masters of their own domains. They wear all the hats (writer, publisher, editor, artist and marketer) and so they need to know how to promote their own brand. The idea of branding is to make something utterly memorable. Our author status and our books are what we're trying to brand and blurbs are almost always what we use to hook readers, especially for series.

In this chapter, we're going to talk about both blurb sizing and blurb branding.

THE ART OF WHITTLING

Let's get our axiom firmly in mind before we go further on the topic of sizing. An effectively good blurb either is effectively good in making a reader open the book or it's not. That's the point and all that matters. A blurb can be good and not effective, or effective and not good, but either it's *both* or it won't work. Ultimately, it doesn't matter a whit if it's long or short or somewhere in-between. You can have a thousand word blurb that's so amazing readers devour it and immediately want to read the book just as you might see a short, punchy blurb that's incredibly well-written but doesn't make you want to read the story inside the pages.

But you have to have various sizing because there are so many restrictions on blurb length these days. Being forced to have a blurb no longer than 150, 100 or a groan-out-loud 75 words can be incredibly limiting. Especially when you combine your series, high-concept, and back cover blurbs (as you should always, everywhere, every single time, if you follow my earlier advice), you'll end up with a formidable word count. This doesn't allow you to have more than a sentence or two for each or, alternately, it means you're forced to cut the series and/or either the high-concept blurb or the back cover one altogether (which can work, but again it's very restrictive).

We talked earlier about how the actual back cover of a physical copy of the book may not allow you to have a much larger word count than what the book information form on distributor and publisher websites accept. Promotion of your books, whether a single title or a series, can also offer meager space for blurbs--and, in this case, that may be wise. Promotional ads are "sound bites" of information, so the shorter and catchier, the better.

The easiest way to handle this situation is to take your longest blurb (and this applies to high-concept, back cover and series blurbs)--which may be you original (and it can conceivably be in excess of 450 words long, as it is always in my case), and whittle it down to the various sizes you may need for all of these applications. I suggest having at least three sizes because they're usually the number maximums you're given: 1) 150 words, 2) 100 words, and 3) 75 words. Along with your original long-form blurbs, with these sizes you've covered pretty much all the bases when it comes to applications you might need them for.

For the 75-word limit, this may mean that you whittle both your high-concept and back cover blurbs to fit into that 75-word limit. If the book is part of a series, you'll have to take the combined three blurbs and somehow get it down to 75-words total (more or less). As I suggested before, one way to do this is to either cut one blurb or the other. For a single-title, maybe your high-concept blurb says all it needs to about the story and you can just go with that. Or you might cut that and carve the back cover blurb down until it hits the 75-word max. For a series blurb, if you have a series high-concept blurb and it does the work you need it to on its own, cut the back cover blurb altogether and whittle the high-concept story blurbs down until, combined with the series blurb, you have around 75 words. Or do that with your back cover blurb sans the high-concept one.

As I've stated a number of times already, I'm a firm believer in the fact that series, high-concept and back cover blurbs should be used together, always, everywhere, every single time. But there have been times when it's hard to do that. Say, a promotional website doesn't allow me the space I need to include everything. Then I need to figure out how I'm going to rearrange things. I have a romantic science fiction horror series that has a fairly large word count--between the three blurbs, it has 424 words. I'm always reluctant to do any cropping with it because I think the combination works so well together. The series blurb basically covers all three books so effectively, I never need to mention any part of "series arc" in the actual story blurbs. The story blurbs can be made very tight at that point because I don't have to worry about whether the series arc can be covered adequately.

However, one caveat that I feel has to be said here about a series blurb: Many times, the back cover of a print book and potentially the publisher, distributor or promotional websites won't allow you to include all you want to for a series book. So when you combine your series blurb, your high-concept blurb, and your back cover blurb--regardless of the size--you might find you have to leave out something vital. For that reason, you have to be careful when taking too much out of one blurb component. For instance, if your series blurb sets the overview for all the individual titles, you might consider leaving out basic details for characters or premise within the individual blurbs. But what if the series blurb is removed? Do you get enough information about the character and premise from the back cover blurbs to be intriguing without that necessary overview that's in the series blurb? Sometimes a crucial element is eliminated that can ruin the impact. For that reason, I do recommend leaving a very short bit in each back cover blurb (maybe one sentence) that covers the pivotal character and premise overview. As an example, in Appendix A, I include Wendy Laing's Jane Doe Mystery Series. The premise of this series is that the heroine in the series is a detective with the ability to communicate with ghosts. This is a secret she had to hide, but it's how she manages to solve so many of her cases where others would fail. This is a crucial premise for the character, including her job, and to have either left out of a book blurb where the series overview isn't included would make the back cover summary extremely confusing. So for each of her revised story blurbs, I include a sentence about that character's job and the premise, though the expanded overview of it is also in the series blurb.

Below, I'll show you how this is done:

Arrow of Time Chronicles
by Karen Wiesner

High-concept series blurb:

> *A timeless universal truth: No simple solutions, no easy answers, and nothing is ever free...* **[15 words]**

Series blurb:

> When mankind realized Earth would soon become uninhabitable, Humans formed a cooperative central nexus in order to save themselves from certain extinction.

Together, they built and transferred their population to massive space habitations in orbit of their planet and as many as possible revolving around the other planetary bodies in the Sol System. They also constructed spacefaring "liveships" in hopes of traveling through the galaxy in search of new homes. Unbelievably after almost a hundred years, their communications sent out into the farthest reaches of the universe to discover other intelligent life secures an audience. Their first allies arrived in mankind's solar system in 2073 and shared their knowledge, technology and resources to not only power their liveships for swift navigation through space corridors that fold space and time but also provided the scientific advancements necessary to eventually heal their dying planet.

Though mankind has a brand-new shaky start, strong potential alliances, and hope for tomorrow, only fifty-eight years into their desperate struggle for survival, a hostile enemy with Napoleonic ambitions emerges as a yet another threat to not only mankind's survival, but also that of their associates who have faced the aliens in times past. Abruptly, the peace the allies have begun to forge is jeopardized as questionable agendas and hidden motives are unveiled. In the wake of these very real, immediate threats a cataclysmic organic menace is only beginning to be recognized, ensuring the total annihilation of every living thing in the universe if, together, they can't find a way to stop it. **[255 words]**

Back cover blurb:

Immutable, Book 1

Spacefaring liveship, the *Aero*, is on a routine mission to the far-flung regions of the galaxy when they receive a distress call from one of their oldest space habitations. The structure has been brutally attacked, inhabitants kidnapped or outright killed. The crew aboard the Aero including Astoria Bertoletti, librarian and planet cataloger, and Raze Salen, mankind's emissary, search for clues to explain the unprecedented tragedy. After several more, similar distress calls, the savage pieces of the mystery begin to emerge--and point to the culpability of humanity's short-sightedness and desperation when they first began seeking out alternate spaces in the galaxy to call home. In the midst of the imminent threat of war Raze and Tori present the immutable evidence of wrongdoing both intentional and inadvertent to mankind's Parliament as well as to their strongest and weakest allies who may have no choice but to desert them in yet another hour of dire need. **[154 words]**

When it's impossible to include all of this, I usually have to start getting creative. My first choice is usually to take out the series blurb altogether, though I do hate to do that. But, between the high-concept series blurb and the story blurb, the gist of what Immutable is about remains understandable.

A timeless universal truth: No simple solutions, no easy answers, and nothing is ever free... **[15 words]**

Spacefaring liveship, the *Aero*, is on a routine mission to the far-flung regions of the galaxy when they receive a distress call from one of their oldest space habitations. The structure has been brutally attacked, inhabitants kidnapped or outright killed. The crew aboard the Aero including Astoria Bertoletti, librarian and planet cataloger, and Raze Salen, mankind's emissary, search for clues to explain the unprecedented tragedy. After several more, similar distress calls, the savage pieces of the mystery begin to emerge--and point to the culpability of humanity's short-sightedness and desperation when they first began seeking out alternate spaces in the galaxy to call home. In the midst of the imminent threat of war Raze and Tori present the immutable evidence of wrongdoing both intentional and inadvertent to mankind's Parliament as well as to their strongest and weakest allies who may have no choice but to desert them in yet another hour of dire need. **[154 words]**

Okay, we're doing good with 169 words total. If I have to get tighter than that, 150 words is generally the cut off, so it's time to whittle the story blurb:

A timeless universal truth: No simple solutions, no easy answers, and nothing is ever free... **[15 words]**

Spacefaring liveship, the *Aero*, is on a routine mission when they receive a distress call from one of their oldest habitations. The structure has been brutally attacked. The crew, including planet cataloger Astoria Bertoletti and mankind's emissary Raze Salen, search for clues to explain the unprecedented tragedy. After several more, similar distress calls, the savage pieces of the mystery begin to emerge--and point to the culpability of humanity's short-sightedness and desperation when they first began seeking out alternate spaces in the galaxy to call home. In the midst of the imminent threat of war Raze and Tori present the immutable evidence of wrongdoing both intentional and inadvertent to mankind's Parliament as well as to their strongest and weakest allies who may have no choice but to desert them in their hour of dire need. **[135 words]**

Exactly 150 words combined. I would be very reluctant to crop this particular series/story blurb any further, but for the sake of example:

No simple solutions, no easy answers, and nothing is ever free... **[11 words]**

The *Aero* receives a distress call from their oldest habitations. *Aero* crew Astoria Bertoletti and Raze Salen search for clues after the terrorist attack. The mystery begins to emerge--and point to the culpability of humanity's desperation when they first began seeking out alternate spaces to call home. With the threat of war imminent, Raze and Tori present the immutable evidence of wrongdoing to mankind's Parliament as well as to their allies who may have no choice but to desert them in their hour of dire need. **[87 words]**

98 words. Aahh! My baby! What have I done to you? But one more ruthless, cruel cut to get to 75 words:

The *Aero* receives a distress call from their oldest habitations, which has been attacked. The mystery emerges--and points to the culpability of humanity's desperation when they first began seeking out alternate spaces to call home. With the threat of war imminent, crew members Tori and Raze present the immutable evidence of wrongdoing to mankind's Parliament as well as to their allies who may have no choice but to desert them. **[71 words]**

Do the individual blurbs and the series itself make sense anymore after all this inhumanity? I'm not sure. But there's no doubt about the fact that, how you present your blurbs when you're forced into a word count limitation necessitates extreme creativity (and a few tears).

Let's take one more look at how I ruthlessly made the word count limitations with my promotional and distribution efforts:

Bloodmoon Cove Spirits Series
by Karen Wiesner
Ghost Story/Paranormal Romance

Series Blurb:

Nestled on Lake Superior in northern Wisconsin is a small, secluded town called Bloodmoon Cove with volatile weather, suspicious folk...and newly awakened ghosts. **[23 words]**

High-concept series blurb:
Don't close your eyes. **[4 words]**

Crooked House, Book 3

High-concept story blurb:

Some doors, once opened, can never be closed again... **[9 words]**

Back Cover Blurb:

Orphan and widow Corinne Zellman is stunned when she receives several urgent letters from a lawyer, telling her she's the only surviving heir of Edward Buchanan, a relative of her recently deceased husband. Though Corinne ignores the first few summons, too grieved to consider them anything but cruel hoaxes, she takes notice when yet another arrives, this time with a family ring identical to the one her husband wore and lost just before he was killed. Stuck in a dead end job and curious about the family the love of her life seldom spoke of, she reluctantly pulls up stakes and heads to Bloodmoon Cove, where the persistent elderly gentleman lives. There, with her best friend Ruby, she finds Crooked House, the family "estate".

Crooked House certainly lives up to its disturbing name, as does Edward Buchanan, who is old and pale and disappears so frequently she can almost believe he's nothing more than a ghost. It isn't long before Corinne begins to suspect that her new family member had ulterior motives for insisting she come live with him. But to believe that is to believe that Rafe Yager, a hardened soldier, is entirely correct when he says Crooked House is dangerous. The longer she stays, the less chance she'll ever leave again.

Ghost hunter Rafe is one of the last descendants of the Mino-Miskwi Native American tribe whose elders disappeared during a ritual at their sacred place at the top of Bloodmoon Mountain. Rafe has come home based on a terrifying vision of wide-eyed, wholesome dreamer Cori losing her soul to an evil she doesn't recognize. Crooked

House is falling and its sinister legacy demands recompense for her husband's death--something that was no accident, as she supposed. Can Rafe save Cori from a sacrifice she never meant to make when she unknowingly came to love a monster? **[309 words]**

This longest version, which includes the series blurb and series high concept blurb, the high-concept story blurb and the back cover blurb is 345 total words. Let's try to get it under 150 this time.

Don't close your eyes. **[4 words]**

Some doors, once opened, can never be closed again... **[9 words]**

Orphan and widow Corinne Zellman is stunned to discover she's the only surviving heir of Edward Buchanan, a relative of her recently deceased husband. In Bloodmoon Cove, she finds Crooked House, the family "estate", which lives up to its disturbing name, as does Edward, who disappears so frequently she can almost believe he's a ghost. It isn't long before Corinne begins to suspect he had ulterior motives for insisting she come. But to believe that is to believe that Rafe Yager, a hardened soldier and ghost hunter, is entirely correct when he says Crooked House is dangerous. The longer she stays, the less chance she'll ever leave again. **[118 words]**

The medium version now contains 131 words total. Okay, finally, let's do the shortest blurb of 75 words or less.

Don't close your eyes. **[4 words]**

Some doors, once opened, can never be closed again... **[9 words]**

Corinne has become the heir of her dead husband's family estate. Crooked House lives up to its disturbing name, as does the last of the line who disappears so often she could believe he's a ghost. But to believe is to accept the claims of ghost hunter, Rafe Yager: The longer she stays in Crooked House, the less chance she'll ever leave. **[62 words]**

75 words achieved. Which is most effective? I almost always believe the longest is the best so I may not be the best judge. I know other people--especially in this day and age of "less is more"--prefer the shortest version possible simply on principle, but I believe even they realize too much may be cropped to leave behind an effectively good blurb that's good for anything other than promotion.

Practice Makes Perfect Session:

Using Appendix A and B (or my blurbs on my Blurb Service website or any other published blurb) along with the Blurb Crafting, Revision, and Whittling Worksheet included here and in Appendix C, try to whittle the combined long versions of high-concept, back cover and series blurbs to the 150, 100 and 75 words range. For now, just do it with books that aren't your own. Blurb whittling is good practice and you'll be less sentimental about carving up someone else's work.

First Pass

High-Concept Blurb

Fill out as completely as possible for the two components that make up this blurb. Remember, the "who" can be a person, a thing, or simply a concept--your main theme.
    Who:
    What:

Blurb:

[_ words]

Back Cover Blurb

Basic Story Information: *Fill out as completely as possible, keeping in mind that you may not use all, much or any of this in your final blurb.*

Title of Book:
Genre(s):
Time Period(s):
Main Setting(s):

Basic Character and Plot Information: *Fill out as completely as possible for the major characters in your story (usually no more than two or three main and one villain).*

Main Character Role (specify hero, heroine, villain, etc.):
First and Last Name:
Age and Job:
Description of the character's personality/hobbies/physical appearance/traumas or hang-ups that factor into his or her story conflicts:

Internal Conflict (i.e., character crisis or what's in jeopardy or at stake):
External Conflict (i.e., plot crisis):

Goals and motivations (i.e., what and why character is compelled to act):

Once you've filled out the form above completely, you can inject your story specifics into this formula (note: fill out one for each major character):

Character 1:
Who __________________________________
(name of character)

wants to _________________________________
(goal to be achieved)
because _________________________________
(motivation for acting)
but who faces _________________________________
(conflict standing in the way).

Character 2:
Who _________________________________
(name of character)
wants to _________________________________
(goal to be achieved)
because _________________________________
(motivation for acting)
but who faces _________________________________
(conflict standing in the way).

Character 3:
Who _________________________________
(name of character)
wants to _________________________________
(goal to be achieved)
because _________________________________
(motivation for acting)
but who faces _________________________________
(conflict standing in the way).

Blurb:

[_ words]

Series Blurb

Basic Series Information: *Fill out as completely as possible, keeping in mind that you may not use all, much or any of this in your final blurb.*

Series Title:
Genre(s):
[Who] Series Tie(s): (circle any or all that apply)
    Recurring or Cast of Characters Series
    Premise/Plot Series
    Setting Series

Basic Series Arcs:
    [What] Conflict or crisis that sets the series in motion:

    [Why] What's the worst case resolution scenario to the crisis situation?

Once you've filled out the form above completely, you can inject your series specifics into this formula:

Who _______________________
(Series Tie)
What ______________________
(Conflict or Crisis)
Why ______________________
(Worst Case Resolution Scenario)

Blurb:

[_ words]

First Revision

Series Blurb

Step 1: Drop your first pass at a series blurb here with the word count listed.

[_ words]

Your first Revision (try to get it down to four lines or less, if you didn't before):

[_ words]

High-Concept Blurb

Step 2: Drop your first pass at a high-concept blurb here with the word count listed.

[_ words]

Your first Revision (try to get it down to two lines, if you didn't before):

[_ words]

Back Cover Blurb

Step 3: Drop your first pass at a back cover blurb here with the word count listed.

[_ words]

Your First Revision (try to get it down to 300 words or less):

[_ words]

Second Revision

Series Blurb

Step 4: Drop your revised series blurb here with the word count listed.

[_ words]

Your Second Revision (try to get it down to three lines or less, if you didn't before):

[_ words]

High-Concept Blurb

Step 5: Drop your revised high-concept blurb here with the word count listed.

[_ words]

Your Second Revision (try to get it down to one line, if you didn't before):

[_ words]

Back Cover Blurb

Step 6: Drop your revised back cover blurb here with the word count listed.

[_ words]

Your Second Revision (try to get it down to 150 words or less):

[_ words]

Third Revision

Series Blurb

Step 7: Drop your 2nd revised series blurb here with the word count listed.

[_ words]

Your Third Revision (try to get it down to two lines, if you didn't before):

[_ words]

High-Concept Blurb

Step 8: Drop your 2nd revised high-concept blurb here with the word count listed.

[_ words]

Your Third Revision (try to get it down to one line, if you didn't before):

[_ words]

Back Cover Blurb

Step 9: Drop your 2nd revised back cover blurb here with the word count listed.

[_ words]

Your Third Revision (try to get it down to 100 words or less):

[_ words]

Fourth Revision

Series Blurb

Step 10: Drop your 3rd revised series blurb here with the word count listed.

[_ words]

Your Fourth Revision (try to get it down to one line, if you didn't before):

[_ words]

High-Concept Blurb

Step 11: Drop your 3rd revised high-concept blurb here with the word count listed.

[_ words]

Your Fourth Revision (try to tighten it a little more, if possible):

[_ words]

Back Cover Blurb

Step 12: Drop your 3rd revised back cover blurb here with the word count listed.

[_ words]

Your Fourth Revision (try to get it down to 75 words or less):

[_ words]

Whittle Down Your Own Blurbs

Using the techniques we've used in this lesson and the Blurb Crafting, Revision, and Whittling Worksheet, try to get your own blurb combinations down to the three optimal sizes. You don't have to achieve an exact 150, 100 and 75 but try to get close. I feel your pain, dear authors, as you performed this horror on your own babies.

BLURB BRANDING

While an author may have little or no control over the process of the publication of her book or series, she can still influence the outcome and specific areas of consideration in order to do this. The place to start is with branding--and this is something that applies to the books, series as well as to the *author* of them. In her article "The Basics of Author Branding" (do an internet search for the article title and author) author Theresa Meyers talks about building an image or perception that's used to create a loyal readership through branding. Essentially, branding is name recognition, creating a distinction for what you're offering. I'd go so far as to say that every author should have an "author branding statement" that she uses in every piece of promotion she undertakes. For instance, my branding statement (another catchy blurb!) is *"Creating realistic, unforgettable characters one story at a time..."* In this statement is a concise summary of what I'm most known for with my fiction: realistic, hauntingly memorable characters. This one simple sentence captures every story I've ever written and everything I will ever write.

Author Branding

Branding is very much an implied promise to consumers that you'll continue offering something similar and you'll do so consistently. While it takes quite a bit of time and effort to build brand recognition (Theresa mentions ten or more impressions in her article, but I've heard it's closer to fourteen these days since the market is so saturated, consumers are harder to entice, and the state of the economy plays such a huge factor in purchasing habits), it's essential that branding is put in place as soon as possible. Create a distinction for your book(s), your author voice, what you want to be known for (go-to author for {fill in the blank}), and what you're willing to provide consistently as an author, and then market it ever afterward. According to Kimberly Grabas in her *How to Build Your Author Brand From Scratch (and*

Why You Need to) article, "a powerful author brand is designed--not stumbled upon by accident." The author is almost always his own designer. Decide what you authentically want to be about, what your books stand for, and continue to evolve the story of your brand.

A series is one of the best places to brand. You want to begin branding your series as soon as you have the first book in the set blurbed. While patrolling listservs for series readers, I overheard comments such as:

"I always check any information on the author or books on their websites, especially if I need to know the order of the series. I don't want to start in the middle and miss any inside jokes or cool continuities."

"Author websites are the first thing I check if I'm interested in a new series."

"I think it would pay for authors and publishers to make it easy to know if a book is part of a series and where each title fits in that series, since each story prepares you for the coming books."

These comments don't necessarily have to be applied only to series titles but all books written by authors. (Re-read the comments with that in mind). Put in these ways, it's logical for publishers and authors to make it as easy as possible to find out about or purchase all author titles including those that fit into a particular series. But sometimes it does seem like they're doing the opposite. Unfortunately, authors don't always have a lot of influence over many aspects of branding, but even if your publisher ultimately doesn't back your series with an aggressive marketing track, nothing is stopping you from discussing upcoming issues in your series with your editor or publisher to get branding running hot and fast, and trying to set a good example by offering as much as you can to your fans on your own website or blog. In both sections below, I'll include methods that authors can employ to promote branding—even if publishers don't cooperate, but keep in mind that each of these practices apply to authors who write single-title books as well as series authors below. Associations and utilization of all the blurbs we've been talking about in this book are crucial for your author, book, and series branding. It is usually with a series that branding is so essential and so we're going to address that now, but keep in mind that many of these principles apply to single-title author branding as well.

Series Branding

Rule 1: Associate the Series With Each Title

To me, this one is so out-and-out obvious, I feel a bit foolish even mentioning it. If your readers don't know that your book is part of a series, what's going to prompt them to look for the next one and the next one and the next one after that? It should be so blatant, yet this is the number one series rule I see broken most frequently, and it's such a missed opportunity. Look at the website of any book distributor, and you'll often have a hard time finding out if a book is even part of a series. A few publishers are diligent about this, but most don't bother.

Make sure the title of the book is always, always, always associated with the series. In other words, never allow yourself or your publisher (if you can help it) to include just the title of your book. For instance, I never refer to my book Shards of Ashley simply by its title. Always, I refer to it as *Shards of Ashley*, Book 5 of the Family Heirlooms Series. Notice several things about this: I include the title of the book, the book number in the series, and the series title. In this way, new readers and long-time fans immediately recognize the information they need to know.

A new trend in the industry that needs to be addressed here is that many distributor websites are becoming sticklers about how your cover and title page have to match in terms of how the title, series and book number are listed. I've had books rejected for distribution because the cover creatively has the title in one place, the series in another, and just the number in some kind of artistic "seal" elsewhere. Because the title page has the book listed as, say, *Shards of Ashley*, Book 5 of the Family Heirlooms Series, the book is rejected as "not matching". This is beyond ridiculous, in my opinion, since they're clearly the same, though automated systems may be too dumb to realize it and you'll have to ask that a human at the place of distribution look into it. When this inquiry has been undertaken in my case, approval is always forthcoming. But authors and publishers need to be aware this is a growing trend and adjust accordingly.

Additionally, my publisher for this book (and my fiction), Writers Exchange, always lists the series name first, followed by the title and the book number in the series, as in: Family Heirlooms Series, Book 5: *Shards of Ashley*. Her very sound logic is that, with the series name first, all the books tend to be listed together (and almost always in the correct order) on websites that list only based on the title in alphabetical order. If you have the title of the book first, the other books in that series can end up on totally different pages, which isn't ideal.

For those readers who try to follow a series, it's extremely helpful to include the book number in the series whenever you talk about a particular title. On the listservs I patrol, I've heard a huge number of series readers say they won't skip around in a series—they start at the beginning and read chronologically. Very few readers will skip around. Having the book number associated with the title (and even on the spine and/or front and back cover, as we'll talk about soon) ensures that readers know exactly where this book falls in the series.

Beyond that, something I mentioned in the introduction of this book and you may have noticed all through this book: I capitalized the word "series" (or "trilogy", "saga" or whatever) in every instance it was used. That's crucial, and I realize that it'll take a shakeup in the publishing industry to get everyone to do this. But "series" is actually part of the book title, and you want readers to know immediately that this story is part of a series. Doing so further solidifies the branding. In other words, I never refer to my Incognito Series as simply Incognito. Always, I add the "Series" tag because this is the full series title and the most effective way to brand it to my readers. If you let the word lag pitifully behind with the lowercase version of "series", you're downplaying the importance of the full series title. Worse, if you leave it off the title altogether, series readers won't even know what they're missing (but you might when your sales aren't what you hope for). Start this habit now and make a point of being consistent in the use of the title of each book and trilogy/series name. Underline this, put it in all caps, but whatever you do don't forget this rule: Make sure the *whole* title of the book is always associated with the series!

Even in the process of working with your editor, continue stressing this point to enforce to her that you see all the stories as part of the series—one book can't be separated from the other because they belong together.

You wouldn't believe how often I had to chase my older publishers to make sure they included the title of the book with the series name and the book number in all the places the book is promoted and distributed. Only my new publisher does it consistently and without fail, and, out of all of the many, many publishers I've had in nearly twenty years, I believe this is the only one who truly understands the power of branding a series. The others must have been getting sick of me complaining about it (I am the original squeaky wheel!), but only after doing this did I get results. I believe it's important enough to keep asking until it's done. As I've mentioned, my fiction is published by small-press publishers, but I often notice the mass market publishers failing to practice this form of branding. I expect above all that this type of publisher must realize that series sell, and they sell better when the book's series title and book number are made clear on every piece of marketing literature, every word of mouth recommendation, and every website mention.

While publishers utilize distributors for getting the books out to the customers, publishers provide all the information necessary for distributors to sell the books. It's the publishers who tend to not provide series information at all, or only incompletely, along with the basic book information. Talk to your editor/publisher about associating the series name and book number for every single title. Make sure this information makes it to distributors consistently.

If your publisher isn't diligent in this regard, you can change your information at Amazon.com, BarnesandNoble.com, and other online distributors. While you're logged in to these sites, the page for your book may have a section labeled with something like "Update This Information". Sometimes publishers won't allow anyone to change the book information, but if you find that you can change it yourself, do so!

Take my advice: If your publisher won't follow through on this particular branding, rigorously follow the advice yourself. For every scrap of promotion you do for the series, make sure you include the complete series information for every title. Absolutely do this for your website. You might even consider putting a list of series on your website with the title in each series and the book number—and maybe even making this list printable. That way, your most avid followers can get the information they need without too much hassle. Remember, you can lose sales by making basic information hard to come by.

Rule 2: Utilize Series Blurbs

In Chapter Two, we discussed creating a series blurb. Almost all of my series have a series blurb I use to promote it. It's necessary to utilize the series blurb as much as possible to create brand awareness for your series. Don't underestimate the appeal of the series blurb. New and longtime series readers alike want to know how the current book connects with others in that series. If the series blurb is effective, those sentences will accurately reflect the premise of every book in the series in a concise, intriguing summary. Series blurbs can sell books just as surely as story blurbs can. An author would never consider skipping a story blurb—a publisher wouldn't either. While some publishers write and use their own series blurbs, the series blurb is often underrated and underutilized—to our detriment.

This is the second most common series branding rule I see

broken. In this case, it's not just the publishers who neglect to utilize the series blurb. Recently, I wanted to find out more information about a certain bestselling author's series. The series had been around for a while, and several books were already available. I went to the publisher's website, the author's website, and even distributor websites trying desperately to find out what the series was about. The story blurbs were fine, but they didn't tell me enough about the connections between the individual books to really appeal to me. (Not to mention that none of the books had numbers, so I had no idea about the order of the series, so finding out where to begin would have been a headache.) When I buy a series, I look first at the series blurb, since that tells me what I'm getting into. If that entices me, I'll read individual story blurbs (in order). If I like those, I'll make a purchase. In this case, the information I needed was nowhere to be found. I got tired of chasing after it, and this author (my apologies if none of this was her fault) lost the sale of all of these particular series' titles.

I do feel bad about that, because I know authors have little if any control over aspects of publication when working with mass-market (and sometimes even small press) publishers. But that particular author did have control of her own website, and she failed to give me the information I needed to make a purchase enticing, or even inevitable.

Utilizing your series blurb is critical to branding. It is part of what convinces a consumer to begin your series. If she likes what she reads, she may buy every single book in the series. But if she doesn't know what she's getting into, she may never bother. If enough consumers have this attitude because the publisher and/or author make it a hassle to obtain vital information, your series will fail to gain readers. A series isn't like a single-title book. If you lose readers from the beginning or anywhere in the series, you've lost them for its entirety. That's major ruin! Some series authors never recover from this.

Talk to your publisher about this, but if they don't do anything, at the very least make sure to provide easily accessible and compelling information about your series on your website.

Rule 3: Encourage Series Recognition

I was talking to a friend of mine who grew up reading Harlequin Superromances. From what I could gather from my friend, this series imprint puts out numerous "continuity miniseries'" that include books from several of their most popular authors. All my friend could remember about this particular series was the logo on the spine. After some research, I also found that this logo was also featured on the back covers of the books, along with a very tight, one-sentence series blurb (which reiterates the importance of including a series blurb on every book in a series and keeping it short and memorable!). After reading a couple of these titles, whenever my friend went to buy books, she would search for this series logo on the spine of the books to make sure she didn't miss future books in that series. She was initially drawn in by reading a single book, but seeing the series logo sucked her in every time. A logo! A tiny, readily identifiable graphic on the spine of a book! It's a brilliant concept...and unfortunately one that tends to be underutilized by many publishers.

Do all books in a series need a logo like this? While I think most authors, like me, would absolutely love that for every series, I think they're only absolutely necessary for books in a very long series, especially if that series has spin-offs and off-shoots and different "worlds" but can fit under one umbrella, and/or it's in some other way complicated. Also, if the series has multiple authors involved in it, you definitely want some kind of distinctive graphic that sets it apart as part of this particular series.

This conversation with my friend reminded me of a reader letter I'd perused in an issue of *RT Book Reviews* in 2010. A reader had been following a particular series and she'd been trying "for ages" to put together a complete list of all the books in that series. The publisher, who had many imprints, published the books in this series across several of the various imprints. At the time this reader was actively purchasing these series books, the publisher had used a "little symbol" on the spine of all the books in the series, making it easy to locate the related books on the shelves in the bookstore. Abruptly, the publisher abandoned that practice. The reader couldn't find the necessary information on the publisher's website, possibly because older books weren't listed or available there. (Harlequin/Silhouette books don't stay on bookstore shelves for long, and that's probably why they also disappear from their website quickly.) Because the series was written by many different authors, the reader couldn't search for upcoming books in the series, since she couldn't know which author's book would be released next. This was a loyal reader who became addicted to a series and went to great lengths to get every single book in that series. The publisher did absolutely nothing to help her gather the information she needed to make purchases. Have you ever heard of anything so sad? Or so avoidable?

So many publishers (and authors) fall off the branding bandwagon in this regard, and I can't fathom why. Creating a ecognizable series logo to go with the series blurb can create instant sales. My friend had loved all previous books in the particular series and she placed any new ones on her automatic buy list. If you can get your publisher to go the extra mile and design a series logo for you that can be placed on the spines and covers of each book in the series, you'll find that it really does help your sales increase.

Also, having similar cover art for each book is a huge help in creating instant recognition for that series. On my current books, I've designed all but one cover (a perk of working with small-press publishers) for which I've been nominated for cover design awards. For my series, I create a series logo and make sure the book cover designs are similar from one to the next. For my Incognito Series, all the books are portrayed in black and white, with a third of the front cover devoted to a vertical black panel that contains the title of the book in a very colorful font (all the books use the same font—the colors for each book are different). The series logo is placed beneath the title. On the spine, I include the book number at the top, the book title and my name down the middle, and a smoking gun near the bottom. The back cover is the same format from one book to the next. When all the books are lined up on a bookshelf, you know instantly that they're part of the same series. The layout for almost all of my series books is very similar from one book to the next, helping to create cover art recognition. I encourage you to check out my website at https://karenwiesner.weebly.com/.com and click on the "Books" link at the top to see examples of series cover similarities and series logos that create branding.

One other way of taking this a step further is to include information inside each book that will allow the reader to follow the series easily. In all of my series books, I include a list of all currently available books in the series (with ISBNs) as well as a teaser blurb for the upcoming book in the series (with the release date).

It's worth a phone call or email to your publisher to ask about getting logos, covers, and front matter that will create instant recognition of your series.

While you probably won't get these things until you're on the bestseller lists, a lot of publishers do create author name recognition logos. In other words, on the covers of all of Nora Robert's books, her name is big and bold—and her name is actually a recognizable logo that's been created by her publisher in an effort to encourage branding.

Finally, another way to create recognition for your series is to create similar titles for the books in you series. We just talked about Nora Roberts: For her Born In Trilogy, the titles were *Born in Fire*, *Born in Ice*, and *Born in Shame*. Fans would have found these easily—especially since series title and order was not only listed on the front covers and some of the back covers, but also in a detailed listing just inside the front covers (and possibly on the spine as well). Jane Toombs also has similar book titles with many of her series: the Temple of Time Series has *Forbidden*, *Forsaken*, *Forlorn*, *Forsworn*, and *Forever*.

While, again, authors have little or no control over whether readers will recognize a book in their series, it doesn't mean you can't push for it as much as possible. If your publisher won't help you in this regard, the least you can do as the author is provide all the information the reader needs on your website or blog.

Writing for small press publishers, I don't have the money to spend on a website with all the bells and whistles, so I do what I can with what I'm capable of working with. I have separate pages on my website for each of my series (including a hot-linked button to each one on the main page). The individual books in the series contain comprehensive information and enticing series and book blurbs so readers can easily figure out the series it belongs to, as well as the book number and availability and distributor details. If the book is available, I include all the links where it can be purchased—instant gratification is key! Another feature on my website are multifaceted search pages to make navigation of my sometimes-overlapping series as easy as possible for my readers. These include an alphabetical character search (which has all of my major and minor characters and how they're linked in my various books and series, along with a list of and links to the titles each character is featured in), a location search (a list of the major settings in my books and the titles they're featured in), and a series search (a basic listing of each title in my many series).

Nora Roberts is another series-oriented author who knows how to keep fans from getting confused. Her website includes everything necessary to follow her many series—and it's easily navigated.

Taking this one step further: I strongly believe in using the combination of high-concept, back cover and series blurbs together in every single promotion you do for a series as well when your book is for sale at a distributor's website. Start now: Associate all the stories in the series as part of the series—one book can't be separated from the other because they belong together.

A series isn't like a single-title book. If you lose readers from the beginning or anywhere in the middle, you've lost them for its entirety. Some series authors never recover from this. Talk to your publisher about this, but if they don't do anything, at the very least make sure to provide easily accessible and compelling information about your series on your own website.

***

Bottom line, the only reason for shortening a blurb that's already effectively good is because we're forced to because of publishing and marketing considerations and limitations, and blurbs are an important part of the branding package of author, books and series. In the next chapter, we'll wrap things up.

<u>CONCLUSION</u>
Crafting Effectively Good Blurbs

"Treat your first sentence like a pick-up line: Many readers don't read past the very first sentence, which is why this should have the biggest impact. [The last sentence should] leave readers curious and wanting more--so much so that they would actually buy the book. [A] good blurb sparks an interest but a great [one] will create intrigue and captivate your potential reader. This could turn her not only into a paying customer but also the latest member of your ever growing fan base." ~Author Society from 17 Tips on How To Write a Blurb That Sells

In this book, we've talked about what a blurb is and where they came from, the purpose of blurbs and the reader's buying process. We've covered the crucial need for high-concept blurbs, back cover blurbs, and series blurbs and went over ways to craft them with a worksheet and formula. We've gone over dozens upon dozens of tips for how to write blurbs and how *not* to. We've discussed when to write them, how long they should be, and talked about specialized types of blurbs for nonfiction, anthologies and children's books. We can tweak and whittle blurbs for various applications and we've learned the ways to brand with blurbs.

We've established in this book that blurbs can make or break sales given that it's one of the first glimpses of the story. We know that readers buy based on an intriguing blurb that convinces them they absolutely have to read the story inside the pages...or they simply set the book down without ever opening it. A blurb is either effectively good or it's not. Work on it until it's both. Additionally, we can see that a winning series blurb can sell not just one book but all of them in that set!

And now we're full-circle. Are you still an author who

dislikes or dreads trying to write back cover blurbs for your stories, or do you feel like you now have the tools now to write your own that sizzles with intrigue and impact?

There's no doubt that learning to write effectively good blurbs is critical to your success as an author. You now know techniques that can help and may even infuse you with the same enthusiasm I have for writing blurbs. Someday, I hope you're wildly, wonderfully *in love* with writing your own book blurbs. Remember, be sizzling in your blurbs if you want your books to sell!

APPENDIX A
Blurb Evaluations

Evaluation 1: Dangerous Waters Series by Dee Lloyd
  Book 1: Change of Plans
  Book 2: Ghost of a Chance
  Book 3: Unquiet Spirits
Evaluation 2: Jane Doe Mystery by Wendy Laing
  Book 1: Flowers from the Grave
  Book 2: Severance Packages
  Book 3: Haunted Heart
Evaluation 3: The Rowland Sisters Trilogy by Catherine Dove
  Book 1: Mr. Harding Proposes
  Book 2: The Lazy Bachelor
  Book 3: Cecilia and the Rake
Evaluation 4: Wild Sorceress Series by Margaret L. Carter and
Leslie Roy Carter
  Book 1: Wild Sorceress
  Book 2: Besieged Adept
  Book 3: Rogue Magess
  Prequel: Legacy of Magic
Evaluation 5: Ancient Scythian Trilogy by Max Overton
  Book 1: Lion of Scythia
  Book 2: The Golden King
  Book 3: Funeral in Babylon
Evaluation 6: Castle Trilogy by J.H. Wear
  Book 1: Fall to Domum
  Book 2: Return to Domum
  Book 3: The New King
Evaluation 7: The Islands of the Sixteen Gods by Stephen Symons
  Book 1: The Amulet of the Hunter God
  Book 2: Beloved of the River Goddess
  Book 3: The Stones of the Sleeping God
  Book 4: The City of the Swan Goddess
  Book 5: The Sons of the Silent God
Evaluation 8: Broken But Mending Series by Dale Mayer

In the exercises that follow, I've convinced some of the bravest-of-brave authors I've revised blurbs for to permit me to use their original blurbs (all of which were published as you see them at one point or another) for each of these published works. So what you'll see are blurbs that are no longer in use but were at one time utilized in all distribution and promotion of the books followed by the revised blurbs for the same book in the cheat sheet section.

Remember the series caveat I mentioned in the blurb sizing chapter: Given that you might not be able to include everything you want to for series, high-concept and back cover blurbs, you don't want to leave out a crucial premises, especially pertaining to characters, in the back cover blurbs. Include at least once sentence if there could be confusion without vital information of that kind, even if the expanded overview of it is also included in the series blurb.

The mixture of genres you'll find to evaluate on the pages that follow are extremely varied. They pretty much run the gamut, and that should give you lots of practice in your blurb evaluation. Additionally, the first seven included are series with all the books currently available in that series. The rest are single titles. I will tell you that many of these authors are ones I've read personally and they're fantastic writers. Some of the blurbs will reflect that while others--dare I say it?--shouldn't be judged on the blurbs.

Your goal? Using the checklist, evaluate these blurbs. I won't tell you which ones actually need revising (though most need at least a little, however slight). What, if anything, is missing? What shouldn't be there? What could be stronger, use more impacting words? What could be shorter and better culled or longer and fleshed out?

So you can see how I revised them, I've included a cheat sheet for all of them in the back of Appendix A, in many cases including the series blurb I wrote/revised along with the book blurbs.

Don't let these be the last blurbs you evaluate with the checklist. If you want much more practice, go to Amazon or

Goodreads and just start dragging out blurbs and using the checklist on them. You may be surprised by the results!

Evaluation 1:
Dangerous Waters Series by Dee Lloyd
http://www.deelloyd.com/
Paranormal Romance

Book 1: Change of Plans

Mike and Sara didn't plan on falling in love...

Mike was determined to change his image from "Mr. Nice Guy" to "dangerous and exciting male on the prowl." He had narrowly missed marrying the wrong woman, who had eloped with her boss before he arrived home from a contract job in Africa. Disillusioned by her broken promise and angry with women in general, Mike plans to find a fun-loving woman to share his honeymoon stateroom.

Sara has never been in love, but she does want a family. She plans to spend the cruise, considering a marriage proposal from Stephen Cafik, a wealthy electronics engineer whose political career her father, a retired state senator, is encouraging.

But someone on the cruise plans to kill Sara. Yet under the romantic tropical moon, the best-laid plans...

Book 2: Ghost of a Chance

Bret's well-ordered life is already off the rails when the lovely but bloody ghost confronts him on a dark, deserted road. His body is almost fully recovered from the attack that nearly killed him but his nerves must be in worse shape than he thought. Seeing ghosts?! He must be losing his grip on reality.

Milly spots the tall, attractive blond the moment he steps into the piano lounge. As she spins her web of magic on the audience, she is intensely aware of the stranger's unwavering gaze. She doesn't realize she is the woman Bret saw on the road—-or is she?

Book 3: Unquiet Spirits

Headstrong Kit Schofield, convinced that the hit-and-run that almost killed her was a random act of violence, heads north to her family resort at Spirit Lake. Not-so-convinced lifelong buddy Bart Thornton joins her as self-appointed bodyguard, much to Kit's chagrin—at first.

Disturbing old secrets and equally unsettling ghosts lurk in the lodge and the calm waters of the deceptively peaceful resort...and a deadly, elusive killer strikes again.

But all this fades into the background when one kiss unleashes unexpected, unwelcome and totally distracting passion.

Two lusty ghosts who drop clues about old murders and insist Kit and Bart are soul mates further confuse their lives.

~*~

Evaluation 2:
Jane Doe Mystery by Wendy Laing
http://www.wendylaing.com/
Paranormal Mystery

Book 1: Flowers from the Grave

The first in the Inspector Jane Doe adult mystery/paranormal series. Inspector Jane Doe, head of Melbourne Homicide is staying in an isolated cliff top cottage. She's recovering from near fatal head injuries received from a serial killer.

Ryan O'Byrne a stranger on the beach befriends her. Jane's idyllic sojourn turns into a nightmare. Who is sending her flowers with threatening notes attached? Is Ryan truly a ghost? Can she trust Ryan as a friend or is he in fact the serial killer, and she his next victim?

Book 2: Severance Packages

Set in the peaceful town of Sunbury, Australia, Jane is once again faced with the prospect of dealing with a serial killer after the grizzly discovery of a dismembered body is made at the local winery...then another at the tip... Who knows how many more 'Severance Packages' will be found?

Book 3: Haunted Heart

This book is set five years on from the second Jane Doe novel, Severance Packages.

Jane's first Cold Case involves an MP's daughter's recent death. He disagrees with the first coroner's verdict of accidental death. The second autopsy reveals that she was murdered. At the same time, Jane's husband, Oliver Tarrant is dealing with a young heart transplant recipient, who is having nightmares of being murdered and Steve Ho is investigating the murder of an eminent heart transplant surgeon, dumped in a local lake.

Eventually, each of these three cases become intermingled. Steve Ho, Oliver Tarrent and Jane are suddenly embroiled together in one of the most haunting cases of their careers.

~*~
Evaluation 3:
The Rowland Sisters Trilogy by Catherine Dove
https://www.catherinedove.com/
Regency Romance

For gentlemen's daughters during the English Regency, life can be a whirl of parties, balls, and outings. But all of this activity is done for a single purpose: to catch a husband. For Georgiana and Cecilia Rowland and their friends, the pressure to find and secure the right husband is complicated by misunderstandings, prejudices, rebellion against social restrictions, uncooperative suitors, and sometimes their own wayward hearts. Read their stories in the "sweet" Regency romances, The Rowland Sisters Trilogy: "Mr. Harding Proposes", "The Lazy Bachelor", and "Cecilia and the Rake".

Book 1: Mr. Harding Proposes

Mr. Richard Harding is an eligible bachelor who has his heart set on marrying his lifelong friend and neighbor, Miss Georgiana Rowland. However, they have been good friends for so long that, when he finally screws up his courage and proposes to her, Georgie thinks he is merely teasing!

Georgiana has good reason to be so distracted. Her younger sister is about to be launched into society, and most of the work and worry falls on Georgie. Also, despite her mother's furious command, she has befriended the scandalous Lady Shipton, which brings both blessings and chaos to the Rowland family and to their kind uncle, Sir Henry. Worse for Mr. Harding, Lady Shipton's charming stepson takes a strong liking to Georgie.

Mr. Harding keeps proposing, again and again, while still trying to support Georgie in her trials. But is it possible for such a good friendship to turn into love?

Book 2: The Lazy Bachelor

Mr. Peregrine Tyndall has often been called the laziest man in London. But he is stirred to the enormous effort of matchmaking when a hunting accident suffered by his cousin, Lord Shipton, makes him realize that he stands in real danger of inheriting an earldom--with all its responsibilities. In his opinion, the perfect girl to marry his cousin and give the earldom another heir than himself would be their childhood friend, Portia Freestone.

Mr. Tyndall doesn't know what formidable obstacles lay before him, however, when he joins a house party at the earl's country home with this match on his mind. In the first place, his normally obliging friend Portia has a secret. She has no wish to marry the earl--she likes him very well, but the man she secretly wishes to marry is Perry himself. An even bigger problem is Miss Frances Armitage. She and her little sister Eleanor had been left in Perry's guardianship, a duty he had benignly and completely neglected. But now Miss Armitage, furious, is about to descend on Lakeford Hall to demand that Perry take up his duties in a responsible manner, even if she has to force him to do it.

Thrust into just the sort of efforts he dislikes most, Mr.

Tyndall tries his best to cope, and in the attempt, gets a great deal more than he bargained for.

Book 3: Cecilia and the Rake

Unpleasant experience has given Miss Cecilia Rowland a strong aversion to rakes, even one so fascinating and gentlemanlike as Lord Ravenshill.

She does her best to ignore his existence, but Fate keeps bringing them together. Even deep in the country, visiting the home of her mother's betrothed husband, Cecilia finds herself in the company of Lord Ravenshill. Not only is he a neighbor of Mr. Clarke's, but Cecilia's stepsister-to-be, Kitty, develops a tendre toward Mr. Guy Dorne, Ravenshill's best friend.

The Viscount Ravenshill is not the sort of man to regret his past, even when he finds himself unaccountably fascinated by the lovely Miss Rowland. He looks on his friend Guy's growing attachment to Kitty Clarke with amusement and resolutely ignores the promptings of his own traitorous heart.

The grim past which made him a ruthless rake also makes him a completely unsuitable match for an innocent girl like Cecilia Rowland.

But when Cecilia and Kitty go to London for the Season, the same Fate that threw Cecilia toward Ravenshill takes an unexpected twist that endangers the loves of both girls.

~*~

Evaluation 4:
Wild Sorceress Series by Margaret L. Carter and Leslie Roy Carter
http://www.margaretlcarter.com
Fantasy

In a world where hostile nations wield magic in combat, twin sorceresses separated at birth and brought up on opposing sides of the war find each other. Together, they face persecution for using wild magic, fight against traitors and assassins, explore family secrets, and discover the hidden origins of magic itself.

Above all, to protect their world, they must deal with ancient, powerful dragons that most people don't even believe exist.

Book 1: Wild Sorceress

In a world where warring nations use magic in combat, years ago young sorceress Aetria's untamed power caused a disaster on the battlefield. Temporarily banished for retraining, she has returned to the army to redeem herself as head of a company of novice mages. She uncovers a traitorous plot by her own commander, renews her bond with her "imaginary" childhood friend, and meets her long-lost twin sister. While also becoming a trusted friend of the commanding general of the army, Aetria unearths secrets of the true nature of the magic she and her comrades wield.

Book 2: Besieged Adept

Adept Aetria, while learning to control her wild sorcery, has defeated a pair of traitors trying to kill her, found a long-lost twin, and uncovered secrets of the source and nature of magic. Now she continues her research while battling the remnants of the Neo-Aggressor rebellion and integrating raw, untrained talent into the Sorcerer Corps. Meanwhile, she discovers deeper secrets of her own family background, along with a surprising new foe and a destiny she never dreamed of. Furthermore, she learns that her "imaginary" dragon friend Rajii actually exists. But so do less friendly dragons. What does their agenda mean for the future of humanity and magic in Aetria's world?

Book 3: Rogue Magess

Sorceresses Aetria and Coleni discover that both their own births and the history of their world have been manipulated in secret by an ancient, powerful race of dragons. Some, like Aetria's lifelong friend Rajii, have benevolent intentions toward humanity, while others want to restore the people of the Domains to total slavery.

All, however, have their own agendas with human beings and mortal magic as pawns.

Emerging from their long-lost mother's hidden home in the deserted Non-Lands, Aetria and Coleni find themselves targeted by assassins under control of the dragons. While the sisters' powers continue to grow, so do the magical gifts of Coleni's baby daughter, but will their magic provide adequate protection?

Meanwhile, still viewed with suspicion for their "wild sorcery", they can't convince most of their rivals and allies, including Aetria's old mentor and the commanding general of the army, that the dragons and the danger they pose are real.

Prequel: Legacy of Magic

Most people in the country of Saphradea admire sorcerers and dream of having magical powers. Not Merina, a young woman who detests magic because she thinks it ruined the life of her mother, a failed sorceress candidate who abandoned her in infancy.

When Merina's fiancé, Trinames, announces he has decided to go for training as a Healer sorcerer, her personal world turns upside down. As heiress to a tract of rich farmland, she wants only to manage her own property and bring up a family in peace, a dream she thought Trinames shared. Yet events conspire to force her into a realm of magic and intrigue she never wanted.

When Trinames gets kidnapped and she strikes out across the wilderness to rescue him, in company with a wandering trader who turns out to be more than he appears, she runs into a crisis that awakens magical powers she shouldn't even possess. Previous-generation, stand-alone prequel to the "Wild Sorceress" trilogy.

~*~

Evaluation 5:
Ancient Scythian Trilogy by Max Overton
http://www.maxovertonauthor.com/
Historical: Ancient Egypt

Book 1: Lion of Scythia

Alexander the Great has conquered the Persian Empire and is marching eastward to India. In his wake he leaves small groups of soldiers to govern great tracts of land and diverse peoples. Nikometros is a young cavalry captain left behind in the lands of the fierce nomadic Scythian horsemen. Captured after an ambush, he must fight for his life and the lives of his surviving men. He seeks an opportunity to escape but owes a debt of loyalty to the chief, and a developing love for the young priestess.

Book 2: The Golden King

The chief of the tribe of nomadic Scythian horsemen is dead, killed by his son's treachery. The priestess, lover of the young cavalry officer, Nikometros, is carried off into the mountains. Nikometros and his friends set off in hard pursuit.

Death rides with them. By the time they return, the tribes are at war. Nikometros must choose between attempting to become chief himself or leaving the people he's come to love and respect to return to his duty as an army officer in the Empire of Alexander.

Book 3: Funeral in Babylon

Alexander the Great has returned from India and set up his court in Babylon. Nikometros and a band of loyal Scythians journey deep into the heart of Persia to join the Royal court. Nikometros finds himself embroiled in the intrigues and wars of kings, generals, and merchant adventurers as he strives to provide a safe haven for his lover and friends. With the fate of an Empire hanging in the balance, Death walks beside Nikometros as events precipitate a Funeral in Babylon...

~*~

Evaluation 6:
Castle Trilogy by J.H. Wear

https://www.jhwear.com/
Medieval Fantasy

Book 1: Fall to Domum

Jon inherited an Irish Castle with a secret- a secret that would send him tumbling to another world called Domum. To return to Earth is a simple matter of obtaining the right crystal. Unfortunately, his journey to find the crystal means learning how to use a sword, avoiding dragons and other creatures that want to kill him, and trusting a thief. Jon wouldn't wish his predicament on anyone, and was unaware his girlfriend Liz had decided to rescue him.

Book 2: Return to Domum

When Lord Troy Sussex buys a recovered gem with unique powers, he believes it will free him from the spell that confines him to his castle. But the strange power the gem possesses has an unexpected result, and the fate of Domum rests with a thief, a sex slave and a warlock in exile.

Book 3: The New King

A hero must be willing to die. Domum is in turmoil when the ruthless Lord Darius vies to become King, overpowering and killing anyone who opposes him. To Liz's dismay Jon accepts the role to lead the undermanned Horstruff defenses. Liz becomes worried Jon doesn't want to return to Earth and plans to give him ultimatum if he wants her, if he can even survive the conflict.

Meanwhile Gilbert's reluctant marriage proposal to Donna takes a surprising turn. As the final battle looms he suddenly finds fate has placed him in the midst of the battle where he has a chance to be a hero.

Evaluation 7:
The Islands of the Sixteen Gods by Stephen Symons

http://www.writers-exchange.com/stephen-symons
Fantasy

Book 1: The Amulet of the Hunter God

The last that Edrun Jaranacad had seen of his beloved Jina, was an arm desperately waving from the raging waters of the flood that was bearing her away. Heartbroken, he decided to leave the safety of his quiet little village to travel the outside world to seek he did not really know what.

The discovery of a small golden jewel, an amulet of Shegadin the Hunter God, convinced Edrun that the Gods were watching over him, guiding him towards some end that only he could see. Edrun soon began to realise that although the Gods might be guiding him as he travelled in dangerous places, in company with even more dangerous people, it would take all of his own strength to reach a destination he could never have foreseen.

Book 2: Beloved of the River Goddess

After a year of torment and pursuit halfway across northwest Kalion, Edrun and Jina have finally found themselves both safe and well-funded. They decide to take a long, leisurely and much-deserved holiday in the fascinating Temple-City of Hazek, while they decide on their future.

Their happy idyll does not last for long. While enjoying a lazy lunch outside a tavern, Edrun, to his horror, finds himself publically hailed as a Lord of the Gathering. The warrior aristocracy of the Islands of the Sixteen Gods are very protective of their status and privileges, and are swift to inflict punishments both brutal and bloody upon those who would usurp their position. Moments later Edrun and Jina discover that their former nemesis Halgar Rassvorea is in Hazek, and has in mind a sadistic revenge against them for the trouble that they caused him in the past.

Immediately any thoughts of a peaceful and prosperous life ahead are shattered as they realise that Hazek is no longer safe for them. They decide to make for Amronulu, the citadel of the Lords of the Kalalutorm whom Edrun befriended after he had defeated them at the battle of Garinesigas. Their plans are soon cast into disarray as, barely having left Hazek, they rescue the fiery Adeta, the daughter of a wealthy merchant, from brigands who are attacking her. Adeta is fleeing an arranged marriage and Ordron insists return her to her betrothed, the arrogant and sadistic Lord Ordron Mailaranarad. But Lord Ordron is anything but grateful, and soon Edrun finds that he must once more fight for his life and that of Jina.

Book 3: The Stones of the Sleeping God

The Stones of the Sleeping God continues the tale of Edrun Jaranacad directly on from The Beloved of the River Goddess.

Edrun and Jina, attended by the loyal Zan, travel to the Kalalutorm Citadel of Amronulu, where they are greeted like long-lost relatives and offered the hospitality of the house for as long as they want. They are now accepted as Lords of the Gathering, members of the ruling aristocracy of the Kalion Islands. Jina begins to heal rapidly, but Edrun, plagued both by questions and by doubts, becomes morose and taciturn.

To help jolly Edrun along, the Kalalutorm brothers and Vaided Mailaranarad, younger brother of Lord Ordron, suggest an expedition to the nearby Forest of Rabti where they can spend a few days hunting, drinking, and chasing milkmaids. They journey to the Forest where they are invited to spend the night in a stone ring sacred to the ancient Forest God, Rabti.

Edrun and his men are ambushed by a group of men-at-arms of the Jemegaidi Clan, resulting in Edrun's capture. He is taken to Chailam Alu to be the 'guest' of Lord Garin, Chieftain of the Jemegaidi. Garin has heard that Edrun enjoys the favour of the Gods, and wants him to join with him in a war to re-conquer the wide lands which once the Jemegaidi ruled without rival. This alliance would involve Edrun marrying Garin's daughter Taren...

Book 4: The City of the Swan Goddess

Edrun, Jina and the council agree that something needs to be done about the mysterious disappearances of young women of the Clans of the DrummGrissa. But late that night, before a plan of action could be agreed, a local guest-house becomes a raging inferno.

All within have perished in the flames, amongst them Harané, a Princess of the powerful Ancaludan Clan and a Priestess of the Goddess Luté who was travelling to Hazek, the City of the Swan Queen.

Investigating, Edrun Sulandax and his companions soon find out that perhaps Harané Ancaludan did not die in the fire after all. There is a conspiracy at work, one that extends into the highest echelons of both the Clans and the Temples, but to dig too deeply might set the whole of the Kalion Islands alight with civil war.

One man, it seems, is the key to everything; Edrun's old enemy Halgar Rassvorea who is determined to finish this young nuisance once and for all.

Book 5: The Sons of the Silent God

No longer does the threat of civil war hang over the Island of the Sixteen Gods. Edrun and his companions can relax for a while in Hazek, the City of Luté, the Swan Queen, before returning to their homes.

But the High Priest and High Priestess complain that brigands are causing trouble in one of the more remote corners of the territory of the Luté. Edrun and his companions offer to do what young Lords of the Gathering are so very good at doing, and eradicate this menace.

All begins well, but a few celebratory drinks, a stumble in the dark, and a crack on the head leave Edrun unconscious, lost in the storm outside. When he awakes he is still in the land of Luté – or is he? Where are his friends? Where is the Inn of the Stranger Maiden? And who are these men, the sinister Brotherhood of the Sword?

Is he dead, journeying on the path of the Sixth Stage? Or have demons of the night taken him? If so, why? And where? And can he ever get back again?

~*~
Evaluation 8:
Broken But...Mending Series by Dale Mayer
https://www.dalemayer.com/
Contemporary Romance

Book 1: Skin

A journey of exploration...
A journey of healing...
A journey of love...
Two people are forced by circumstances into a therapy class to help them deal with their problems. They are strangers. Forced to be partners. Naturally opposites.

Kane is dealing with anger of betrayal at the deepest level, needing to find his way back to forgiveness. Tania is a previous rape victim hoping to deal with her fear of intimacy so she can have a loving relationship.

Tania's medium of expression - her camera.

Her subject – the human body – Kane's physical body.

Looking through the lens of a camera, she learns to find beauty and compassion...and the strength to find wholeness...with him.

Book 2: Scars

Some scars are visible...
Some scars are hidden...
The worst scars are buried deep inside...
Robin and Sean are existing in their private worlds. Hiding in plain sight, not really living, definitely not thriving. They both need to move forward... if they can.

Yet the price of success is pain as they confront issues that have plagued them for years. They're so different, with such opposite problems. Yet they complement each other - or at least they will, if they can work through their issues and find each other.

This is a story of pain and sorrow, joy and success... and... love.

Book 3: Scales (of Justice)

She thinks she escaped Justice
He is still waiting for Justice to happen.
She's afraid her day of reckoning is near.
He's afraid his day of reckoning will never arrive.
Will love balance the scales of Justice?

Paris and Weaver's story will be out soon in this 3 installment of the Broken but... Mending series.

~*~

Evaluation 9:
The Shadows of Mallachrom by Michelle Levigne
http://www.mlevigne.com/
Science Fiction

Far on the edge of settled space, the colony world Mallachrom is mostly wilderness. The growth of Human settlements have been slowed by fear and secrets and deception. Years ago, during an invasion by the alien Talroqi, most of the adults were killed, and most of the children vanished, spirited away to safety by the sentient canines known as Shadows.

Those children came back from the wilderness changed, bound to the planet in ways they can't, or won't, explain. Called the Taken, they live on the edges of civilization and the new government of Mallachrom fears them. The colony's leaders want to exterminate the Shadows, and claim the Taken are dangerous, under the influence of the Shadows. The Taken don't trust the government. They know what is really happening out in the wilderness, and guard secrets and dangers that most Mallachrom colonists will never know.

A war is poised on the horizon. On the surface, it is a battle for control of a planet, the extermination of a sentient species. The truth is that if Mallachrom falls, so might the Human race.

Book 1: Blue Fire, A Novel

The hive-minded insectoid Talroqi have been at war with Humans for generations. Rover captain Rhianni Day grew up with her father's team. Memories of Mallachrom, the colony world where she was born, and the boy who was her best friend, are a burden of guilt on her soul. Far from the battle lines, Mallachrom should have been safe – yet after the Rovers left the colony world, the aliens invaded. That sense of guilt weighed on her father, and on his death that burden is passed to Rhianni.

She is ordered to return to Mallachrom and investigate what really happened in the Talroqi invasion, especially the strange stories about the children who survived – carried away to safety by the sentient canines called Shadows. The government of Mallachrom fears these children, called the Taken. Rhianni has only good memories of the Shadows. Even more important: Petroc Ash, her childhood friend, is a Taken. Rhianni will do her duty, but Mallachrom is no longer home. She intends to find out the truth, leave, and never return.

Petroc leads the Taken. His responsibilities to the Taken and their secrets are too great to risk, even for Rhianni. Their childhood bond has grown even stronger, despite her long absence. Loving her will bind her to Mallachrom forever -- and could kill her.

The quest to learn the truth, to understand the duty the Shadows placed on the Taken, and protect the Taken from destruction nearly separates Petroc and Rhianni forever. Trusting their instincts and each other shatters the last barriers and creates an alliance that could save Mallachrom. The question is if their partnership has come in time. The Shadows have a task for Rhianni that has been waiting since she was born. The Talroqi sense this, and try to warp her to their long-range plan. If she fails, not just Mallachrom but the entire Human race could fall.

Book 2: That Synching Feeling, A Novella

Rover Pilot Nureen Keala, Rhianni Day's best friend, is on patrol on the other side of the galaxy from Mallachrom. She would rather be supporting Rhianni's mission, but the bureaucrats aren't cooperating. Responding to a distress call puts Nureen in the wrong place at the wrong time. She falls through a vortex into another universe that has never heard of the Rovers or the war against the Talroqi.

On a space station belonging to the Trefarian Empire, Tedrin Creed has been waiting for the vortex to open again. Five years ago, Talroqi ships attacked his ship. After sending his crew away to safety, he defeated the Talroqi before the vortex sucked down his ship. He has been lying to the Empire's people ever since, waiting for the vortex to open, so he can go home. When a ship and a pilot claiming to be a Rover fall through, his chance has finally come.

Problem: This ship is like no Rover ship he has ever seen, and the pilot doesn't like him, or believe he is who he says he is. Nureen has every reason to distrust this man who claims to be Tedrin Creed. She knows all about him. He was her grandfather's best friend, and died a hero fifty years ago.

Time is the problem, in several ways. The vortex and the way home will only be open for a short period of time. Can they learn to trust each other and escape the dangers of the Empire before time runs out?

Book 3: Starblue, A Novel

Starblue Ash, daughter of Rhianni Day and Petroc Ash, is well aware of the burden of her heritage. She has sworn never to join the Rovers or leave Mallachrom. Blue learns the hard way that swearing never to do something just challenges the universe to work against her.

Her two closest friends are the twins, Neona and Keegan Creed, children of Nureen Keala and Tedrin Creed. The three have shared a psionic bond since childhood. The twins are Rover pilots. Commander General Day of the Rovers is determined to make Blue a Rover, because she is the last of their family line. If he has to use her friends against her, he will.

Fate intervenes when a team of Rovers discovers a world inhabited by creatures uncannily similar to the Shadows of Mallachrom. The Creed twins' duty takes them to this world, to investigate. Neona is entranced by the creatures, called Shades. When the Shades make mental captives of Neona and other Rovers, the bond between the twins is stretched to the point of breaking. Blue's bond with the twins might be the only hope they have of freeing the prisoners.

Blue leaves Mallachrom and joins Keegan in chasing down the ship taken by the Shades and their mental puppets. The long journey deepens their bond. If they survive this crisis, they might change the universe.

~*~

Evaluation 10:
Retreat House by Sarah Yasin
https://www.sarahyasin.com/
Romantic Gothic Thriller

At an overnight youth group retreat on an island in Maine, six teenagers play an outdoor game of hide and seek in the dark, leaving Holly, their chaperone, alone in the house. None of the kids notices when the power goes out, and soon a teen enters the darkened house with a knife wound. The party's over, and Holly tries to wrangle the kids together to hide from the attacker. In the dark, she fails to locate all the retreatants. Mainland cell phone towers don't reach the island, and help is not on the way. With the bond of fellowship, Holly and the kids must outsmart the attacker once he invades the house. Retreat House explores life questions of trust and integrity, and plumbs the darkness we all face when we hide from others.

~*~

Evaluation 11:

Mind's Eye - The Imagery of Remembered Scenes by Wendy Laing
http://www.wendylaing.com/
Poetry

A collection of poems written by Wendy over the years, full of images from childhood, family, pets the Australian countryside around her, with a touch of homespun philosophy.

~*~

Evaluation 12:
Time Thieves by Dale Mayer
Time-Travel Romantic Suspense

Time has a way of solving many problems – but it also has a way of creating many more...

Sari grew up with a secret that involved her missing father... The only other person who knows the truth refuses to acknowledge it. Sari can't forget what happened. Ever. She lost someone she loved.

Fifteen years later, the possibility of reversing the series of events drives her to keep searching for answers. Especially now that she's finally returned to where it all happened and with the people – one in particular – that she'd been forced to leave behind.

Fifteen years ago, Ward was devastated when Sari's mother fled to France with Sari. Even at ten, they'd been sweethearts. But the mystery of what happened back then had lain fallow... waiting for someone to stir up the soil. And damn if Sari wasn't the best at doing just that...

Sari and Ward are out of time. Can they solve the mystery of what happened? Or do they become the next victims...

~*~

Evaluation 13:
Second Chances by Dale Mayer
Contemporary Romance

Go ahead. Take Charge of your life. Move forward...if you can...

Changing her future means letting go of her past. Karina heads to a weekend seminar and discovers the speaker is the person she needs to move on from. But she soon realizes bigger issues are facing her...

Brian has moved on, at least he'd believed he had... until he sees Karina in his audience...and realizes he's been lying to himself.

Passion pulls them together, love binds them together, but a revengeful enemy determines to keep the two apart...and destroy them both.

~*~

Evaluation 14:
Riana's Revenge by Dale Mayer
Romantic Fantasy Suspense Short Story

This short story was first published in the anthology *Every Witch Way But Wicked*.

A young hydromancer must win a challenge to save her place as rightful heir to her elemental House. When she discovers her ex - the man she still loves - is one of the judges, she wonders just how many enemies she's really fighting.

Riana has lived her life hidden away from the envious eyes of those who would take over her house and all that comes with it. As long as her mother, the powerful elder lived, the house was untouchable. When she died, secrecy was...everything.

Then someone found out...

~*~

Evaluation 15:
Gem Stone, A Gemma Stone Mystery by Dale Mayer
Romantic Suspense Young Adult

A juvie kid trying to stay on the right path stumbles into trouble...

Gemma takes her camera everywhere. From juvie hall to a halfway home, the new hobby gives her a focus she'd never had before and… hope in a future.

Until she takes pictures of something that could get her killed. And not just her…after she and another juvie girl are chased by a stranger to the halfway home that same night, the other girl goes missing and Gemma knows she needs help. But who can she trust? Not the authorities that's for sure.

Trusting them is impossible for a girl with her damaged history, and besides, who cares about a troubled kid…especially when trouble just naturally seems to find her.

~*~
Evaluation 16:
Age of Jeweled Intelligence Series by Christina Greenaway
http://www.christinagreenaway.com/
Visionary Fiction

MANKIND MUST EVOLVE AND TRANSCEND TO THE NEXT
UNIVERSE BEFORE EARTH'S SUN STAR BURNS OUT

On the journey into life, every soul deposits atoms of brilliance from its highest awareness into Time—the mastermind that oversees the evolution of mankind. One man is entrusted to carry Time Blade, the weapon that can cut, stop, or reverse Time to prevent actions that could annihilate the human family.

Book 2: Time Blade

Rebel high school grad Sky Hunter, sets out to see the world. He'll work odd jobs to support himself—live by the hand of chance.

Chance challenges Sky's resolve, as he crosses the River Tamar in Cornwall. His soul guides appears—Tamara spirit of the river. Tamara tells Sky eons ago he lived in the dazzling Age of Jeweled Intelligence. When disaster ended that world, he made a sacred vow to one day restore that Intelligence on Earth. That promise has come due. Sky must time-travel back to a past life and learn how to meet it.

In his ancient life, Sky lives as the emissary for Time on Earth. He carries Time Blade. Engaged to wed the beautiful and tempestuous Princess Sol'aria, he struggles to juggle work and passion. The astral energy of rubies powers this extraordinary civilization—airships, industries, and all the comforts of home. Rubies evoke creativity, love, and happiness. Everyone thrives, but evil lurks. Dark Master, ruler of the underworld, riles up the people, telling them they deserve to reap the riches the emerald kingdom. Time warns mankind is not ready to handle the astral fire of emeralds. Greed wins the day.

Sky spends five harrowing days in his ancient life, fighting Dark Master and wielding Time Blade in an effort to save that world. Returning to his present-day life, Sky is challenged to win back guardianship of Time Blade and keep his ancient promise to restart the Age of Jeweled Intelligence on Earth.

~*~

Evaluation 17:

Greenspell: A Fantasy Anthology by Kathy Ann Trueman

https://www.kathytrueman.com/

Fantasy/Anthology

A sorceress unravels a spell and gets a result she never expected; a young girl wins a contest and gets to speak with a god; a secret vampire fears she'll be blamed for the depredations of another of her kind; a minstrel travels with a witch who has a pair of very unusual cart horses--these are what the reader will find in this anthology of fantasy short stories. Although each story is different, they have one thing in common--they all feature female protagonists.

This anthology includes "The Sow's Ear", which was originally published in Marion Zimmer Bradley's *Sword and Sorceress* anthology series.

~*~

Evaluation 18:

Crimson Dreams by Margaret L. Carter

Fantasy Romance (Vampire)

The summer when Heather was eighteen, her dream beast's nightly visits warded off loneliness and swept her away in flights of ecstasy. Now, returning to the mountains to sell her dead parents' vacation cabin, she finds her "beast" again. But he turns out to be more than a dream. She meets Devin in the flesh, apparently not a day older. His first human lover, centuries in the past, died horribly because of her devotion to him. Does he dare to expose another mortal woman to that risk?

~*~

Evaluation 19:
Hearts Desires and Dark Embraces by Margaret L. Carter
Fantasy Romance Anthology

When Margaret L. Carter first read Dracula at the age of twelve, her spontaneous reaction was to wonder how the undead Count saw the events in which he was portrayed as the villain. She has always been fascinated with the "monster's" viewpoint and relationships between human and nonhuman beings. Most of the stories in this collection can be described as romances, and all involve love and passion in some form. Here you will encounter vampires, elves, ghosts, and at least one human-monster hybrid. The vampire stories in the first half of the book are part of an ongoing series in which the creatures we know as vampires belong to a naturally evolved, nonhuman species secretly living among us. Readers can get better acquainted with them in *Crimson Dreams*, *Sealed in Blood*, and *Passion in the Blood*.

~*~

Evaluation 20:
From the Dark Places by Margaret L. Carter
Paranormal Romance

When Father Michel Emeric and Dr. Ray Benson warn young widow Kate Jacobs of occult danger stalking her, she dismisses them as deranged fanatics. The eerie disappearance of her four-year-old daughter, Sara, changes her mind. Ray and Father Mike rescue Kate's child, but the fight has only begun. Dark powers from beyond our world want to destroy Kate and her daughter and prevent the birth of a future child foretold to have extraordinary psychic powers and a destiny as a great warrior against evil. Kate must develop her latent wild talents and allow Sara to do the same, in a universe weirder--and more dangerous-- than she has ever imagined.

~*~

Evaluation 21:
Passion in the Blood by Margaret L. Carter
Paranormal Romance (Vampire)

Cordelia and her twin sister don't realize the mother who left them soon after their birth bequeathed them a dark bloodline. They are half vampire. Although human in most respects, they have certain psychic gifts. A friend of their late father's, Karl, a vampire, has been watching over their family for generations to honor his love for their distant ancestor. When her sister is kidnapped and Cordelia must beg for help from Karl, she learns the truth about his vampirism and her own heritage. In the process, she and Karl form a blood bond that leads to deeper intimacy than either one expected.

~*~

Evaluation 22:
Sealed in Blood by Margaret L. Carter
Paranormal Romance (Vampire)

Science fiction conventions attract some strange people, but Sherri Hudson never expected to spend a con weekend helping a sexy man in a cape steal photos of a winged alien. When the photographer is murdered, and Nigel Jamison reveals to Sherri that the "alien" is actually his sister, the situation gets intriguingly complicated. Unwillingly swept up in Nigel's quest to rescue his sister, Sherri can't help being fascinated with him. By the time she finds out he's a vampire, the fascination has become mutual--and too strong to resist.

~*~

Evaluation 23:
Sealing the Dark Portal by Margaret L. Carter
Fantasy Romance

Almost nothing Rina remembers about her life is true. Rather than an ordinary librarian, she is a sorceress who fled from another world to ours when creatures from an alien dimension devastated her home and killed her family. Now they have pursued her to our world, summoned by a sorcerer who plans to open a portal and invite monstrous entities from the void between dimensions to overrun this planet. Rina's former bodyguard, a cat shapeshifter who was once her lover and still yearns for her, helps her true memories to awaken. She must come to terms with the truth about her past so that together they can save their new home from the fate of their old one.

~*~

Evaluation 24:
Shadow of the Beast by Margaret L. Carter
Paranormal Romance

After the mysterious deaths of her brother and sister at the fangs of what looks like a feral dog, Jenny Cameron develops nightmares and blackouts. The quest for the truth about herself leads to her long-lost father, who deserted the family before her birth. He seeks redemption for the curse he carries, but has his bloody past condemned him beyond salvation? When Jenny discovers the secret of her dark heritage, she must face the possibility that she cannot trust herself enough to be with the man she loves, and she may have to destroy her own father. Fearing she has inherited the violence that rages in him, she must struggle to find her true self under the shadow of the beast.

~*~

Evaluation 25:

Windwalker's Mate by Margaret L. Carter
Paranormal Romance

Shannon's little boy Daniel has disturbing psychic powers. He talks to the wind--and it listens. All Shannon wants is a normal life. She wants to forget the cult of the Windwalker, a dark god from another dimension, and the terrifying night when her child was conceived. But her first love, Nathan, son of the cult leader, contacts her for the first time since that horrific ceremony. He claims his father is stalking Shannon and Daniel. Whose child is Daniel, Nathan's or the Windwalker's? Nathan's father plans to use Daniel to open a gate between dimensions and unleash chaos on our world. To save her child and become reconciled with her first love, Shannon must embrace the strange powers she has rejected.

~*~

Evaluation 26:
Different Blood: The Vampire as Alien by Margaret L. Carter
Nonfiction

Different blood flows in their veins--but our blood quenches their thirst. From Bram Stoker's 1897 creation of Count Dracula, portrayed as a foreign invader bent on the conquest of England, the literary vampire has symbolized the Other, whether his or her otherness arises from racial, ethnic, sexual, or species difference. Even before the bloodsucking Martians of H. G. Wells' *War of the Worlds*, however, popular fiction contained a few vampires who were members of alien species rather than supernatural undead. Even more intriguing than interplanetary invaders are humanoid and quasi-humanoid beings who have evolved to live on Earth among us, often camouflaged as our own kind. The boom in vampire fiction that began in the 1970s engendered a variety of "alien" vampires, many of them portrayed as sympathetic characters. The science fiction vampire is especially suited to the presentation of vampirism as morally neutral rather than inherently evil. *Different Blood* surveys the literary vampire as alien, whether extraterrestrial or a different species evolved on Earth, from the mid-1800s to the 1990s, and analyzes the many uses to which science fiction and fantasy authors have put this theme. Their works explore issues of species, race, ecological responsibility, gender, eroticism, xenophobia, parasitism, symbiosis, intimacy, and the bridging of differences. An extensive bibliography lists dozens of novels and short stories on the "vampire as alien" theme, many of them still in print.

~*~

Evaluation 27:
Dance of Desolation by Jenna Whittaker
https://jennawhittaker-author.weebly.com/
Fantasy

Shren has been locked in his own mansion's cellar for seven years before one day, he finds the door unlocked, and his house--once filled with parties that his captors, his traitorous servants, threw--silent and empty. Upon closer inspection, Shren finds that his home has only one difference from the days before his imprisonment--a painting gracing one of the walls, a painting of a man with eyes bleeding pitch black. A magicworker has been in his home.

Shren leaves, seeking to escape the wrath of the magicworker, should they return. It is then that he discovers their origin, that they are far more insidious and dangerous than he'd ever imagined, and he is inexorably drawn into a journey to stop the magicworkers from taking and corrupting his people as they did in the land they were created.

~*~

Evaluation 28:
Dreamscape by Jenna Whittaker
Fantasy

Set in a fantasy world full of sects fighting against each other, a man from an alternate dimension of the gods is sent to earth to save it from a threat it does not yet know. Khalos had powers he didn't even realise, and when they awakened, they destroyed his world. After a fire, started from his rage, burned down his childhood home, Khalos' innocence died in the ashes. He began a long journey to a city where he may be safe--and others may be safe from him--meeting up with a woman who worked with dark forces from the future.

~*~

Evaluation 29:
Watership by Jenna Whittaker
Science Fiction

The world was dying, so scientists worked to create a safe haven in the centre of the earth; hollowing it out for the future generations to live safely.

When the creatures created to watch over the people detected the failsafe program had activated, and that their hollow world was about to collapse, they took them to a sentient, biological spaceship, set with the coordinates to take them to a new world.

But with the aliens who helped the scientists in the past come back to change the course of the ship, things soon spiral out of control.

~*~

Evaluation 30:
The Last Immortal by Jenna Whittaker
Fantasy: Dystopian

Death was alien to them. The people of the world never knew death for as long as any could recall; yet when their world slowed on its axis, the atmosphere disintegrating, the immortals felt death for the first time.

A wasting sickness ravaged their species. The old could not fight it, and the young who survived were permanently scarred by it, unable to ever bear children. Yet when it seemed that the sickness had passed, further destruction was laid upon them; the earth shattered. What was once a whole world became a mass of small shards of land held together, barely, with never-ending chasms separating them.

But when an immortal girl appears, Kyrilee, who cannot catch the wasting sickness, she tells a tale of dreaming thousands of years past, of giving birth to a cat. Most dismiss her as mad, but some believe she is the one they have been searching for. The one who holds the key to curing the sickness, who can bring the people together once more.

Kyrilee finds that she is no immortal, but instead a mortal body with an immortal soul, constantly reincarnating throughout the ages.

When she discovers the cats, the descendants of the one she birthed in her dream, and she realises it wasn't a dream at all. These creatures hold the key to restoring the earth. She must take this key from them before they enslave the humans.

Cheat Sheet
(Karen's Revised Versions)

Evaluation 1:
Dangerous Waters Series by Dee Lloyd

Dashing heroes set out to protect the women of their dreams as they travel by boat over the Caribbean and the Bahamas, even to a clear lake in Muskoka, where romance--and deception--will take them all into Dangerous Waters.

Book 1: Change of Plans

Mike and Sara didn't plan on falling in love...

Determined to change his image from "Mr. Nice Guy" to "dangerous and exciting male on the prowl" after a near miss that almost had him marrying the wrong woman, Mike is disillusioned and angry with women in general. His fiancée eloped with her boss while he was away completing a contract job in Africa, and he can only think, *Good riddance!* Now all he has to do is find a fun-loving woman to share his honeymoon stateroom...

Sara has never been in love, but she does want a family. She decides to take a cruise so she can consider the marriage proposal of Stephen Cafik, a wealthy electronics engineer whose political career her retired state senator father is encouraging.

But someone else on board the ship has plans--ones that involve killing Sara...

Book 2: Ghost of a Chance

Bret's well-ordered life is already off the rails when a lovely but bloody ghost confronts him on a dark, deserted road. Recovering from a recent injury that nearly killed him, he's convinced his nerves must be in worse shape than he believed if he's starting to see ghosts.

When Bret steps into the piano lounge, he sees a beauty on

the stage, weaving a spell for her audience. Milly's performance doesn't suffer, but she's intensely aware of the stranger's unwavering gaze on her from the audience.

Bret is convinced Milly is the ghostly, bloody woman he saw on the road. But how can she be?

Book 3: Unquiet Spirits

Headstrong Kit Schofield heads north to her family resort at Spirit Lake, convinced the hit-and-run that almost killed her was a random act of violence. Not-so-convinced, lifelong buddy Bart Thornton joins her as a self-appointed bodyguard, much to Kit's chagrin--at first.

Two lusty ghosts drop clues about old murders and insist that Kit and Bart are soul mates. One kiss proves it, unleashing unexpected, unwelcome and totally distracting passion between them.

Disturbing old secrets and equally unsettling ghosts lurk in the lodge as well as in the calm waters of the deceptively peaceful resort. In the calm, a deadly, elusive killer strikes again...

~*~

Evaluation 2:
Jane Doe Mystery by Wendy Laing

As the daughter of a policeman who died in the line of duty, Inspector Jane Doe, head of Melbourne Homicide, is single-mindedly driven to seek justice for all. But Jane is no ordinary detective. She can communicate with the ghosts of murder victims. Not wanting to be dismissed as mentally unstable, she must keep her secret from all but her husband and her senior officer, using each victim's information to subtly direct her team in the right direction on each case. Jane realizes she's the only thing standing between a killer being brought to justice and a monster getting off scot-free. But, with each case she solves, her fear that the police hierarchy will accidentally discover her secret forces her to walk a fine line indeed.

Book 1: Flowers from the Grave

Recovering from near fatal head injuries received from a serial killer, who is still at large, Inspector Jane Doe, head of Melbourne Homicide, is staying in an isolated clifftop cottage. Ryan, a stranger on the beach, befriends her. But Jane's idyllic sojourn turns into a nightmare. Flowers arrive with threatening notes attached. Worse, she can't help but believe that Ryan is some kind of ghost, and, if he is, is he friend or foe? Has the serial killer she apprehended in the name of justice returned to finish what he started and make her his next victim?

Book 2: Severance Packages

Set in the peaceful town of Sunbury, Australia, Inspector Jane Doe, head of Melbourne Homicide, once again deals with a serial killer after grisly, dismembered body parts are discovered at a local winery and the rubbish dump. Jane has to act fast to stop any more of these 'severance packages' from being delivered.

Book 3: Haunted Heart

Head of Melbourne Homicide, Inspector Jane Doe's first Cold Case involves the recent death of a daughter of a Member of Parliament. After he disagrees with the first coroner's verdict of accidental death, the MP secures a second autopsy that reveals his daughter was murdered. At the same time, Jane's husband Oliver is dealing with a young heart transplant recipient who's having nightmares of being murdered. Elsewhere, another law enforcement officer, Steve Ho, investigates the murder of an eminent heart transplant surgeon found in a local lake. Jane, Oliver and Steve become embroiled in a case that will surely haunt them all for years to come.

~*~

Evaluation 3:
The Rowland Sisters Trilogy by Catherine Dove

For the daughter of a gentleman during the English Regency, life can be a whirlwind of parties, balls and outings--all to catch a suitable husband. For Georgiana and Cecilia Rowland and their friends, finding and securing the right husband is further complicated by misunderstandings, prejudices, rebellion against social restrictions, uncooperative suitors...and sometimes their own wayward hearts.

Book 1: Mr. Harding Proposes

Eligible bachelor Mr. Richard Harding has his heart set on marrying his lifelong friend and neighbor, Miss Georgiana Rowland. However, the two have been good friends for so long that, when he finally screws up his courage and proposes to her, Georgie thinks he's merely teasing!

Georgiana has good reason to be so distracted. Her younger sister is about to be launched into society and most of the work and worry falls on Georgie. Also, despite her mother's furious command, she's befriended the scandalous Lady Shipton, which brings both blessing and chaos to the Rowland family and to their kind uncle, Sir Henry. Worse for Mr. Harding, Lady Shipton's charming stepson takes a strong liking to the beguiling Georgie.

Mr. Harding keeps proposing, again and again, while still trying to support Georgie in her trials. Is it possible for such a good friendship to turn into love?

Book 2: The Lazy Bachelor

Mr. Peregrine Tyndall has often been called the laziest man in London. Even still, stirred to the enormous task of matchmaking when a hunting accident suffered by his cousin makes him realize he stands in real danger of inheriting an earldom--with all its tedious responsibilities. In his opinion, the perfect girl to marry his cousin and give the earldom another heir than himself would be their childhood friend, Portia Freestone.

Mr. Tyndall doesn't know what formidable obstacles lay before him in this endeavour. However, when he joins a house party at the earl's country home with this match on his mind, everything seems to go wrong. In the first place, his normally obliging friend Portia has a secret. She has no wish to marry the earl--she likes him very well but the man she secretly wishes to marry is Mr. Tyndall himself. An even bigger problem is Miss Frances Armitage. She and her little sister Eleanor had been left in his guardianship, a duty he has benignly and completely neglected up to now. A furious Miss Armitage is about to descend on Lakeford Hall to demand that Mr. Tyndall take up his duties to her and her sister in a responsible manner--even if she has to force him to do it!

Thrust into just the sort of efforts he dislikes most, Mr. Tyndall tries his best to cope, and, in the attempt, gets a great deal more than he bargained for.

Book 3: Cecilia and the Rake

Unpleasant experience has given Miss Cecilia Rowland a strong aversion to rakes, even one so fascinating and gentlemanlike as Lord Ravenshill. She does her best to ignore his existence, but Fate keeps bringing them together. Even deep in the country, visiting the home of her mother's betrothed husband, Cecilia finds herself in the company of Lord Ravenshill. Not only is he a neighbor of Mr. Clarke's, but Cecilia's stepsister-to-be, Kitty, develops a tendre toward Mr. Guy Dorne, Ravenshill's best friend.

The Viscount Ravenshill is not the sort of man to regret his past, even when he finds himself unaccountably fascinated by the lovely Miss Rowland. He looks on his friend Guy's growing attachment to Kitty Clarke with amusement and resolutely ignores the promptings of his own traitorous heart. The grim past which made him a ruthless rake also makes him a completely unsuitable match for an innocent girl like Cecilia Rowland. Nevertheless, when Cecilia and Kitty go to London for the Season, the same Fate that threw Cecilia toward Ravenshill takes an unexpected twist that endangers the loves of both girls.

~*~

Evaluation 4:
Wild Sorceress Series by Margaret L. Carter and Leslie Roy Carter

In a world where hostile nations wield magic in combat, twin sorceresses separated at birth and brought up on opposing sides of the war find each other. Together, they face persecution for using wild magic, fight against traitors and assassins, explore family secrets, and discover the hidden origins of magic itself. Above all, to protect their world, they must deal with ancient, powerful dragons that most people don't even believe exist.

Book 1: Wild Sorceress

In a world where warring nations use magic in combat, years ago young sorceress Aetria's untamed power caused a disaster on the battlefield. Temporarily banished and retrained, she's returned to the army to redeem herself as head of a company of novice mages. She uncovers a traitorous plot by her own commander, renews her bond with her "imaginary" childhood friend, and meets her long-lost twin sister. While also becoming a trusted friend of the commanding general of the army, Aetria unearths secrets of the true nature of the magic she and her comrades wield.

Book 2: Besieged Adept

While learning to control her wild sorcery, Adept Aetria has defeated a pair of traitors trying to kill her, found a long-lost twin, and uncovered secrets of the source and nature of magic. Now she continues her research while battling the remnants of the Neo-Aggressor rebellion and integrating raw, untrained talent into the Sorcerer Corps. Meanwhile, she discovers deeper secrets of her own family background, along with a surprising new foe and a destiny she never dreamed of. Furthermore, she learns that her "imaginary" dragon friend Rajii actually exists...but so do less friendly dragons. What does their agenda mean for the future of humanity and magic in Aetria's world?

Book 3: Rogue Magess

Sorceresses Aetria and Coleni discover that both their own births and the history of their world have been manipulated in secret by an ancient, powerful race of dragons. Some, like Aetria's lifelong friend Rajii, have benevolent intentions toward humanity while others want to restore the people of the Domains to total slavery. All, however, have their own agendas with human beings and mortal magic as pawns.

Emerging from their long-lost mother's hidden home in the deserted Non-Lands, Aetria and Coleni find themselves targeted by assassins under control of the dragons. While the sisters' powers continue to grow, so do the magical gifts of Coleni's baby daughter, but will their magic provide adequate protection?

Meanwhile, still viewed with suspicion for their "wild sorcery", they can't convince most of their rivals and allies, including Aetria's old mentor and the commanding general of the army, that the dragons and the danger they pose are real.

Prequel: Legacy of Magic

Most people in the country of Saphradea admire sorcerers and dream of having magical powers. Not Merina, a young woman who detests magic because she thinks it ruined the life of her mother, a failed sorceress candidate who abandoned her in infancy.

When Merina's fiancé, Trinames, announces he's decided to go for training as a Healer sorcerer, her personal world turns upside down. Merina is heiress to a tract of rich farmland, and she wants only to manage her own property and bring up a family in peace--a dream she thought Trinames shared. Yet events conspire to force her into a realm of magic and intrigue she never wanted.

When Trinames is kidnapped and she strikes out across the wilderness to rescue him, in company with a wandering trader who turns out to be more than he appears, she runs into a crisis that awakens magical powers she shouldn't even possess.

~*~
Evaluation 5:
Ancient Scythian Trilogy by Max Overton

Captured by the warlike, tribal Scythians who bicker amongst themselves and bitterly resent outside interference, a fiercely loyal captain in Alexander the Great's Companion Cavalry Nikometros and his men are to be sacrificed to the Mother Goddess. Lucky chance--and the timely intervention of Tomyra, priestess and daughter of the Massegetae chieftain--allows him to defeat the Champion. With their immediate survival secured, acceptance into the tribe...and escape...is complicated by the captain's growing feelings for Tomyra--death to any who touch her--and the chief's son Areipithes who not only detests Nikometros and wants to have him killed or banished but intends to murder his own father and take over the tribe.

Book 1: Lion of Scythia

Alexander the Great has conquered the Persian Empire and is marching eastward to India. In his wake he leaves small groups of soldiers to govern great tracts of land and diverse peoples. Nikometros is one young cavalry captain left behind in the lands of the fierce, nomadic Scythian horsemen. Captured after an ambush, Nikometros must fight for his life and the lives of his surviving men. Even as he seeks an opportunity to escape, he finds himself bound by a debt of loyalty to the chief...and his own developing love for the young priestess.

Book 2: The Golden King

The chief of the tribe of nomadic Scythian horsemen is dead, killed by his son's treachery. The priestess, lover of the young cavalry officer, Nikometros, is carried off into the mountains. Nikometros and his friends set off in hard pursuit.

Death rides with them. By the time they return, the tribes are at war. Nikometros must choose between attempting to become chief himself or leaving the people he's come to love and respect to return to his duty as an army officer in the Empire of Alexander.

Book 3: Funeral in Babylon

Alexander the Great has returned from India and set up his court in Babylon. Nikometros and a band of loyal Scythians journey deep into the heart of Persia to join the Royal court. Nikometros finds himself embroiled in the intrigues and wars of kings, generals, and merchant adventurers as he strives to provide a safe haven for his lover and friends. With the fate of an Empire hanging in the balance, Death walks beside Nikometros as events precipitate a Funeral in Babylon...

~*~
Evaluation 6:
Castle Trilogy by J.H. Wear

In the medieval land of Domum, mythical creatures and reckless magic threaten to unravel its very existence. In this fantastical place, crystals also have extraordinary abilities. A set of the legendary Locus Crystals are rumored to give the holder invincibility and may be the most awesome and dangerous treasure to gain...or lose.

Book 1: Fall to Domum

Jon McKinney is anything but an ordinary Boston university student on the path toward a career in computer science, but he's spent his life feeling like he should be more than he is. When he inherits a castle in Ireland from his presumably drowned Uncle Gordon, he leaves behind his education and his girlfriend to see what awaits him on the other side of the world. Once there, he meets the fascinating and beautiful Liz O'Doul and discovers a strange crystal he mistakenly believes is merely a good luck charm. Liz tells him Miller Castle has a long and colourful history of strange creatures lurking about its stone walls, but Jon doesn't believe it...until Liz catches a dwarf named Gilbert trying to steal unmentionables from her suitcase. Jon pursues the creature up the steep staircases of the castle. But, just as he catches Gilbert, the two of them tumble out the window and through a magical gateway.

Jon finds himself trapped in a medieval world where dragons, gargoyles and demon-like creatures actually exist. For a college student who's more comfortable with a football in his hand than a sword, the idea of saving anyone, least of all himself, is ludicrous. To return to Earth, John will need to obtain an exceptionally rare Voltaire Crystal. Meanwhile, Liz has followed Jon to Domum and encounters her own difficulties in reuniting with him.

There is only one way back to where they came from, and the impossible quest they must undertake to return will require much more than a hapless plunge from a towering window.

Book 2: Return to Domum

In the magical land of Domum, Lord Troy Sussex seeks to purchase a Dracon Crystal to free himself from an improperly executed, perpetual youth spell that's forced his confinement on his castle property. Gilbert, a dwarf and a thief, has the gem he needs and shortsightedly sells it to the notorious playboy. But the reversal spell Lord Troy casts with the crystal has unexpected consequences. Domum begins to transform into the world it was before humans arrived, destroying anyone or anything in its path. The only way to prevent utter ruin is at the origin point.

Beset by numerous complications along the way, Gilbert and one of Lord Troy's slaves journey to the Castle Miller with its gateway between Domum and Earth, where they enlist the aid of Jon and Gordon Miller, magic practitioner Council Madoc, and two physics students. Few could have predicted the fate of Domum would rest in the hands of a thief, a sex slave, and a warlock in exile.

Book 3: The New King

When slavery, mass slaughter and annihilation are inevitable, a hero must be willing to give of himself sacrificially--or die fighting...

Domum has barely recovered from the destruction that almost led to total eradication when the evil Lord Darius seizes control of the land with his vast army that includes a horde of fearsome dragons. Those who defy him are executed while submission brings bondage. Proving he's all but unstoppable, Darius murders the reigning king and takes his place.

Lord Perry and his loyal supporters are all that stand between the dictator and certain victory. Jon McKinney--once an ordinary college student from Boston who stumbled blindly through a portal into Domum--has been promoted to the status of Lord and given the responsibility of defending Horstruff Castle. Jon's fiancée Liz O'Doul has endured her own struggles in this medieval world where dragons, gargoyles and demon-like creatures exist alongside powerful magic that can heal or damage to the extreme. She and Jon escaped once, but Jon was lured back once before to help save the land from extinction. This isn't her world and she wants nothing more than to return to Earth and a normal life. Her only choice is to give Jon an ultimatum. Torn, Jon realizes that to walk away now is to leave Domum to its grim fate.

Poised on the brink of war, five of the legendary Locus Crystals rumored to impart to the holder invincibility have been discovered. Jon possesses the sixth and final Locus Crystal and offers it to Lord Perry. Used together, the crystals become a weapon capable of unparalleled death and destruction, making the user indestructible. Such a powerful tool should only be used as the very last resort...

~*~

Evaluation 7:
The Islands of the Sixteen Gods by Stephen Symons

At my request for a series blurb, the author provided this for a series blurb:

All Edrun and Jina had ever wanted was to get married, raise children and have a long, happy and uneventful life in their native village, at the very last walking together hand in hand through the Gate of the Sixth Path into eternity. But the Gods of the Kalion Islands had other plans for Edrun and Jina. Dark forces were stirring up strife and discord that threatened to explode into destruction even more terrible than the chaos of the Temple Wars of bitter memory. Neither Edrun nor Jina alone could stop that. But together...?

My revision:

All Edrun and Jina ever wanted was to get married, raise children and have a long, happy and uneventful life in their native village, at the very last walking together hand in hand through the Gate of the Sixth Path into eternity. But the Gods of the Kalion Islands have other plans for Edrun and Jina. Dark forces are stirring up strife and discord that threatens to explode into destruction even more terrible than the chaos of the Temple Wars, still a bitter memory. Neither Edrun nor Jina alone can stop that. But together...?

Book 1: The Amulet of the Hunter God

The last thing Edrun Jaranacad saw of his beloved Jina was an arm desperately waving from the raging waters of the flood bearing her away. Heartbroken, he decided to leave the safety of his quiet little village to travel the outside world.

The discovery of a small golden jewel, an amulet of Shegadin the Hunter God, convinces Edrun the Gods are indeed watching over him, guiding him toward an end he could never have foreseen.

Book 2: Beloved of the River Goddess

After a year of torment and pursuit halfway across northwest Kalion, Edrun and Jina have finally found themselves both safe and well-funded. They decide to take a much-deserved holiday in the fascinating Temple-City of Hazek while they decide on their future.

While enjoying a lazy lunch outside a tavern, to his horror, Edrun finds himself publically hailed as a Lord of the Gathering. The warrior aristocracy of the Islands of the Sixteen Gods are very protective of their status and privileges and are swift to inflict punishments upon those who would usurp their position. Moments later, Edrun and Jina discover a former nemesis is also in Hazek and has in mind a sadistic revenge against them for the trouble they caused him in the past.

Making for a citadel that was once a safe haven for them, their plans are soon cast into disarray when they're forced to rescue the fiery daughter of a wealthy merchant from attacking brigands. Once more Edrun and Jina find themselves in a fight for their lives.

Book 3: The Stones of the Sleeping God

Edrun and Jina travel to the Kalalutorm Citadel of Amronulu, where they're greeted like long-lost relatives and offered the hospitality of the house for as long as they want. Now accepted as Lords of the Gathering, members of the ruling aristocracy of the Kalion Islands, Jina begins to heal rapidly but Edrun, plagued by questions and doubts, becomes morose and taciturn.

To help jolly Edrun along, an expedition to the nearby Forest of Rabti where they can spend a few days hunting, drinking, and chasing milkmaids is suggested by friends. Once there, they're invited to spend the night in a stone ring sacred to the ancient Forest God but are ambushed and Edrun captured by Lord Garin, a chieftain. Garin has heard that Edrun enjoys the favour of the Gods and wants him to join with him in a war to re-conquer the wide lands his people once ruled without rival. This alliance would involve Edrun marrying Garin's daughter Taren...

Book 4: The City of the Swan Goddess

Edrun, Jina and the council agree that something needs to be done about the mysterious disappearances of young women of the Clans of the DrummGrissa. But late that night, before a plan of action can be agreed, a local guest-house becomes a raging inferno. All within perish; amongst them Harané, a Princess of a powerful clan and a Priestess of the Goddess Luté who was travelling to Hazek. Is there a conspiracy at work, one that extends into the highest echelons of both the Clans and the Temples? Digging too deeply might set the whole of the Kalion Islands alight with civil war. One man, it seems, is the key to everything--Edrun's old enemy Halgar Rassvorea, who's determined to finish Edrun off once and for all.

Book 5: The Sons of the Silent God

No longer does the threat of civil war hang over the Island of the Sixteen Gods. Edrun and his companions can relax for a while before returning to their homes. But the High Priest and Priestess complain that brigands are causing trouble in one of the more remote corners of the territory of the Luté. Edrun and his companions offer to eradicate this menace, but instead Edrun ends up stumbling in the dark with a crack on the head, lost in a storm. When he awakes, he is still in the land of Luté...or is he? Where are his friends? Where is the Inn of the Stranger Maiden? And who are these men--the sinister Brotherhood of the Sword? Edrun is forced to wonder if he is, in fact, dead, journeying on the path of the Sixth Stage, and, if so, can he ever get back again?

~*~

Evaluation 8:
Broken But Mending Series by Dale Mayer
Note that I suggested a change in the series title and for Book 3 (for consistency).

A university psychologist runs unorthodox seminars for select pairs of students that are broken by emotional issues. Given specialized projects to undertake together, the two delve into their deepest, dark pain in a radical approach to healing.

Book 1: Skin

Forced to deal with very deep and individual problems, Kane and Tania--strangers who are complete opposites--agree to a therapy that includes only the two of them and that initially seems radical and a little scary.

Kane was ruthlessly betrayed by someone he trusted. The anger he can't seem to exorcise prevents him from grasping the only thing that can mend the damage: forgiveness.

Tania was raped, and her inability to deal with the trauma has kept her from the intimacy she nevertheless longs for in a romantic relationship. She's spent the years since the brutal attack she endured hiding behind her favored medium of expression. With her camera, she's kept the world at a distance, but the therapy requires her to step infinitely closer to her subject. As she immerses herself in Kane's skin--and his very male, physical body--Tania learns about beauty, compassion, strength, and wholeness.

Together, two broken souls take a journey of exploration, love, and ultimately healing.

Book 2: Scars

Some scars are on the surface, others are in hiding, but the worst ones are buried so deep they refuse to be brought to the light...

Forced to deal with very deep and individual problems, Robin and Sean--strangers who are complete opposites--agree to a therapy that includes only the two of them and that initially seems radical and a little scary.

Separately, they've existed in private worlds, hiding in plain sight, not living and certainly not thriving. To move forward, they'll have to confront issues that have plagued them for most of their lives. Despite their differences, they discover they complement each other, and, in finding themselves, they also find each other...

Book 3: Scales

What can balance the scales of justice when hearts are shattered, pain is inflicted and damage is dealt beyond repair?

Paris escaped a situation that some would consider a crime. She worries constantly that the day of reckoning is coming for her around every corner. Weaver seeks justice with the avidity of a hunter seeking prey. His biggest fear is that the day of reckoning he deserves will never come.

Forced to deal with very deep and individual problems, Paris and Weaver--strangers who are complete opposites--agree to a therapy that includes only the two of them and that initially seems radical and a little scary.

Against shattered hearts, inflicted pain and irreparable damage, can love balance the scales of justice?

~*~

Evaluation 9:
The Shadows of Mallachrom by Michelle Levigne

Far on the edge of settled space, the colony world Mallachrom is mostly wilderness. The slow growth of Human settlements is due to fear, secrets, and deception. Years ago, during an invasion by the alien Talroqi, many adults were killed while most of the children vanished, spirited away to safety by the sentient canines known as Shadows.

Those children came back from the wilderness changed, bound to the planet in ways they can't, or won't, explain. Called the Taken, they live on the edges of civilization. The new government on Mallachrom fears them enough to want to exterminate the Shadows and claim the Taken are dangerous--under the corrupt influence of Shadows. The Taken have no illusions about what's really happening out in the wilderness and refuse to trust the government. Alone, they guard secrets and elude dangers that most Mallachrom colonists will never be forced to face.

Poised on the horizon is a war that looks on the surface to be nothing less and nothing more than a battle for control of a planet and the extermination of a sentient species. But at its core is the truth that, if Mallachrom should fall, so might the entire Human race.

Book 1: Blue Fire, A Novel

The hive-minded insectoid Talroqi have been at war with Humans for generations. Rover captain Rhianni Day was born on Mallachrom but grew up close to the battle lines with her father's team. Far from the war, Mallachrom should have been safe yet, after the Rovers left the colony world, the aliens invaded. The burden of guilt weighed on her father to his death, then passed to her.

Rhianni is ordered to return to Mallachrom and investigate what really happened in the Talroqi invasion, especially the strange stories of the children who survived and were carried away to safety by the sentient canines called Shadows. Those children, called the Taken, are deeply feared by the Mallachrom government. Rhianni has only good memories of the Shadows. More importantly, her childhood friend, Petroc Ash, is the leader of the Taken. Rhianni will do her duty, but Mallachrom is no longer home to her. She intends to find out the truth, leave, and never return.

Petroc's responsibility for the Taken and their secrets is too great to risk, even for Rhianni. Despite her long absence, their childhood bond has grown even stronger. Staying together will bind her to Mallachrom forever...and may inadvertently lead to her death and the fall of the entire Human race.

Book 2: That Synching Feeling, A Novella

Rover Pilot Nureen Keala, Rhianni Day's best friend, is on patrol on the other side of the galaxy from Mallachrom and Rhianni's mission there. Responding to a distress call puts Nureen in the wrong place at the wrong time. She falls through a vortex into another universe where the Rovers and the war against the Talroqi don't exist.

On a space station belonging to the Trefarian Empire, Tedrin Creed has waited impatiently for the vortex to open again. Five years ago, Talroqi ships attacked his ship. After sending his crew away to safety, he defeated the Talroqi before the vortex sucked down his ship. He's been playing a dangerous game, feigning loyalty to the Empire ever since, all the while longing to go home. When a ship and a pilot claiming to be a Rover fall through, his chance finally comes.

But this ship is like no Rover ship Tedrin has ever seen, and the pilot doesn't like him, let alone believe anything he says. Nureen has every reason to distrust him. She knows all about Tedrin Creed--he was her grandfather's best friend and died a hero fifty years ago. Unfortunately, the vortex and the way home through it will only remain open for a short time. Can they learn to trust each other and escape the dangers of the Empire before it's too late?

Book 3: Starblue, A Novel

Starblue Ash, daughter of Rhianni Day and Petroc Ash, is well aware of the burden of her heritage. She's sworn never to join the Rovers or leave Mallachrom, but she's about to learn the hard way that making vows just challenges the universe to work against her.

Blue's two closest friends are Rover pilot twins Neona and Keegan Creed, children of Nureen Keala and Tedrin Creed. Since childhood, the three have shared a psionic bond. Given that she's the last of their family line, Commander General Day is determined to make Blue a Rover, too. If he has to use her friends against her to get her to comply, he will.

Fate intervenes when a team of Rovers discovers a world inhabited by creatures called Shades, who resemble the Shadows of Mallachrom. When the Shades make mental captives of Neona and other Rovers, the bond between the twins and Blue might be the only hope they have of freeing the prisoners.

~*~
Evaluation 10:
Retreat House by Sarah Yasin

Secrets hidden in darkness become exposed in the light...

Twenty-five-year-old Holly is co-leader of her church's youth group, but many in the congregation believe she's too young to supervise the kids and question her competence. Holly has never felt she fit in anywhere. The energy she derives from worship is similar to the feelings she shares with the only man she's ever loved, Adam, a former Marine who's seen combat and suffers from PTSD, nerve damage, and an inability to venture out into the world where there are too many threats to assess. Finding out she's pregnant puts Holly's position in the church in jeopardy and ensures that her secret love affair with Adam will have to be unveiled sooner rather than later.

When Holly suggests an overnight youth group retreat at her uncle's beachfront house on Pine Cliff Island, six teenagers show up for a night of clean, fun fellowship. They explore hidden annexes in the house followed by a lobster cookout and s'mores, bonfire ghost stories, and a game of nighttime hide-and-seek outdoors. When the power abruptly goes out, no one notices...until one of the teenagers returns to the darkened house with a knife wound. The party is over.

Most of the resident island snowbirds have flown south, cell phone service is nonexistent, car tires have been slashed, and a madman lies in wait in the darkness at every turn. Holly attempts to gather all the kids to make their escape by dinghy, and unexpectedly Adam shows up--a major step for him since he rarely leaves home--with no clue Holly's youth group retreat was in progress. He lands square in the middle of a maniac's nightmare. The race to survive long enough to escape may depend solely on teamwork...and knowing who to trust.

~*~
Evaluation 11:
Mind's Eye - The Imagery of Remembered Scenes by Wendy

Laing

A collection of poems encompassing one life filled with images from childhood, family, pets, the Australian countryside around, and delivered with a touch of homespun philosophy.

~*~
Evaluation 12:
Time Thieves by Dale Mayer

Time is said to heal problems, even while it creates even more than it fixes...

Sari grew up realizing a secret that involved her missing father, and the only other person who knows the truth refuses to acknowledge it. But Sari refuses to forget something that led to the loss of a person she loved deeply and has never been the same without. In search of answers, Sari returns to the people and place where the events happened fifteen years before. She's determined to find a way to do the impossible: Reverse the past.

Ward was devastated when Sari's mother fled France with her daughter a decade and a half ago. Though Sari and Ward had only been ten at the time, they'd been sweethearts. But her father's disappearance and the mystery surrounding the situation has lain dormant all this time, just waiting for someone to stir things up again. The one thing Ward had always known about the girl he loves is that she'll do whatever it takes to reach her goals. If anyone can figure out how to go back in time and right the wrongs, it's Sari. Ward can only follow and do what he can to help her. But her father's disappearance wasn't due to mere circumstance or chance. The past holds deadly secrets...and even more dangerous enemies...

~*~
Evaluation 13:
Second Chances by Dale Mayer

Take charge of your life--if you dare...

Karina knows that the only way to change her future is to let go of the past. But, in a brutally ironic twist, when she heads to a weekend seminar for counseling, she discovers that the lead speaker is the very person she came here to make a clean break from!

Brian had convinced himself he'd moved on with his life after his relationship with Karina shattered, but, after he recognizes her in the audience of his counseling symposium, he realizes he's been lying to himself to cope with his devastating loss. What right does he have to give lofty guidance about moving forward in life when he needs to take his own advice most of all?

Even after all their time apart, passion draws Karina and Brian together, love refused to die...and a vengeful enemy is deadly serious about ripping them apart again--this time for good.

~*~

Evaluation 14:
Riana's Revenge by Dale Mayer

Originally published *in Every Witch Way But Wicked Anthology*.

To claim her position as the rightful heir to her elemental house, a hydromancer who specializes in water divination must succeed in the challenge to decide her authority. In the precarious position of being the target of those envious to take over her house and the power contained within, Riana has lived her life hidden away. As long as her mother, the powerful Elder, remained alive, the ancient house stood untouchable to those many who long to breach the secrets buried there. Upon her death, everything Riana is and has could be taken away if she can't prove herself worthy of her illustrious legacy. When Riana discovers that her ex-husband, a man she still loves, is one of the judges to the challenge to her house, Riana fears her enemies may be numerous...and unstoppable.

~*~

Evaluation 15:

Gem Stone, A Gemma Stone Mystery by Dale Mayer

After landing in a juvenile detention center, Gemma is determined to stay on the right path to ensure a promising future for herself. But trouble seems dogged-determined to find her wherever she goes...

Gemma's positive new hobby has her taking her camera everywhere--from juvie hall to a halfway house--and she finally has focus and ambition like she's never experienced before. That she might take a picture of something that could get her killed never occurs to her...until she and her new friend from the halfway home are chased back to their facility and her friend disappears not long afterward.

Gemma knows she needs help, but trusting people, especially those in authority, is hard for her. That mistrust is the source of her damaged past. Pessimism swamps her--after all, who cares about an offender who seems to find trouble without having to look for it? But Gemma's had a taste of hope and she's determined to see it through, regardless of the danger solving this mystery is guaranteed to land her in.

~*~

Evaluation 16:
Age of Jeweled Intelligence Series by Christina Greenaway

Will mankind evolve and transcend to the next universe before Earth's sun star burns out? Only Time will tell...

Seven jewel kingdoms exist. Previously on an earlier planet, mankind was allowed the use of all aspects of the seven kingdoms until a supernova destroyed their civilization. Goddesses rule the Jeweled Spheres and decide when man has evolved sufficiently to handle other jeweled powers. Sadly, in the first age, man went against the edicts of the goddesses. The Age of Jeweled Intelligence came to a cataclysmic end. Those left behind wrote sacred futures that promised atonement and threw them into the Great River of Life.

When a promise comes due, it surfaces and a writer of that future is called to the area, where the spirit of the river, Tamara, greets them. Thus begins the journey to transcendence...

Book 2: Time Blade

Time is the mastermind that oversees human evolution. In order to save the inhabitants on the planet, one singular man is entrusted to carry the Time Blade, a weapon capable of cutting, stopping and even reversing Time.

Having graduated high school, Sky Hunter is a rebel eager to see the world and trusting to chance to support himself. As he crosses the River Tamar in Cornwall, chance challenges his resolve when Tamara, spirit of the river, appears to him. She tells him that eons ago, he lived in the dazzling Age of Jeweled Intelligence and wrote a sacred future promising to raise Mt. Rube back to Earth in order to restart the age and restore Transcendent Intelligence. His vow has come due.

In his ancient life, Sky is Time's Earth emissary and bearer of the Time Blade. The astral energy of rubies--evoking creativity, love and happiness--powers this extraordinary civilization that thrives with airships, industries, and every imaginable creature comfort. But, deep in the underworld, evil lurks. Dark Master seeks to instigate the people to defy Time's warning that mankind hasn't yet evolved enough to handle the astral fire of emeralds.

With only a few days to fulfill his oath, Sky has no idea where to start in juggling the passions involved in being engaged to wed a princess along with the dangerous work of fighting Dark Master. He knows only that he and the Time Blade are all that stand between the restoration of the age...and certain annihilation.

~*~

Evaluation 17:
Greenspell: A Fantasy Anthology by Kathy Ann Trueman

In this collection of fantasy short stories all featuring female protagonists, you'll find diverse, imaginative tales, including:

A sorceress unravels a spell and gets a result she could never have expected...

A young girl wins a contest--her prize: to speak with a god...

A vampire in hiding fears she'll be blamed for the reckless depredations of another of her kind...

A minstrel travels with a witch who has a pair of very unusual cart horses...

As a bonus, this anthology includes "The Sow's Ear", originally published in Marion Zimmer Bradley's acclaimed *Sword and Sorceress* series.

~*~

Evaluation 18:
Crimson Dreams by Margaret L. Carter

The summer when Heather was eighteen, her dream beast's nightly visits warded off loneliness and swept her away in flights of ecstasy. Now, returning to the mountains to sell her dead parents' vacation cabin, she finds her "beast" again. But he turns out to be more than a dream. She meets Devin in the flesh, apparently not a day older. His first human lover, centuries in the past, died horribly because of her devotion to him. Does he dare expose another mortal woman to that risk?

~*~

Evaluation 19:
Hearts Desires and Dark Embraces by Margaret L. Carter

When Margaret L. Carter first read Dracula at the age of twelve, her spontaneous reaction was to wonder how the undead Count saw the events in which he was portrayed as the villain. She's always been fascinated with the "monster's" viewpoint and relationships between human and nonhuman beings. Most of the stories in this collection can be described as romances, and all involve love and passion in some form. Here you'll encounter vampires, elves, ghosts, and at least one human-monster hybrid. The vampire stories in the first half of the book are part of an ongoing series in which the creatures we know as vampires belong to a naturally evolved, nonhuman species secretly living among us. Readers can get better acquainted with them in *Crimson Dreams*, *Sealed in Blood*, and *Passion in the Blood*.

~*~

Evaluation 20:
From the Dark Places by Margaret L. Carter

When Father Michel Emeric and Dr. Ray Benson warn young widow Kate Jacobs of occult danger stalking her, she dismisses them as deranged fanatics. The eerie disappearance of her four-year-old daughter, Sara, changes her mind. Ray and Father Mike rescue Kate's child, but the fight has only begun. Dark powers from beyond our world want to destroy Kate and Sara and prevent the birth of a future child foretold to have extraordinary psychic powers and a destiny as a great warrior against evil. Kate must develop her latent wild talents and allow Sara to do the same, in a universe weirder--and more dangerous--than she's ever imagined.

~*~

Evaluation 21:
Passion in the Blood by Margaret L. Carter

Cordelia and her twin sister don't realize the mother who left them soon after their birth bequeathed them a dark bloodline. They're half vampire. Although human in most respects, they possess certain psychic gifts. A friend of their late father's, Karl, also a vampire, has been watching over their family for generations in honor of his love for their distant ancestor. When her sister is kidnapped and Cordelia must beg for help from Karl, she learns the truth about his vampirism and her own heritage. In the process, she and Karl form a blood bond that leads to deeper intimacy than either one could have anticipated.

~*~
Evaluation 22:
Sealed in Blood by Margaret L. Carter

Science fiction conventions attract some strange people, but Sherri Hudson never expected to spend a con weekend helping a sexy man in a cape steal photos of a winged alien. When the photographer is murdered and Nigel Jamison reveals to Sherri that the "alien" is actually his sister, the situation gets intriguingly complicated. Unwillingly swept up in Nigel's quest to rescue his sister, Sherri can't help being fascinated with him. By the time she finds out he's a vampire, the fascination has become mutual--and too strong to resist.

~*~
Evaluation 23:
Sealing the Dark Portal by Margaret L. Carter

Almost nothing Rina remembers about her life is true. Rather than the ordinary librarian she believes herself to be, she's actually a sorceress who fled from another world to ours when creatures from an alien dimension devastated her home and killed her family. Now they've pursued her to our world, summoned by a sorcerer who plans to open a portal and invite monstrous entities from the void between dimensions to overrun this planet. Rina's former bodyguard, a cat shapeshifter who was once her lover and still yearns for her, helps her true memories to awaken. She must come to terms with the truth about her past so that together they can save their new home from the fate of their old one.

~*~
Evaluation 24:
Shadow of the Beast by Margaret L. Carter

After the mysterious deaths of her brother and sister at the fangs of what looks like a feral dog, Jenny Cameron develops nightmares and blackouts. The quest for the truth about herself leads to her long-lost father, who deserted the family before her birth. He seeks redemption for the curse he carries, but has his bloody past condemned him beyond salvation? When Jenny discovers the secret of her dark heritage, she's no longer sure she can trust her dangerous nature enough to be with the man she loves, and she may ultimately be forced to destroy her own father. Fearing she has inherited the violence that rages in him, she struggles to find her true self under the shadow of the beast.

~*~

Evaluation 25:
Windwalker's Mate by Margaret L. Carter

Shannon's little boy Daniel has disturbing psychic powers. He talks to the wind--and it listens. All Shannon wants is a normal life. She wants to forget the cult of the Windwalker, a dark god from another dimension, and the terrifying night when her child was conceived. But her first love, Nathan, son of the cult leader, contacts her for the first time since that horrific ceremony. He claims his father is stalking Shannon and Daniel. Whose child is Daniel, Nathan's or the Windwalker's? Nathan's father plans to use Daniel to open a gate between dimensions and unleash chaos on our world. To save her child and become reconciled with her first love, Shannon may have no choice but embrace the strange powers she previously rejected.

~*~

Evaluation 26:
Different Blood: The Vampire as Alien by Margaret L. Carter

Different blood flows in their veins--but our blood quenches their thirst. From Bram Stoker's 1897 creation of Count Dracula, portrayed as a foreign invader bent on the conquest of England, the literary vampire has symbolized the Other, whether his or her otherness arises from racial, ethnic, sexual, or species difference. Even before the bloodsucking Martians of H. G. Wells' *War of the*

Worlds, however, popular fiction contained a few vampires who were members of alien species rather than supernatural undead.

Even more intriguing than interplanetary invaders are humanoid and quasi-humanoid beings who have evolved to live on Earth among us, often camouflaged as our own kind. The boom in vampire fiction that began in the 1970s engendered a variety of "alien" vampires, many of them portrayed as sympathetic characters. The science fiction vampire is especially suited to the presentation of vampirism as morally neutral rather than inherently evil.

Different Blood surveys the literary vampire as alien, whether extraterrestrial or a different species evolved on Earth, from the mid-1800s to the 1990s, and analyzes the many uses to which science fiction and fantasy authors have put this theme. Their works explore issues of species, race, ecological responsibility, gender, eroticism, xenophobia, parasitism, symbiosis, intimacy, and the bridging of differences. An extensive bibliography lists dozens of novels and short stories on the "vampire as alien" theme, many of which are still in print.

~*~

Evaluation 27:
Dance of Desolation by Jenna Whittaker

Shren has been locked in his own mansion's cellar for seven years before he unexpectedly finds the door unlocked. His house--once filled with parties that his captors and traitorous servants threw--is now silent and empty. Upon closer inspection, Shren notes only one difference to his home from the days before his imprisonment: A painting graces one of the walls of a man with eyes bleeding pitch black. Chilled, Shren knows then that a magicworker has been in his home.

Seeking to escape the wrath of the magicworker, should he return, Shren flees his home. In his flight, he discovers the origin of the magicworkers--more insidious and dangerous than he could have imagined. Shren is inexorably drawn to stop the magicworkers from capturing and corrupting his people...as they

231

did those who lived in the land where they were first created.

~*~
Evaluation 28:
Dreamscape by Jenna Whittaker

Set in a fantasy-world full of sects fighting against one another, a man from an alternate dimension of the gods is sent to Earth to save mankind from a threat they don't yet know but soon will...

Khalos's untapped powers when, once awakened, destroyed his world. A fire kindled by his rage burned down his childhood home, and his innocence died in the ashes. To find safety from those who fear his powers, Khalos begins a long journey to a city he's heard harbors those with powers like his. Along the way, he meets up with a woman who may be working with dark forces from the future...

At my request for a revision, the author provided this:

Khalos's untapped powers destroyed his world. A fire kindled by his rage burned down his childhood home, and his innocence died in the ashes. To find safety from those who fear his powers, Khalos begins a long journey to a city he's heard harbours those with powers like his. Along the way, he meets up with a woman who may be working with dark forces from the future.

Despite those trying to keep him from this knowledge, Khalos discovers he is from an alternate dimension of the gods, and has been sent to earth to save it from a threat it does not yet know...but it soon will. His powers stem from his origins, and Khalos begins to search for control over them, and to use them to save his world and his gods from the most deadly threat it has ever faced: a race of sentient technology from the future, returning to the past to conquer the earth—and then the realms beyond.

My revision:

Khalos's untapped powers destroyed his world. A fire kindled by his rage burned down his childhood home, and his innocence died in the ashes. To find safety from those who fear his powers, Khalos begins a long journey to a city he's heard harbours those with powers like his. Along the way, he meets up with a woman who may be working with dark forces from the future.

Despite those trying to keep him from the knowledge, Khalos discovers he is from an alternate dimension of the gods and has been sent to Earth to save it from a threat humanity does not yet know...but soon will. His powers stem from his origins, and Khalos begins to search for control over them as well as to use them to save his world and his gods from the most deadly threat they have ever faced. A race of sentient technology from the future has returned to the past to conquer the Earth—and then the realms beyond.

~*~
Evaluation 29:
Watership by Jenna Whittaker

To save their dying world, scientists and a race of ostensibly benevolent aliens worked to create a safe haven in the centre of the planet, hollowing it out for future generations to live safely. Creatures were also created to watch over the people and alert them if their hollow world was about to collapse. When the failsafe program activated, the creatures guided the people to a sentient, biological spaceship already programmed with the coordinates to take them to a new world. Little do they realize that the aliens they assumed were helping them in the past have changed the course of the ship...

~*~
Evaluation 30:
The Last Immortal by Jenna Whittaker

Death was an alien concept for them...
The people of the world weren't aware death existed since

it'd never happened as long as anyone could recall. So, when the planet slowed on its axis and the atmosphere disintegrated, the immortals felt death for the first time.

Wasting sickness ravaged their species. The elderly perished while the young that survived were permanently scarred, unable to bear children. But the worst was yet to come. The world shattered and the pieces became shards of land barely held together and separated by never-ending chasms.

Kyrilee is believed to be the last immortal, immune to the wasting disease. She tells the survivors of dreaming thousands of years past, of giving birth to a cat. While most dismiss her as mad, some believe she's the one who holds the key to curing their sickness and can bring the people together once more.

The truth is far stranger: Kyrilee has a mortal body with an immortal soul, constantly reincarnating throughout the ages. When she discovers the feline descendants of the one she birthed in her dream, she realises her reverie was no mere dream. These creatures hold the key to restoring the world...and they intend to enslave the immortal species.

APPENDIX B
All-in-One High-Concept and Series Blurb Crafting, Blurb Revision, and Blurb Sizing Exercises

Exercise 1: The Midnight Line, A Jack Reacher Novel by Lee Child
Example 1 by Karen Wiesner: The Midnight Line, A Jack Reacher Novel by Lee Child

Exercise 2: Among Wolves, Book 1: Children Of The Mountain Series by R.A. Hakok
Example 2 by Karen Wiesner: Among Wolves, Book 1: Children Of The Mountain Series by R.A. Hakok

Exercise 3: The Storm Sister, Book 2: The Seven Sisters Series by Lucinda Riley
Example 3 by Karen Wiesner: The Storm Sister, Book 2: The Seven Sisters Series by Lucinda Riley

Exercise 4: Obsession by Amanda Robson
Example 4 by Karen Wiesner: Obsession by Amanda Robson

Exercise 5: Sleeping Beauties by Stephen King and Owen King
Example 5 by Karen Wiesner: Sleeping Beauties by Stephen King and Owen King

Exercise 6: Neverwhere by Neil Gaiman
Example 6 by Karen Wiesner: Neverwhere by Neil Gaiman

Okay, let's have some blurb whittling fun, as well as crafting series and high concept blurbs, and finally revising back cover blurbs--all in one exercise! On the pages that follow, I've included the back cover blurbs of several popular books (the first three are part of a series, the last three aren't). If the book is part of a series, I've found a potential basis for a series blurb (see my notes about where I got it from in each one), which you'll see first.

The worksheet for this is a little different than the one you'd use for your own blurb crafting and whittling in Appendix A since some of the work was already done for us by the authors/publishers. Other than trying to come up with a high-concept blurb (if there wasn't one already written for it) we're skipping to the Second Revision section. This is all about practice. Keep that in mind. If you're just reading this and not doing the exercises, it can get repetitious, but the intention with this workbook of sorts is to learn how to shave blurbs into the optimal sizes needed. It's not meant for simple reading and, if you were only reading, you would likely find it annoying to have the original blurb included so many times with each exercise. Because you're doing this as an exercise, though, you need that blurb close by for an easy reference during each pass, and that's why it's included for every single step in the whittling.

First, read the original blurbs as they're given. I included them exactly as they are from distributor or publisher websites-- complete with errors, if any. While you read, try to think of a high-concept blurb for the story (or find one--you can usually find it right there, buried in the back cover blurb) if there isn't already one. After that, try to crop each component (series if it is part of one, high-concept, and back cover blurb) *three times*, separately (following the instructions and worksheet template included) in order to achieve the ideal sizes necessary. I'll add a "caveat" about the value of sizing at the end of this page.

Because this is about practice, work in stages as you tighten and whittle and potentially bring more impact each time unless you feel the series and high-concept blurbs have already reached the optimal point. Sometimes it may seem like you're not doing much, but even shaving a handful of sentences off is progress.

The steady removal of excess words and trying to meet the three optimal word counts you may need is an art that you only learn by performing the stages, even incremental ones, so don't give up even if it feels like you're not doing much.

Take a break between passes. Honestly, your eyes will glaze over during this process and probably multiple times. You want to go away from the blurb so you can come back to it later and get a fresh perspective on it.

One other thing to note is that I haven't actually read many of the books contained in these exercises. Conceivably, I made assumptions that might be incorrect and I would only discover that after reading the book. For the purposes of these exercises, it doesn't really matter whether the assumptions I made in revising and whittling are incorrect. The exercises are mere practice, with the point being to eventually write, revise and whittle your own back cover blurbs--and who knows your own story better than you do? So making presumptions won't be a factor for your own blurbs.

At the end of each exercise, you'll find my example versions of all three passes at the blurbs for each exercise, followed by a "final blurb combo (series, high concept and back cover blurb together)" with the whittled word count.

When you're done going over each pass (including my examples), take a wide view of all of them. While our goal here is to practice crafting various types of blurbs as well as whittling them down, you might want to ask yourself: Which of the blurb passes do you feel is the most effectively good? Original, first, second or third pass? Evaluate your own work, then read my example and evaluate that. I've provided my own assessment of which blurb is the most effectively good as well. There's no right or wrong here--just preference, something you need to be aware of in any case when it comes to a reader's eclectics tastes.

Exercise 1:
Jack Reacher Series by Lee Child

Potential Series Blurb (taken from Wikipedia):

A former major in the United States Army Military Police Corps, Jack Reacher roams the United States taking odd jobs and investigating suspicious and frequently dangerous situations. **[26 words]**

The Midnight Line, Book 22

Original Back Cover Blurb:

Reacher takes a stroll through a small Wisconsin town and sees a class ring in a pawn shop window: West Point 2005. A tough year to graduate: Iraq, then Afghanistan. The ring is tiny, for a woman, and it has her initials engraved on the inside. Reacher wonders what unlucky circumstance made her give up something she earned over four hard years. He decides to find out. And find the woman. And return her ring. Why not?

So begins a harrowing journey that takes Reacher through the upper Midwest, from a lowlife bar on the sad side of small town to a dirt-blown crossroads in the middle of nowhere, encountering bikers, cops, crooks, muscle, and a missing persons PI who wears a suit and a tie in the Wyoming wilderness.

The deeper Reacher digs, and the more he learns, the more dangerous the terrain becomes. Turns out the ring was just a small link in a far darker chain. Powerful forces are guarding a vast criminal enterprise. Some lines should never be crossed. But then, neither should Reacher. **[178 words]**

First Revision

Step 1: Revise the series blurb.

A former major in the United States Army Military Police Corps,

Jack Reacher roams the United States taking odd jobs and investigating suspicious and frequently dangerous situations. **[26 words]**

Your First Revision:

[_ words]

Step 2: Read the original back cover blurb below, searching for a potential high-concept blurb since there wasn't one in the original blurb. Once you have one, put it in the section for it below. Fill in the blanks for how many words it is.

Potential High-Concept Blurb:

[_ words]

Step 3: Revise the original back cover blurb below. Try to make it about 150 words. When you're done, fill in the blanks for how many words you end up with. Leave it alone after that and come back later for your second pass.

Original Back Cover Blurb:

Reacher takes a stroll through a small Wisconsin town and sees a class ring in a pawn shop window: West Point 2005. A tough year to graduate: Iraq, then Afghanistan. The ring is tiny, for a woman, and it has her initials engraved on the inside. Reacher wonders what unlucky circumstance made her give up something she earned over four hard years. He decides to find out. And find the woman. And return her ring. Why not?

So begins a harrowing journey that takes Reacher through the upper Midwest, from a lowlife bar on the sad side of small town to a dirt-blown crossroads in the middle of nowhere, encountering bikers, cops, crooks, muscle, and a missing persons PI who wears a suit and a tie in the Wyoming wilderness.

The deeper Reacher digs, and the more he learns, the more

dangerous the terrain becomes. Turns out the ring was just a small link in a far darker chain. Powerful forces are guarding a vast criminal enterprise. Some lines should never be crossed. But then, neither should Reacher. **[178 words]**

Your Revised Back Cover Blurb:

[_ words]

Second Revision

Step 4: Now that you've had some time away from the revised blurb, let's revise and crop each element into something even tighter with more impact. First, take the series blurb you revised in the first pass and whittle it down a little more. Fill in the blank for the word count when you're done.

Your 2nd Pass at the Revised Series Blurb (optional):

[_ words]

Step 5: Now take the high-concept blurb you revised in the first pass and whittle it down a little more. Fill in the blank for the word count when you're done.

Your 2nd Pass at the High-Concept Blurb (no more than one line):

[_ words]

Step 6: Finally, take the back cover blurb you revised in the first pass and whittle it down a little more, trying to get it around 100 words. Fill in the blank for the word count when you're done.

Your 2nd Pass at the Back Cover Blurb:

[_ words]

Third Revision

Step 7: Take some time away after the second pass. By this point, you'll have a very tight series and high-concept blurb so no need to redo those unless you feel they need it. I've included sections for it just in case. Focus on getting the back cover blurb down to 75 words or less here. Fill in the blank for the word count when you're done.

Your 3rd Pass at the Revised Series Blurb (optional):

[_ words]

Your 3rd Pass at the High-Concept Blurb (optional):

[_ words]

Your 3rd Pass at the Back Cover Blurb:

[_ words]

Your evaluation:
Which pass (original, 1st, 2nd of 3rd) do you believe is the most effectively good?
Which one most made you want to read the book?

Example 1 by Karen Wiesner
Jack Reacher Series by Lee Child

Potential Series Blurb:

A former major in the United States Army Military Police Corps, Reacher roams the United States taking odd jobs and investigating suspicious and frequently dangerous situations. **[26 words]**

The Midnight Line, Book 22

Original Back Cover Blurb:

Reacher takes a stroll through a small Wisconsin town and sees a class ring in a pawn shop window: West Point 2005. A tough year to graduate: Iraq, then Afghanistan. The ring is tiny, for a woman, and it has her initials engraved on the inside. Reacher wonders what unlucky circumstance made her give up something she earned over four hard years. He decides to find out. And find the woman. And return her ring. Why not?

So begins a harrowing journey that takes Reacher through the upper Midwest, from a lowlife bar on the sad side of small town to a dirt-blown crossroads in the middle of nowhere, encountering bikers, cops, crooks, muscle, and a missing persons PI who wears a suit and a tie in the Wyoming wilderness.

The deeper Reacher digs, and the more he learns, the more dangerous the terrain becomes. Turns out the ring was just a small link in a far darker chain. Powerful forces are guarding a vast criminal enterprise. Some lines should never be crossed. But then, neither should Reacher. **[178 words]**

Karen's First Revision

Revised Series Blurb:

Jack Reacher, former Army major, rambles the country incognito, taking odd jobs while investigating suspicious and dangerous situations. **[18 words]**

High-Concept Series Blurb (taken from the last two sentences in the original back cover blurb):

Some lines--and some men--should never be crossed. **[9 words]**

While strolling through a small Wisconsin town, Jack Reacher sees a West Point 2005 class ring in a pawn shop window. Given what happened in Iran, then Afghanistan, that year, he muses it was a tough year to graduate. The small size and initials intrigue him--what unlucky circumstance made the owner give up what she earned? He decides to find out.

In order to locate the woman, Reacher travels through the upper Midwest from a lowlife bar to a dirt-blown crossroads in the middle of nowhere, encountering bikers, cops, crooks, muscle, and a missing persons PI who wears a suit and a tie in the wilderness. The deeper Reacher digs, the more dangerous the terrain becomes when the ring proves to be a small link in a very dark chain of powerful forces guarding a wide-spread criminal enterprise. **[139 words]**

Karen's Second Revision

Revised Series Blurb:
Former Army major Jack Reacher rambles the country incognito while investigating suspicious, dangerous situations. **[14 words]**

Revised High-Concept Series Blurb:

Some lines--and men--should never be crossed. **[8 words]**

Jack Reacher sees a West Point 2005 class ring in a pawn shop window of a small town. Given what happened in Iran and Afghanistan that year, he muses it was a tough year to graduate. The small size and initials intrigue him--what unlucky circumstance made someone give this up?

In order to locate the owner, Reacher travels through the

upper Midwest from a lowlife bar to a middle-of-nowhere crossroads. The deeper Reacher digs, the more dangerous the terrain becomes. The ring proves to be a small link in a chain of wide-spread criminal activity. **[96 words]**

Karen's Third Revision

Revised Series Blurb:

Former Army major Jack Reacher rambles the country incognito, finding danger everywhere. **[12 words]**

Revised High-Concept Series Blurb:

Some lines--and men--should never be crossed. **[8 words]**
Jack Reacher sees a West Point 2005 class ring in a pawn shop window. The small size and initials intrigue him--what unlucky circumstance made someone give this up? In order to locate the owner, Reacher travels through the upper Midwest from a lowlife bar to a middle-of-nowhere crossroads. The deeper Reacher digs, the more dangerous the terrain. The ring proves to be a small link in a chain of criminal activity. **[72 words]**

Karen's Final Blurbs

Former Army major Jack Reacher rambles the country incognito, finding danger everywhere.

Some lines--and men--should never be crossed.
Jack Reacher sees a West Point 2005 class ring in a pawn shop window. The small size and initials intrigue him--what unlucky circumstance made someone give this up? In order to locate the owner, Reacher travels through the upper Midwest from a lowlife bar to a middle-of-nowhere crossroads. The deeper Reacher digs, the more dangerous the terrain. The ring proves to be a small link in a chain of criminal activity. **[92 words**

TOTAL]

Karen's evaluation:
Which pass (original, 1st, 2nd of 3rd) do you believe is the most
effectively good?
Which one most made you want to read the book?

The original was sloppy. My first revision at least fixed the
awkwardness of the original. My second revision, I feel, is the
most effectively good of all the versions I did. It definitely made
me want to read the book. My final pass felt like I was revising the
heart and soul out of all elements just to meet a word count.

Your evaluation of my revised versions:
Which pass (original, 1st, 2nd of 3rd) do you believe is the most
effectively good?
Which one most made you want to read the book?

Exercise 2:
Children Of The Mountain Series by R.A. Hakok

Potential Series Blurb (taken from a customer review on Amazon):

Gabriel's first grade class went to the White House on that day for a tour. When atomic bombs begin raining down on the Eastern Seaboard, they are evacuated, along with the President, to a remote bunker deep within a mountain in the Maryland hillsides. This is the story of what happens to that class of first graders ten years after the event. **[62 words]**

Among Wolves, Book 1

Original Back Cover Blurb:

There's only one place left that's safe. It's the last place you should be. Gabriel remembers the Last Day. He and Mags had been on a tour of the White House with the rest of Miss Kimble's first-graders when it happened. They fled with the President to a long-abandoned bunker, even as the first of the bombs began to fall. Ten years have passed, and now Gabriel is almost grown. He still lives deep inside the mountain, waiting for the world to thaw. But outside the storms continue to rage, and supplies are running low. The President says it will be okay, because they are the Chosen Ones. But Gabriel isn't so sure. Gabriel's their scavenger, and he's seen what it's like out there. Then one day Gabriel finds a bloodstained map. The blood's not a problem, nor are the frozen remains of the person it once belonged to. Gabriel's used to seeing dead bodies. There's far worse to be found in any Walmart or Piggly Wiggly you care to wander into. Except this one he recognizes, and it shouldn't be all the way out here. Now all Gabriel can think is how he's going to make it back to the bunker and let the President know what he's found. But Gabriel's troubles are only just beginning. For things are not as they seem inside the mountain, and soon he will face a much larger problem: how to get Mags and the others out. **[244 words]**

First Revision

Step 1: Revise the series blurb.

[_ words]

Your First Revision:

[_ words]

Step 2: Read the original back cover blurb below, searching for a potential high-concept blurb since there wasn't one in the original blurb. Once you have one, put it in the section for it below. Fill in the blanks for how many words it is.

Potential High-Concept Blurb:

[_ words]

Step 3: Revise the original back cover blurb below. Try to make it about 150 words. When you're done, fill in the blanks for how many words you end up with. Leave it alone after that and come back later for your second pass.

Original Back Cover Blurb:

There's only one place left that's safe. It's the last place you should be. Gabriel remembers the Last Day. He and Mags had been on a tour of the White House with the rest of Miss Kimble's first-graders when it happened. They fled with the President to a long-abandoned bunker, even as the first of the bombs began to fall. Ten years have passed, and now Gabriel is almost grown. He still lives deep inside the mountain, waiting for the world to thaw. But outside the storms continue to rage, and supplies are running low. The President says it will be okay, because they are the

Chosen Ones. But Gabriel isn't so sure. Gabriel's their scavenger, and he's seen what it's like out there. Then one day Gabriel finds a bloodstained map. The blood's not a problem, nor are the frozen remains of the person it once belonged to. Gabriel's used to seeing dead bodies. There's far worse to be found in any Walmart or Piggly Wiggly you care to wander into. Except this one he recognizes, and it shouldn't be all the way out here. Now all Gabriel can think is how he's going to make it back to the bunker and let the President know what he's found. But Gabriel's troubles are only just beginning. For things are not as they seem inside the mountain, and soon he will face a much larger problem: how to get Mags and the others out. **[244 words]**

Your Revised Back Cover Blurb:

[_ words]

Second Revision

Step 4: Now that you've had some time away from the revised blurb, let's revise and crop each element into something even tighter with more impact. First, take the series blurb you revised in the first pass and whittle it down a little more. Fill in the blank for the word count when you're done.

Your 2nd Pass at the Revised Series Blurb (optional):

[_ words]

Step 5: Now take the high-concept blurb you revised in the first pass and whittle it down a little more. Fill in the blank for the word count when you're done.

Your 2nd Pass at the High-Concept Blurb (no more than one line):

[_ words]

Step 6: Finally, take the back cover blurb you revised in the first pass and whittle it down a little more, trying to get it around 100 words. Fill in the blank for the word count when you're done.

Your 2nd Pass at the Back Cover Blurb:

[_ words]

Third Revision

Step 7: Take some time away after the second pass. By this point, you'll have a very tight series and high-concept blurb so no need to redo those unless you feel they need it. I've included sections for it just in case. Focus on getting the back cover blurb down to 75 words or less here. Fill in the blank for the word count when you're done.

Your 3rd Pass at the Revised Series Blurb (optional):

[_ words]

Your 3rd Pass at the High-Concept Blurb (optional):

[_ words]

Your 3rd Pass at the Back Cover Blurb:

[_ words]

Your evaluation:
Which pass (original, 1st, 2nd of 3rd) do you believe is the most effectively good?
Which one most made you want to read the book?

Example 2 by Karen Wiesner
Children Of The Mountain Series by R.A. Hakok

Potential Series Blurb:

Gabriel's first grade class went to the White House on that day for a tour. When atomic bombs begin raining down on the Eastern Seaboard, they are evacuated, along with the President, to a remote bunker deep within a mountain in the Maryland hillsides. This is the story of what happens to that class of first graders ten years after the event. **[62 words]**

Among Wolves, Book 1

Original Back Cover Blurb:

There's only one place left that's safe. It's the last place you should be. Gabriel remembers the Last Day. He and Mags had been on a tour of the White House with the rest of Miss Kimble's first-graders when it happened. They fled with the President to a long-abandoned bunker, even as the first of the bombs began to fall. Ten years have passed, and now Gabriel is almost grown. He still lives deep inside the mountain, waiting for the world to thaw. But outside the storms continue to rage, and supplies are running low. The President says it will be okay, because they are the Chosen Ones. But Gabriel isn't so sure. Gabriel's their scavenger, and he's seen what it's like out there. Then one day Gabriel finds a bloodstained map. The blood's not a problem, nor are the frozen remains of the person it once belonged to. Gabriel's used to seeing dead bodies. There's far worse to be found in any Walmart or Piggly Wiggly you care to wander into. Except this one he recognizes, and it shouldn't be all the way out here. Now all Gabriel can think is how he's going to make it back to the bunker and let the President know what he's found. But Gabriel's troubles are only just beginning. For things are not as they seem inside the mountain, and soon he will face a much larger problem: how to get Mags and the others out. **[244 words]**

Karen's First Revision

Original Series Blurb:

Gabriel's first grade class went to the White House on that day for a tour. When atomic bombs begin raining down on the Eastern Seaboard, they are evacuated, along with the President, to a remote bunker deep within a mountain in the Maryland hillsides. This is the story of what happens to that class of first graders ten years after the event. **[69 words]**

First Revision:

A first-grade class is touring the White House when atomic bombs begin raining down on the Eastern Seaboard and they're evacuated with the President to a remote bunker deep within a mountain in the Marilyn hillsides. Ten years after the event, life for all has drastically changed. **[69 words]**

High-Concept Series Blurb (taken from the first two sentences in the original back cover blurb):

There's only one place left that's safe. It's the last place you should be. **[14 words]**

First Revision:

The only place left that's safe is the last place anyone would want to be. **[15 words]**

Back Cover blurb:

Original Back Cover Blurb:

There's only one place left that's safe. It's the last place you should be. Gabriel remembers the Last Day. He and Mags had been on a tour of the White House with the rest of Miss Kimble's first-graders when it happened. They fled with the President to a long-abandoned bunker, even as the first of the bombs began to fall. Ten years have passed, and now Gabriel is almost grown. He still lives deep inside the mountain, waiting for the world to thaw. But outside the storms continue to rage, and supplies are running low. The President says it will be okay, because they are the Chosen Ones. But Gabriel isn't so sure. Gabriel's their scavenger, and he's seen what it's like out there. Then one day Gabriel finds a bloodstained map. The blood's not a problem, nor are the frozen remains of the person it once belonged to. Gabriel's used to seeing dead bodies. There's far worse to be found in any Walmart or Piggly Wiggly you care to wander into. Except this one he recognizes, and it shouldn't be all the way out here. Now all Gabriel can think is how he's going to make it back to the bunker and let the President know what he's found. But Gabriel's troubles are only just beginning. For things are not as they seem inside the mountain, and soon he will face a much larger problem: how to get Mags and the others out. **[244 words]**

Back Cover Blurb:

First Revision (150 word limit):

Gabriel remembers the Last Day. He and his best friend Mags had been on a tour of the White House with the rest of Miss Kimble's first-graders. Even as the first of the bombs began to fall, the class fled with the President to a long-abandoned bunker deep inside the mountain. Ten years later, the storms continue to rage outside, supplies are running low, and the President assures them they're the Chosen Ones--they will survive. As a scavenger, Gabriel isn't as optimistic; he's seen what it's like outside. One day Gabriel finds a bloodstained map on a body--a body that shouldn't be where it is. Desperate as he is to make it back to the bunker, Gabriel's no longer sure who to trust. Inside the mountain, are things as they seem? If not, how can he get Mags and the others out? **[144 words]**

Karen's Second Revision

First Pass Series Blurb:

A first-grade class is touring the White House when atomic bombs begin raining down on the Eastern Seaboard and they're evacuated with the President to a remote bunker deep within a mountain in the Marilyn hillsides. Ten years after the event, life for all has drastically changed. [69 words]

Series Blurb Second Revision:

While a first-grade class is touring the White House, atomic bombs rain down and they're evacuated with the President to a remote bunker deep in the Marilyn hillsides. **[28 words]**

First Pass High-Concept Blurb:

The only place left that's safe is the last place anyone would want to be. **[15 words]**

High-Concept Blurb Second Revision:

The only safe place is the last place you ever want to be. **[13 words]**

First Pass Back Cover Blurb:

Gabriel remembers the Last Day. He and his best friend Mags had been on a tour of the White House with the rest of Miss Kimble's first-graders. Even as the first of the bombs began to fall, the class fled with the President to a long-abandoned bunker deep inside the mountain. Ten years later, the storms continue to rage outside, supplies are running low, and the President assures them they're the Chosen Ones--they will survive. As a scavenger, Gabriel isn't as optimistic; he's seen what it's like outside. One day Gabriel finds a bloodstained map on a body--a body that shouldn't be where it is. Desperate as he is to make it back to the bunker, Gabriel's no longer sure who to trust. Inside the mountain, are things as they seem? If not, how can he get Mags and the others out? **[144 words]**

Back Cover Blurb Second Revision (100 word limit):

Gabriel remembers the Last Day, when he and the other first-graders were touring the White House. When the bombs fell, the class fled with the President to a bunker deep inside the mountain. Ten years later, the President assures them they're the ones chosen to survive. As a scavenger, Gabriel finds a bloodstained map on a body that shouldn't be where it is. Desperate as he is to make it back to the bunker, Gabriel's no longer sure who to trust. Are things as they seem inside the mountain? If not, how can he get the others out? **[98 words]**

Karen's Third Revision

Second Pass Series Blurb:

While a first-grade class is touring the White House, atomic bombs rain down and they're evacuated with the President to a remote bunker deep in the Marilyn hillsides. **[28 words]**

Series Blurb Second Revision:

While a first-grade class tours the White House, atomic bombs rain down and they and the President are evacuated to a remote bunker in the Marilyn hillsides. **[27 words]**

Second Pass High-Concept Blurb:

The only safe place is the last place you ever want to be. **[13 words]**

High-Concept Blurb Second Revision:

The only safe place is the last place you want to be. **[12 words]**

Second Pass Back Cover Blurb:

Gabriel remembers the Last Day, when he and the other first-graders were touring the White House. When the bombs fell, the class fled with the President to a bunker deep inside the mountain. Ten years later, the President assures them they're the ones chosen to survive. As a scavenger, Gabriel finds a bloodstained map on a body that shouldn't be where it is. Desperate as he is to make it back to the bunker, Gabriel's no longer sure who to trust. Are things as they seem inside the mountain? If not, how can he get the others out? **[98 words]**

Back Cover Blurb Second Revision (75 word limit):

Ten years later after the Last Day--when Gabriel and his first-grade class fled with the President to a bunker inside the mountain after bombs fell--the President assures them they're the Chosen Ones. As a scavenger, Gabriel finds a bloodstained map on a body that shouldn't be where it is and he's no longer sure who to trust. If things aren't as they seem inside the mountain, how can he get the others out? **[75 words]**

Karen's Final Blurbs

While a first-grade class tours the White House, atomic bombs rain down and they and the President are evacuated to a remote bunker in the Marilyn hillsides.

The only safe place is the last place you want to be.
Ten years later after the Last Day--when Gabriel and his first-grade class fled with the President to a bunker inside the mountain after bombs fell--the President assures them they're the Chosen Ones. As a scavenger, Gabriel finds a bloodstained map on a body that shouldn't be where it is and he's no longer sure who to trust. If things aren't as they seem inside the

mountain, how can he get the others out? **[114 words TOTAL]**

Karen's evaluation:

Which pass (original, 1st, 2nd of 3rd) do you believe is the most effectively good?
Which one most made you want to read the book?

The original was pretty poorly written from start to finish, with far too many extraneous details instead of crucial ones that were needed near the end (but of course I could only work with what was provided in the original so I couldn't add those necessary items). You may have noticed the words counts for the series and high-concept blurbs actually went up at first as I tried to make the blurbs into something better. (And, in defense, the series blurb was taken from an Amazon customer review, so that was a bit of cheating.) I was able to whittle them down later. I actually preferred the first series blurb I wrote because I felt like, with that one, no more information about the events ten years before actually needed to go into the back cover blurb. But the second revision I did was much tighter (and the one I think is the most effectively good). My second pass at the high-concept blurb was the best, and my first revision of the back cover blurbs was best (so a combination of those two might be ideal). The extraneous details were taken out and what was left was just enough to be intriguing. While the "final combo" of all blurbs was the least word count total, it wasn't the most effectively good in my opinion, since there were too few details to truly lure me into wanting to read the book.

Your evaluation of my revised versions:

Which pass (original, 1st, 2nd of 3rd) do you believe is the most effectively good?
Which one most made you want to read the book?

Exercise 3:
The Seven Sisters Series by Lucinda Riley

Potential Series Blurb (taken in part from the author's Seven Sisters Series website):

A series inspired by the mythology surrounding The Pleiades star cluster (also known as the Seven Sisters). Six sisters gather in their childhood home of Atlantis, a beautiful castle on the shores of Lake Geneva, after the death of their adoptive father, the elusive billionaire they call Pa Salt. Discovering that he has mysteriously already been buried at sea, each sister is handed a tantalizing clue about her true heritage. But who is Pa Salt? Why was he buried at sea so quickly? Why are there only six sisters? And why did he adopt them in the first place? **[99 words]**

The Storm Sister, Book 2

Original Back Cover Blurb:

Ally D'Aplièse is about to compete in one of the world's most perilous yacht races when she hears the news of her adoptive father's sudden, mysterious death. Rushing back to meet her five sisters at their family home, she discovers that her father—an elusive billionaire affectionately known to his daughters as Pa Salt—has left each of them a tantalizing clue to their true heritage.

But the timing couldn't be worse: Ally had only recently fallen into a new and deeply passionate love affair, but with her life now turned upside down, she decides to leave the open seas and follow the trail that her father left her, which leads her to the icy beauty of Norway...

There, Ally begins to discover her roots and how her story is inextricably bound to that of a young unknown singer, Anna Landvik, who lived over a century before and sang in the first performance of Grieg's iconic music set to Ibsen's play Peer Gynt. As Ally learns more about Anna, she also begins to question who her father, Pa Salt, really was—and why is the seventh sister missing? **[188 words]**

First Revision

Step 1: Revise the series blurb.

[_ words]

Your First Revision:

[_ words]

Step 2: Read the original back cover blurb below, searching for a potential high-concept blurb since there wasn't one in the original blurb. Once you have one, put it in the section for it below. Fill in the blanks for how many words it is.

Potential High-Concept Blurb:

[_ words]

Step 3: Revise the original back cover blurb below. Try to make it about 150 words. When you're done, fill in the blanks for how many words you end up with. Leave it alone after that and come back later for your second pass.

Original Back Cover Blurb:

Ally D'Aplièse is about to compete in one of the world's most perilous yacht races when she hears the news of her adoptive father's sudden, mysterious death. Rushing back to meet her five sisters at their family home, she discovers that her father—an elusive billionaire affectionately known to his daughters as Pa Salt—has left each of them a tantalizing clue to their true heritage.

But the timing couldn't be worse: Ally had only recently

fallen into a new and deeply passionate love affair, but with her life now turned upside down, she decides to leave the open seas and follow the trail that her father left her, which leads her to the icy beauty of Norway...

There, Ally begins to discover her roots and how her story is inextricably bound to that of a young unknown singer, Anna Landvik, who lived over a century before and sang in the first performance of Grieg's iconic music set to Ibsen's play Peer Gynt. As Ally learns more about Anna, she also begins to question who her father, Pa Salt, really was—and why is the seventh sister missing? **[188 words]**

Your Revised Back Cover Blurb:

[_ words]

Second Revision

Step 4: Now that you've had some time away from the revised blurb, let's revise and crop each element into something even tighter with more impact. First, take the series blurb you revised in the first pass and whittle it down a little more. Fill in the blank for the word count when you're done.

Your 2nd Pass at the Revised Series Blurb (optional):

[_ words]

Step 5: Now take the high-concept blurb you revised in the first pass and whittle it down a little more. Fill in the blank for the word count when you're done.

Your 2nd Pass at the High-Concept Blurb (no more than one line):

[_ words]

Step 6: Finally, take the back cover blurb you revised in the first pass and whittle it down a little more, trying to get it around 100 words. Fill in the blank for the word count when you're done.

Your 2nd Pass at the Back Cover Blurb:

[_ words]

Third Revision

Step 7: Take some time away after the second pass. By this point, you'll have a very tight series and high-concept blurb so no need to redo those unless you feel they need it. I've included sections for it just in case. Focus on getting the back cover blurb down to 75 words or less here. Fill in the blank for the word count when you're done.

Your 3rd Pass at the Revised Series Blurb (optional):

[_ words]

Your 3rd Pass at the High-Concept Blurb (optional):

[_ words]

Your 3rd Pass at the Back Cover Blurb:

[_ words]

Your evaluation:
Which pass (original, 1st, 2nd of 3rd) do you believe is the most effectively good?
Which one most made you want to read the book?

Example 3 by Karen Wiesner
The Seven Sisters Series by Lucinda Riley

Potential Series Blurb (taken in part from the author's Seven Sisters Series website):

A series inspired by the mythology surrounding The Pleiades star cluster (also known as the Seven Sisters). Six sisters gather in their childhood home of Atlantis, a beautiful castle on the shores of Lake Geneva, after the death of their adoptive father, the elusive billionaire they call Pa Salt. Discovering that he has mysteriously already been buried at sea, each sister is handed a tantalizing clue about her true heritage. But who is Pa Salt? Why was he buried at sea so quickly? Why are there only six sisters? And why did he adopt them in the first place? **[99 words]**

The Storm Sister, Book 2

Original Back Cover Blurb:

Ally D'Aplièse is about to compete in one of the world's most perilous yacht races when she hears the news of her adoptive father's sudden, mysterious death. Rushing back to meet her five sisters at their family home, she discovers that her father—an elusive billionaire affectionately known to his daughters as Pa Salt—has left each of them a tantalizing clue to their true heritage.

But the timing couldn't be worse: Ally had only recently fallen into a new and deeply passionate love affair, but with her life now turned upside down, she decides to leave the open seas and follow the trail that her father left her, which leads her to the icy beauty of Norway...

There, Ally begins to discover her roots and how her story is inextricably bound to that of a young unknown singer, Anna Landvik, who lived over a century before and sang in the first performance of Grieg's iconic music set to Ibsen's play Peer Gynt. As Ally learns more about Anna, she also begins to question who her father, Pa Salt, really was—and why is the seventh sister missing? **[188 words]**

Karen's First Revision

Original Series Blurb:

A series inspired by the mythology surrounding The Pleiades star cluster (also known as the Seven Sisters). Six sisters gather in their childhood home of Atlantis, a beautiful castle on the shores of Lake Geneva, after the death of their adoptive father, the elusive billionaire they call Pa Salt. Discovering that he has mysteriously already been buried at sea, each sister is handed a tantalizing clue about her true heritage. But who is Pa Salt? Why was he buried at sea so quickly? Why are there only six sisters? And why did he adopt them in the first place? **[99 words]**

First Revision:

Inspired by the mythology surrounding The Pleiades star cluster (also known as the Seven Sisters). Six sisters gather in their childhood home of Atlantis, a beautiful castle on the shores of Lake Geneva, after the death of their adoptive father, the elusive billionaire they called Pa Salt. Discovering he's already been buried at sea, each sister is handed a tantalizing clue about her true heritage. Who was Pa Salt? Why was he buried so quickly? Why did he adopt the six of them in the first place? **[87 words]**

High-Concept Series Blurb (taken from the first sentence in second paragraph of the original back cover blurb):

But the timing couldn't be worse. **[6 words]**

First Revision:

The timing couldn't be worse... **[5 words]**

Back Cover blurb:

Original Back Cover Blurb:

Ally D'Aplièse is about to compete in one of the world's most perilous yacht races when she hears the news of her adoptive father's sudden, mysterious death. Rushing back to meet her five sisters at their family home, she discovers that her father—an elusive billionaire affectionately known to his daughters as Pa Salt—has left each of them a tantalizing clue to their true heritage.

But the timing couldn't be worse: Ally had only recently fallen into a new and deeply passionate love affair, but with her life now turned upside down, she decides to leave the open seas and follow the trail that her father left her, which leads her to the icy beauty of Norway...

There, Ally begins to discover her roots and how her story is inextricably bound to that of a young unknown singer, Anna Landvik, who lived over a century before and sang in the first performance of Grieg's iconic music set to Ibsen's play Peer Gynt. As Ally learns more about Anna, she also begins to question who her father, Pa Salt, really was—and why is the seventh sister missing? **[188 words]**

Back Cover Blurb:

First Revision (150 word limit):

Ally D'Aplièse is about to compete in one of the world's most perilous yacht races when she hears the news of her adoptive father's sudden, mysterious death. Rushing back to meet her five sisters at their family home, she discovers her father—affectionately known as Pa Salt—has left each of them a tantalizing clue to their true heritage. Despite that Ally had only recently fallen into a new, deeply passionate love affair, she decides to follow the trail her father left her.

In Norway's icy beauty, Ally discovers her roots and how

she's inextricably bound to a young unknown singer who lived over a century before. As Ally learns more, she also begins to question who Pa Salt really was...and if she has a seventh sister who's missing. **[129 words]**

Karen's Second Revision

First Pass Series Blurb:

Inspired by the mythology surrounding The Pleiades star cluster (also known as the Seven Sisters). Six sisters gather in their childhood home of Atlantis, a beautiful castle on the shores of Lake Geneva, after the death of their adoptive father, the elusive billionaire they called Pa Salt. Discovering he's already been buried at sea, each sister is handed a tantalizing clue about her true heritage. Who was Pa Salt? Why was he buried so quickly? Why did he adopt the six of them in the first place? **[87 words]**

Series Blurb Second Revision:

Inspired by the mythology surrounding The Pleiades star cluster (also known as the Seven Sisters). Six sisters gather in their childhood home of Atlantis on the shores of Lake Geneva after the death of their adoptive father, the elusive billionaire they called Pa Salt. Discovering he's already been buried at sea, each sister is handed a tantalizing clue about her true heritage. **[62 words]**

First Pass High-Concept Blurb:

The timing couldn't be worse... **[5 words]**

High-Concept Blurb Second Revision:

No change made.

First Pass Back Cover Blurb:

Ally D'Aplièse is about to compete in one of the world's most perilous yacht races when she hears the news of her adoptive father's sudden, mysterious death. Rushing back to meet her five sisters at their family home, she discovers her father—affectionately known as Pa Salt—has left each of them a tantalizing clue to their true heritage. Despite that Ally had only recently fallen into a new, deeply passionate love affair, she decides to follow the trail her father left her.

In Norway's icy beauty, Ally discovers her roots and how she's inextricably bound to a young unknown singer who lived over a century before. As Ally learns more, she also begins to question who Pa Salt really was...and if she has a seventh sister who's missing. **[129 words]**

Back Cover Blurb Second Revision (100 word limit):

Ally D'Aplièse is about to compete in a yacht race when she hears the news of her adoptive father's sudden death. Rushing back to meet her five sisters at their family home, she discovers Pa Salt left each of them a clue to their true heritage. Despite a new love affair, she decides to follow the trail.

In Norway, Ally discovers her roots and how she's bound to an unknown singer who lived over a century before. As Ally learns more, she questions who Pa Salt really was...and if she has a seventh sister who's missing. **[96 words]**

Karen's Third Revision

Second Pass Series Blurb:

Inspired by the mythology surrounding The Pleiades star cluster (also known as the Seven Sisters). Six sisters gather in their childhood home of Atlantis on the shores of Lake Geneva after the death of their adoptive father, the elusive billionaire they called Pa Salt. Discovering he's already been buried at sea, each sister is handed a tantalizing clue about her true heritage. **[62 words]**

Series Blurb Second Revision:

Six sisters gather in their childhood home after the death of their adoptive father and each sister is given a tantalizing clue about her true heritage. **[26 words]**

Second Pass High-Concept Blurb:

The timing couldn't be worse... **[5 words]**

High-Concept Blurb Second Revision:

No change made.

Second Pass Back Cover Blurb:

Ally D'Aplièse is about to compete in a yacht race when she hears the news of her adoptive father's sudden death. Rushing back to meet her five sisters at their family home, she discovers Pa Salt left each of them a clue to their true heritage. Despite a new love affair, she decides to follow the trail.

In Norway, Ally discovers her roots and how she's bound to an unknown singer who lived over a century before. As Ally learns more, she questions who Pa Salt really was...and if she has a seventh sister who's missing. **[96 words]**

Back Cover Blurb Second Revision (75 word limit):

When Ally D'Aplièse hears the news of her adoptive father's sudden death, she rushes to meet her five sisters. At their family home, she discovers Pa Salt left a clue to her true heritage. In Norway, Ally discovers her roots and how she's bound to an unknown singer who lived over a century before. As Ally learns more, she questions who Pa Salt really was...and if she has a seventh sister who's missing. **[73 words]**

Karen's Final Blurbs

Six sisters gather in their childhood home after the death of their adoptive father and each sister is given a tantalizing clue about her true heritage.

The timing couldn't be worse...
When Ally D'Aplièse hears the news of her adoptive father's sudden death, she rushes to meet her five sisters. At their family home, she discovers Pa Salt left a clue to her true heritage. In Norway, Ally discovers her roots and how she's bound to an unknown singer who lived over a century before. As Ally learns more, she questions who Pa Salt really was...and if she has a seventh sister who's missing.
[104 words TOTAL]

Karen's evaluation:
Which pass (original, 1st, 2nd of 3rd) do you believe is the most effectively good?
Which one most made you want to read the book?

The original blurb was fairly well-written though a tiny bit repetitious and "padded" so the goal became tightening with impacting words after the first pass. I feel my first pass was the most compelling, though each one after that still retained a lot of intrigue.

Your evaluation of my revised versions:
Which pass (original, 1st, 2nd of 3rd) do you believe is the most effectively good?
Which one most made you want to read the book?

Exercise 4:
Obsession by Amanda Robson

Original Back Cover Blurb:

He's not your husband. He's hers.

One evening, a wife asks her husband a question: who else would you go for, if you could? It is a simple question – a little game – that will destroy her life.

Carly and Rob are a happy couple. They share happy lives with their children and their close friends Craig and Jenny. They're lucky. But beneath the surface, no relationship is simple: can another woman's husband and another man's wife ever just be good friends?

Little by little, Carly's question sends her life spiraling out of control, as she begins to doubt everything she thought was true. Who can she trust? The man she has promised to stick by forever, or the best friend she has known for years? And is Carly being entirely honest with either of them?

Obsession is a dark, twisting thriller about how quickly our lives can fall apart when we act on our desires. **[155 words]**

First Revision

Step 1: Read the original back cover blurb below, searching for a potential high-concept blurb since there wasn't one in the original blurb. Once you have one, put it in the section for it below. Fill in the blanks for how many words it is.

Potential High-Concept Blurb:

[_ words]

Step 2: Revise the original back cover blurb below. Try to make it about 150 words. When you're done, fill in the blanks for how many words you end up with. Leave it alone after that and come back later for your second pass.

Original Back Cover Blurb:

He's not your husband. He's hers.

One evening, a wife asks her husband a question: who else would you go for, if you could? It is a simple question – a little game – that will destroy her life.

Carly and Rob are a happy couple. They share happy lives with their children and their close friends Craig and Jenny. They're lucky. But beneath the surface, no relationship is simple: can another woman's husband and another man's wife ever just be good friends?

Little by little, Carly's question sends her life spiraling out of control, as she begins to doubt everything she thought was true. Who can she trust? The man she has promised to stick by forever, or the best friend she has known for years? And is Carly being entirely honest with either of them?

Obsession is a dark, twisting thriller about how quickly our lives can fall apart when we act on our desires. **[155 words]**

Your Revised Back Cover Blurb:

[_ words]

Second Revision

Step 3: Now that you've had some time away from the revised blurb, let's revise and crop each element into something even tighter with more impact. First, take the high-concept blurb you revised in the first pass and whittle it down a little more. Fill in the blank for the word count when you're done.

Your 2nd Pass at the High-Concept Blurb (no more than one line):

[_ words]

Step 4: Finally, take the back cover blurb you revised in the first pass and whittle it down a little more, trying to get it around 100 words. Fill in the blank for the word count when you're done.

Your 2nd Pass at the Back Cover Blurb:

[_ words]

Third Revision

Step 5: Take some time away after the second pass. By this point, you'll have a very tight high-concept blurb so no need to redo that unless you feel it needs it. I've included a section for it just in case. Focus on getting the back cover blurb down to 75 words or less here. Fill in the blank for the word count when you're done.

Your 3rd Pass at the High-Concept Blurb (optional):

[_ words]

Your 3rd Pass at the Back Cover Blurb:

[_ words]

Your evaluation:
Which pass (original, 1st, 2nd of 3rd) do you believe is the most effectively good?
Which one most made you want to read the book?

Example 4 by Karen Wiesner
Obsession by Amanda Robson

Original Back Cover Blurb:

He's not your husband. He's hers.

One evening, a wife asks her husband a question: who else would you go for, if you could? It is a simple question – a little game – that will destroy her life.

Carly and Rob are a happy couple. They share happy lives with their children and their close friends Craig and Jenny. They're lucky. But beneath the surface, no relationship is simple: can another woman's husband and another man's wife ever just be good friends?

Little by little, Carly's question sends her life spiraling out of control, as she begins to doubt everything she thought was true. Who can she trust? The man she has promised to stick by forever, or the best friend she has known for years? And is Carly being entirely honest with either of them?

Obsession is a dark, twisting thriller about how quickly our lives can fall apart when we act on our desires. **[155 words]**

Karen's First Revision

Step 1: Read the original back cover blurb below, searching for a potential high-concept blurb since there wasn't one in the original blurb. Once you have one, put it in the section for it below. Fill in the blanks for how many words it is.

Potential High-Concept Blurb (this was actually on the front cover of the book but not within the book description itself):

He's not your husband. He's hers. **[6 words]**

Step 2: Revise the original back cover blurb below. Try to make it about 150 words. When you're done, fill in the blanks for how many words you end up with. Leave it alone after that and come back later for your second pass.

Original Back Cover Blurb:

He's not your husband. He's hers.
One evening, a wife asks her husband a question: who else would you go for, if you could? It is a simple question – a little game – that will destroy her life.

Carly and Rob are a happy couple. They share happy lives with their children and their close friends Craig and Jenny. They're lucky. But beneath the surface, no relationship is simple: can another woman's husband and another man's wife ever just be good friends?

Little by little, Carly's question sends her life spiraling out of control, as she begins to doubt everything she thought was true. Who can she trust? The man she has promised to stick by forever, or the best friend she has known for years? And is Carly being entirely honest with either of them?

Obsession is a dark, twisting thriller about how quickly our lives can fall apart when we act on our desires. **[155 words]**

First Pass Back Cover Blurb:

One night, Carly asks her husband a question: If you could have more than one woman, who else would you go for? A simple question--maybe even a game...one that will ultimately destroy her life.

Carly and Rob are a happy couple. They share rich, fulfilling lives with their children and close friends Craig and Jenny. But, beneath the surface, no relationship is simple. Can another woman's husband and another man's wife ever just be good friends?

Little by little, Carly's innocent question sends her life spiraling out of control as she begins to doubt everything she believed to be true. Who can she trust? The man she's promised to stick by forever? Or the best friend she's known for years? Is Carly herself being entirely honest with either of them?

Obsession is dark, twisting, and our lives can fall apart quickly when we act on our desires... **[148 words]**

Karen's Second Revision

First Pass High-Concept Blurb:

He's not your husband. He's hers. **[6 words]**

Second Pass High-Concept Revision:

No change made.

First Pass Back Cover Blurb:

One night, Carly asks her husband a question: If you could have more than one woman, who else would you go for? A simple question--maybe even a game...one that will ultimately destroy her life.

Carly and Rob are a happy couple. They share rich, fulfilling lives with their children and close friends Craig and Jenny. But, beneath the surface, no relationship is simple. Can another woman's husband and another man's wife ever just be good friends?

Little by little, Carly's innocent question sends her life spiraling out of control as she begins to doubt everything she believed to be true. Who can she trust? The man she's promised to stick by forever? Or the best friend she's known for years? Is Carly herself being entirely honest with either of them?

Obsession is dark, twisting, and our lives can fall apart quickly when we act on our desires... **[148 words]**

Second Pass Back Cover Blurb:

Carly and Rob are a happy couple. They share rich, fulfilling lives with their children and close friends. One night, Carly asks him a question: If you could have more than one woman, who else would you go for? A simple question--maybe even a game...one that will ultimately destroy her life.

Little by little, Carly's innocent question sends her life spiraling out of control as she begins to doubt everything she believed to be true. Who can she trust? Obsession is dark, twisting, and our lives can fall apart quickly when we act on our desires... **[97 words]**

Karen's Third Revision

Third Pass High-Concept Blurb:

He's not your husband. He's hers. **[6 words]**

Third Pass High-Concept Revision:

No change made.

Second Pass Back Cover Blurb:

Carly and Rob are a happy couple. They share rich, fulfilling lives with their children and close friends. One night, Carly asks him a question: If you could have more than one woman, who else would you go for? A simple question--maybe even a game...one that will ultimately destroy her life.

Little by little, Carly's innocent question sends her life spiraling out of control as she begins to doubt everything she believed to be true. Who can she trust? Obsession is dark, twisting, and our lives can fall apart quickly when we act on our desires... **[97 words]**

Third Pass Back Cover Blurb:

Carly and Rob are a happy couple. One night, she asks him, If you could have more than one woman, who else would you go for? A simple question...one that will ultimately destroy her life.

Little by little, Carly's question sends her life spiraling out of control as she begins to doubt everything she believed to be true. Obsession is dark, twisting, and our lives can fall apart quickly when we act on our desires... **[75 words]**

Karen's Final Blurbs

He's not your husband. He's hers.

Carly and Rob are a happy couple. One night, she asks him, If you could have more than one woman, who else would you go for? A simple question...one that will ultimately destroy her life.

Little by little, Carly's question sends her life spiraling out of control as she begins to doubt everything she believed to be true. Obsession is dark, twisting, and our lives can fall apart quickly when we act on our desires... **[81 words TOTAL]**

Karen's evaluation:
Which pass (original, 1st, 2nd of 3rd) do you believe is the most effectively good?
Which one most made you want to read the book?

Ironically, the high-concept blurb was included on the front cover of the book, but not in the book description. That is one killer high-concept blurb that needed no revision--anything else would have destroyed the effectively good impact--and it should be used everywhere, not just the front cover for maximum lure. Additional, the original back cover blurb was extremely compelling. However, it wasn't well-written in any sense of the word. It was sloppy and awkward. So a revision of that was necessary to bring out the best of it. I personally liked the first pass version of it because it contained the most information (and, after that high-concept blurb, I definitely wanted to know more).

Your evaluation:
Which pass (original, 1st, 2nd of 3rd) do you believe is the most effectively good?
Which one most made you want to read the book?

Exercise 5:
Sleeping Beauties by Stephen King and Owen King

Original Back Cover Blurb:

In this spectacular father/son collaboration, Stephen King and Owen King tell the highest of high-stakes stories: what might happen if women disappeared from the world of men?

In a future so real and near it might be now, something happens when women go to sleep: they become shrouded in a cocoon-like gauze. If they are awakened, if the gauze wrapping their bodies is disturbed or violated, the women become feral and spectacularly violent. And while they sleep they go to another place, a better place, where harmony prevails and conflict is rare.

One woman, the mysterious "Eve Black," is immune to the blessing or curse of the sleeping disease. Is Eve a medical anomaly to be studied? Or is she a demon who must be slain? Abandoned, left to their increasingly primal urges, the men divide into warring factions, some wanting to kill Eve, some to save her. Others exploit the chaos to wreak their own vengeance on new enemies. All turn to violence in a suddenly all-male world.

Set in a small Appalachian town whose primary employer is a women's prison, Sleeping Beauties is a wildly provocative, gloriously dramatic father-son collaboration that feels particularly urgent and relevant today. **[155 words]**

First Revision

Step 1: Read the original back cover blurb below, searching for a potential high-concept blurb since there wasn't one in the original blurb. Once you have one, put it in the section for it below. Fill in the blanks for how many words it is.

Potential High-Concept Blurb:

[_ words]

Step 2: Revise the original back cover blurb below. Try to make it about 150 words. When you're done, fill in the blanks for how many words you end up with. Leave it alone after that and come back later for your second pass.

Original Back Cover Blurb:

In this spectacular father/son collaboration, Stephen King and Owen King tell the highest of high-stakes stories: what might happen if women disappeared from the world of men?

In a future so real and near it might be now, something happens when women go to sleep: they become shrouded in a cocoon-like gauze. If they are awakened, if the gauze wrapping their bodies is disturbed or violated, the women become feral and spectacularly violent. And while they sleep they go to another place, a better place, where harmony prevails and conflict is rare.

One woman, the mysterious "Eve Black," is immune to the blessing or curse of the sleeping disease. Is Eve a medical anomaly to be studied? Or is she a demon who must be slain? Abandoned, left to their increasingly primal urges, the men divide into warring factions, some wanting to kill Eve, some to save her. Others exploit the chaos to wreak their own vengeance on new enemies. All turn to violence in a suddenly all-male world.

Set in a small Appalachian town whose primary employer is a women's prison, Sleeping Beauties is a wildly provocative, gloriously dramatic father-son collaboration that feels particularly urgent and relevant today. **[155 words]**

Your Revised Back Cover Blurb:

[_ words]

Second Revision

Step 3: Now that you've had some time away from the revised blurb, let's revise and crop each element into something even tighter with more impact. First, take the high-concept blurb you revised in the first pass and whittle it down a little more. Fill in the blank for the word count when you're done.

Your 2nd Pass at the High-Concept Blurb (no more than one line):

[_ words]

Step 4: Finally, take the back cover blurb you revised in the first pass and whittle it down a little more, trying to get it around 100 words. Fill in the blank for the word count when you're done.

Your 2nd Pass at the Back Cover Blurb:

[_ words]

Third Revision

Step 5: Take some time away after the second pass. By this point, you'll have a very tight high-concept blurb so no need to redo that unless you feel it needs it. I've included a section for it just in case. Focus on getting the back cover blurb down to 75 words or less here. Fill in the blank for the word count when you're done.

Your 3rd Pass at the High-Concept Blurb (optional):

[_ words]

Your 3rd Pass at the Back Cover Blurb:

[_ words]

Your evaluation:
Which pass (original, 1st, 2nd of 3rd) do you believe is the most effectively good?
Which one most made you want to read the book?

Example 5 by Karen Wiesner
Sleeping Beauties by Stephen King and Owen King

Original Back Cover Blurb:

In this spectacular father/son collaboration, Stephen King and Owen King tell the highest of high-stakes stories: what might happen if women disappeared from the world of men?

In a future so real and near it might be now, something happens when women go to sleep: they become shrouded in a cocoon-like gauze. If they are awakened, if the gauze wrapping their bodies is disturbed or violated, the women become feral and spectacularly violent. And while they sleep they go to another place, a better place, where harmony prevails and conflict is rare.

One woman, the mysterious "Eve Black," is immune to the blessing or curse of the sleeping disease. Is Eve a medical anomaly to be studied? Or is she a demon who must be slain? Abandoned, left to their increasingly primal urges, the men divide into warring factions, some wanting to kill Eve, some to save her. Others exploit the chaos to wreak their own vengeance on new enemies. All turn to violence in a suddenly all-male world.

Set in a small Appalachian town whose primary employer is a women's prison, Sleeping Beauties is a wildly provocative, gloriously dramatic father-son collaboration that feels particularly urgent and relevant today. **[199 words]**

First Revision

Potential High-Concept Blurb (this was buried in the first sentence of the original back cover blurb):

What might happen if women disappeared from the world of men? **[11 words]**

Original Back Cover Blurb:

In this spectacular father/son collaboration, Stephen King and

Owen King tell the highest of high-stakes stories: what might happen if women disappeared from the world of men?

In a future so real and near it might be now, something happens when women go to sleep: they become shrouded in a cocoon-like gauze. If they are awakened, if the gauze wrapping their bodies is disturbed or violated, the women become feral and spectacularly violent. And while they sleep they go to another place, a better place, where harmony prevails and conflict is rare.

One woman, the mysterious "Eve Black," is immune to the blessing or curse of the sleeping disease. Is Eve a medical anomaly to be studied? Or is she a demon who must be slain? Abandoned, left to their increasingly primal urges, the men divide into warring factions, some wanting to kill Eve, some to save her. Others exploit the chaos to wreak their own vengeance on new enemies. All turn to violence in a suddenly all-male world.

Set in a small Appalachian town whose primary employer is a women's prison, Sleeping Beauties is a wildly provocative, gloriously dramatic father-son collaboration that feels particularly urgent and relevant today. **[199 words]**

First Pass Back Cover Blurb:

In the future, women who go to sleep become shrouded in a cocoon-like gauze. If awakened or disturbed, the women become feral and violent. Asleep, they go to better place where harmony prevails and conflict is rare.

"Eve Black" is mysteriously immune to the blessing or curse of the sleeping disease. Is Eve a medical anomaly to be studied? Or is she a demon that must be slain? Abandoned, left to their increasingly primal urges, the men divide into warring factions, some wanting to kill Eve, some to save her. Others exploit the chaos to wreak their own vengeance on new enemies. All turn to violence in a suddenly all-male world. **[111 words]**

Karen's Second Revision

First Pass High-Concept Blurb:

What might happen if women disappeared from the world of men? **[11 words]**

Second Pass High-Concept Revision:

No change made.

First Pass Back Cover Blurb:

In the future, women who go to sleep become shrouded in a cocoon-like gauze. If awakened or disturbed, the women become feral and violent. Asleep, they go to better place where harmony prevails and conflict is rare.

"Eve Black" is mysteriously immune to the blessing or curse of the sleeping disease. Is Eve a medical anomaly to be studied? Or is she a demon that must be slain? Abandoned, left to their increasingly primal urges, the men divide into warring factions, some wanting to kill Eve, some to save her. Others exploit the chaos to wreak their own vengeance on new enemies. All turn to violence in a suddenly all-male world. **[111 words]**

Second Pass Back Cover Blurb:

In the future, women who go to sleep become shrouded in a cocoon. If awakened or disturbed, they become feral and violent. Asleep, they go to better place where harmony prevails and conflict is rare.

"Eve Black" is mysteriously immune to the sleeping disease. Is she a medical anomaly to be studied or a demon that must be slain? Abandoned, left to their increasingly primal urges, the men divide into warring factions, some wanting to kill Eve, some to save her. In a suddenly all-male world, with nothing to stop them, chaos is exploited and violence is out of control. **[100 words]**

Karen's Third Revision

Third Pass High-Concept Blurb:

What might happen if women disappeared from the world of men? **[11 words]**

Third Pass High-Concept Revision:
No change made.

Second Pass Back Cover Blurb:

In the future, women who go to sleep become shrouded in a cocoon. If awakened or disturbed, they become feral and violent. Asleep, they go to better place where harmony prevails and conflict is rare.

"Eve Black" is mysteriously immune to the sleeping disease. Is she a medical anomaly to be studied or a demon that must be slain? Abandoned, left to their increasingly primal urges, the men divide into warring factions, some wanting to kill Eve, some to save her. In a suddenly all-male world, with nothing to stop them, chaos is exploited and violence is out of control. **[100 words]**

Third Pass Back Cover Blurb:

In the future, sleeping women become shrouded in a cocoon. If awakened, they become feral. In sleep's better place, harmony prevails and conflict is rare. Eve Black is mysteriously immune to the sleeping disease. Is she a medical anomaly or a demon that must be slain?

Abandoned to their primal urges, the men divide into warring factions. In an all-male world, with nothing to stop them, chaos is exploited and violence is out of control. **[75 words]**

Karen's Final Blurbs

What might happen if women disappeared from the world of men?
In the future, sleeping women become shrouded in a cocoon. If awakened, they become feral. In sleep's better place, harmony prevails and conflict is rare. Eve Black is mysteriously immune to the sleeping disease. Is she a medical anomaly or a demon that

must be slain?

Abandoned to their primal urges, the men divide into warring factions. In an all-male world, with nothing to stop them, chaos is exploited and violence is out of control. **[86 words TOTAL]**

Karen's evaluation:

Which pass (original, 1st, 2nd of 3rd) do you believe is the most effectively good?

Which one most made you want to read the book?

The original blurb was buried under a lot of non-impacting word choices. I feel like the first pass revision had the most impact though it could be tighter--as the second, lean, mean version was. I also have to comment that I think this book may be geared more toward men. To me, it was like politics and war--I have absolutely no interest in either. This books sounds like something that only men would "get", so the blurb failed to connect with me from original to final revision.

Your evaluation:

Which pass (original, 1st, 2nd of 3rd) do you believe is the most effectively good?

Which one most made you want to read the book?

Exercise 6:
Neverwhere by Neil Gaiman

Original Back Cover Blurb:

Richard Mayhew is a young London businessman with a good heart whose life is changed forever when he stops to help a bleeding girl—an act of kindness that plunges him into a world he never dreamed existed. Slipping through the cracks of reality, Richard lands in Neverwhere—a London of shadows and darkness, monsters and saints, murderers and angels that exists entirely in a subterranean labyrinth. Neverwhere is home to Door, the mysterious girl Richard helped in the London Above. Here in Neverwhere, Door is a powerful noblewoman who has vowed to find the evil agent of her family's slaughter and thwart the destruction of this strange underworld kingdom. If Richard is ever to return to his former life and home, he must join Lady Door's quest to save her world—and may well die trying. **[151 words]**

First Revision

Step 1: Read the original back cover blurb below, searching for a potential high-concept blurb since there wasn't one in the original blurb. Once you have one, put it in the section for it below. Fill in the blanks for how many words it is.

Potential High-Concept Blurb (this was on what I believe was the first edition front cover of the book but nowhere else):

Under the streets of London lies a world most people could never dream of... **[14 words]**

Step 2: Revise the original back cover blurb below. Try to make it about 150 words. When you're done, fill in the blanks for how many words you end up with. Leave it alone after that and come back later for your second pass.

Original Back Cover Blurb:

Richard Mayhew is a young London businessman with a good heart whose life is changed forever when he stops to help a bleeding girl—an act of kindness that plunges him into a world he never dreamed existed. Slipping through the cracks of reality, Richard lands in Neverwhere—a London of shadows and darkness, monsters and saints, murderers and angels that exists entirely in a subterranean labyrinth. Neverwhere is home to Door, the mysterious girl Richard helped in the London Above. Here in Neverwhere, Door is a powerful noblewoman who has vowed to find the evil agent of her family's slaughter and thwart the destruction of this strange underworld kingdom. If Richard is ever to return to his former life and home, he must join Lady Door's quest to save her world—and may well die trying. **[151 words]**

Your Revised Back Cover Blurb:

[_ words]

Second Revision

Step 3: Now that you've had some time away from the revised blurb, let's revise and crop each element into something even tighter with more impact. First, take the high-concept blurb you revised in the first pass and whittle it down a little more. Fill in the blank for the word count when you're done.

Your 2nd Pass at the High-Concept Blurb (no more than one line):

[_ words]

Step 4: Finally, take the back cover blurb you revised in the first pass and whittle it down a little more, trying to get it around 100 words. Fill in the blank for the word count when you're done.

Your 2nd Pass at the Back Cover Blurb:

[_ words]

Third Revision

Step 5: Take some time away after the second pass. By this point, you'll have a very tight high-concept blurb so no need to redo that unless you feel it needs it. I've included a section for it just in case. Focus on getting the back cover blurb down to 75 words or less here. Fill in the blank for the word count when you're done.

Your 3rd Pass at the High-Concept Blurb (optional):

[_ words]

Your 3rd Pass at the Back Cover Blurb:

[_ words]

Your evaluation:
Which pass (original, 1st, 2nd of 3rd) do you believe is the most effectively good?
Which one most made you want to read the book?

Example 6 by Karen Wiesner
Neverwhere by Neil Gaiman

Original Back Cover Blurb:

Richard Mayhew is a young London businessman with a good heart whose life is changed forever when he stops to help a bleeding girl—an act of kindness that plunges him into a world he never dreamed existed. Slipping through the cracks of reality, Richard lands in Neverwhere—a London of shadows and darkness, monsters and saints, murderers and angels that exists entirely in a subterranean labyrinth. Neverwhere is home to Door, the mysterious girl Richard helped in the London Above. Here in Neverwhere, Door is a powerful noblewoman who has vowed to find the evil agent of her family's slaughter and thwart the destruction of this strange underworld kingdom. If Richard is ever to return to his former life and home, he must join Lady Door's quest to save her world—and may well die trying. **[151 words]**

Karen's First Revision

Potential High-Concept Blurb (this was on what I believe was the first edition front cover of the book but nowhere else):

Under the streets of London lies a world most people could never dream of... **[14 words]**

Original Back Cover Blurb:

Richard Mayhew is a young London businessman with a good heart whose life is changed forever when he stops to help a bleeding girl—an act of kindness that plunges him into a world he never dreamed existed. Slipping through the cracks of reality, Richard lands in Neverwhere—a London of shadows and darkness, monsters and saints, murderers and angels that exists entirely in a subterranean labyrinth. Neverwhere is home to

Door, the mysterious girl Richard helped in the London Above. Here in Neverwhere, Door is a powerful noblewoman who has vowed to find the evil agent of her family's slaughter and thwart the destruction of this strange underworld kingdom. If Richard is ever to return to his former life and home, he must join Lady Door's quest to save her world—and may well die trying. **[151 words]**

First Pass Back Cover Blurb:

An act of kindness plunges Richard Mayhew, a young London businessman with a good heart, into a world he never dreamed existed. When he stops to help a bleeding girl, his life is changed forever. Slipping through the cracks of reality, Richard lands in Neverwhere—a London of shadows and darkness, monsters and saints, murderers and angels that exists entirely in a subterranean· labyrinth. Neverwhere is home to Door, the mysterious girl Richard helped in the London Above. Here in Neverwhere, Door is a powerful noblewoman who has vowed to find the evil agent of her family's slaughter and thwart the destruction of this strange underworld kingdom. If Richard is ever to return to his former life and home, he must join Lady Door's quest. But to save her world, he may well die trying. **[135 words]**

Karen's Second Revision

First Pass High-Concept Blurb:

Under the streets of London lies a world most people could never dream of... **[14 words]**

Second Pass High-Concept Revision:

No change made.

First Pass Back Cover Blurb:

An act of kindness plunges Richard Mayhew, a young London businessman with a good heart, into a world he never dreamed existed. When he stops to help a bleeding girl, his life is changed forever. Slipping through the cracks of reality, Richard lands in Neverwhere—a London of shadows and darkness, monsters and saints, murderers and angels that exists entirely in a subterranean labyrinth. Neverwhere is home to Door, the mysterious girl Richard helped in the London Above. Here in Neverwhere, Door is a powerful noblewoman who has vowed to find the evil agent of her family's slaughter and thwart the destruction of this strange underworld kingdom. If Richard is ever to return to his former life and home, he must join Lady Door's quest. But to save her world, he may well die trying. **[135 words]**

Second Pass Back Cover Blurb:

When Richard Mayhew stops to help a bleeding girl, his life is changed forever. Slipping through the cracks of reality, Richard lands in Neverwhere—a London of shadows and darkness, monsters and saints, murderers and angels that exists entirely in a subterranean labyrinth. Neverwhere is home to Door, the mysterious girl Richard helped, actually a powerful noblewoman bent on finding the evil agent who slaughtered her family and intends to destroy Neverwhere. If Richard is to ever return to his former life, he must join Lady Door's quest to save her world--but he may well die trying. **[98 words]**

Karen's Third Revision

Third Pass High-Concept Blurb:

Under the streets of London lies a world most people could never dream of... **[14 words]**

Third Pass High-Concept Revision:

No change made.

Second Pass Back Cover Blurb:

When Richard Mayhew stops to help a bleeding girl, his life is changed forever. Slipping through the cracks of reality, Richard lands in Neverwhere—a London of shadows and darkness, monsters and saints, murderers and angels that exists entirely in a subterranean labyrinth. Neverwhere is home to Door, the mysterious girl Richard helped, actually a powerful noblewoman bent on finding the evil agent who slaughtered her family and intends to destroy Neverwhere. If Richard is to ever return to his former life, he must join Lady Door's quest to save her world--but he may well die trying. **[98 words]**

Third Pass Back Cover Blurb:

When Richard Mayhew stops to help a bleeding girl, he slips through the cracks into Neverwhere—a London of shadows and darkness, monsters and saints, murderers and angels. Neverwhere is home to Door whom he helped, actually a powerful noblewoman bent on finding the evil agent who slaughtered her family and intends to destroy Neverwhere. To return to his former life, he must join the quest to save her world--but he may die trying. **[75 words]**

Karen's Final Blurbs

Under the streets of London lies a world most people could never dream of...

When Richard Mayhew stops to help a bleeding girl, he slips through the cracks into Neverwhere—a London of shadows and darkness, monsters and saints, murderers and angels. Neverwhere is home to Door whom he helped, actually a powerful noblewoman bent on finding the evil agent who slaughtered her family and intends to destroy Neverwhere. To return to his former life, he must join the quest to save her world-

-or die trying. **[87 words TOTAL]**

Karen's evaluation:

Which pass (original, 1st, 2nd of 3rd) do you believe is the most effectively good?
Which one most made you want to read the book?

The original blurb was excellent. My first revision made is more impacting and lean, but I think both are compelling enough to be effectively good. Further passes only cropped out the unique flavor and some of the intrigue.

Your evaluation:

Which pass (original, 1st, 2nd of 3rd) do you believe is the most effectively good?
Which one most made you want to read the book?

APPENDIX C
Blurb Aids

Worksheet 1: High-Concept, Back Cover, and Series Blurb
Worksheet
Worksheet 2: Blurb Evaluation Checklist
Worksheet 3: Blurb Crafting, Revision, and Whittling Worksheet

High-Concept, Back Cover, and Series Blurb Worksheet

High-Concept Blurb

Fill out as completely as possible for the two components that make up this blurb. Remember, the "who" can be a person, a thing, or simply a concept--your main theme.

Who:
What:

Back Cover Blurb

Basic Story Information: *Fill out as completely as possible, keeping in mind that you may not use all, much or any of this in your final blurb.*

Title of Book:
Genre(s):
Time Period(s):
Main Setting(s):

Basic Character and Plot Information: *Fill out as completely as possible for the major characters in your story (usually no more than two or three main and one villain).*

Main Character Role (specify hero, heroine, villain, etc.):

First and Last Name:

Age and Job:

Description of the character's personality/ hobbies/physical appearance/traumas or hang-ups that factor into his or her story conflicts:

Internal Conflict (i.e., character crisis or what's in jeopardy or at stake):

External Conflict (i.e., plot crisis):

Goals and motivations (i.e., what and why character is compelled to act):

Once you've filled out the form above completely, you can inject your story specifics into this formula (note: fill out one for *each* major character):

Who ________________________ (*name of character*)
wants to __________________ (*goal to be achieved*)
because __________________(*motivation for acting*)
but who faces _________ (*conflict standing in the way*).

Series Blurb

Basic Series Information: *Fill out as completely as possible, keeping in mind that you may not use all, much or any of this in your final blurb.*

Series Title:
Genre(s):
[Who] Series Tie(s):
　　Recurring or Cast of Characters Series
　　Premise/Plot Series
　　Setting Series

Basic Series Arcs:
　　[What] Conflict or crisis that sets the series in motion:

　　[Why] What's the worst case resolution scenario to the crisis situation?

Once you've filled out the form above completely, you can inject your series specifics into this formula:

Who _____________________________ (*Series Tie*)
What __________________________ (*Conflict or Crisis*)
Why ______________ (*Worst Case Resolution Scenario*)

Blurb Order

Use and utilize the separate parts of every blurb, together always, everywhere, every single time!

1. Series Blurb
2. High-Concept Blurb
3. Back Cover Blurb

Blurb Evaluation Checklist

Pros

On the "Pro" Blurb Evaluation Checklist, we only want to see checks in the "Yes" column. Any checks in the "No" column should send you back to the blurb to fix the problem pinpointed.

Pro	Yes	No	Comments
Are the main characters actually named in the back cover blurb?			
Are there short, concise "descriptor punches" included in the blurb for the main characters?			
Is there a simple, descriptive inference of time and place in the blurb?			
Is the blurb written in present tense?			
Is the blurb written in third-person POV?			
Is the genre evident in the blurb (preferably without actually saying what it is)?			
Does the blurb capture the mood/tone/language inside the book?			
Are the stakes made clear with just enough hyperbole to induce excitement?			
Is the reason for the title of the book evident or inferred in the blurb?			
Are strong, compelling, impacting words and short sentences used in the blurb?			
Does the blurb make sense?			
Are hints of three elements of good fiction--character, plot			

(internal and external) and setting--included in a blurb?			
Are the characters goals and motivations clear and concise in the blurb?			
Does the blurb give just enough information/intrigue to make the reader want to continue the journey by reading the book?			
Is a series installment blurb written as if it's the only book in the series? Can it stand alone and make sense of the story inside separate from the other books in the series?			
If the book is part of a series, are all story arcs kept within the individual back cover blurbs while the series arc is clearly defined in the series blurb?			
Is the back cover blurb of a series book written so that book and the series itself are accessible and *welcome* new readers, regardless of where they're starting from?			
Has the blurb been revised multiple times so it's as tight and impacting as possible? Is it available in a variety of sizes, preferably 150, 100, and 75 words?			
If the book is part of a series, does it have a series blurb, a high-concept blurb, and a back cover blurb that are used in every promotion, at every distributor's website?			
If the book is a single-title, does it have a high-concept blurb and			

a back cover blurb that are used in every promotion, at every distributor's website?			
Has the blurb gotten feedback from critique partners, readers or beta-testers?			
Has the blurb raised intriguing questions in reader's mind that can only be answered by reading the book?			
Is the blurb effectively good (i.e., not just well-written but capable of convincing readers to part with hard-earned dollars to read)?			

Cons

On the "Con" Blurb Evaluation Checklist, we only want to see checks in the "No" column. Any checks in the "Yes" column should send you back to the blurb to fix the problem pinpointed.

Con	Yes	No	Comments
Are there more than 3 characters mentioned in the back cover blurb?			
Is the blurb in any way misleading?			
Are there any unimportant, unexplained, overblown details mentioned needlessly in the blurb?			
Are there provocative questions asked in the blurb that you already know the answer to?			
Are there more than two questions in a row in the blurb?			
Do any of the sentences in the blurb read as if the author was			

asked: "What is your story about? Tell me in a single sentence."			
Are there long, hard-to-digest sentences used in the blurb?			
Is dialogue (or dialogue tags) used in the blurb?			
Is the blurb, in whole or part, actually an excerpt from the book?			
Are you struggling to find the conflict in the blurb because maybe it's a mirror of what's lacking in the story?			
Is the blurb overburdened by too much information or complicated concepts? Is there an assumption that everyone knows what something in the blurb means when they might not? Would you have to read the *book* to understand the *blurb*?			
Is the blurb so lean on details, it fails to draw interest?			
Is there anything in the blurb that could be confusing?			
Does the blurb read more like a synopsis than a brief summary?			
Does the blurb include colloquialisms or clichés?			
If the blurb isn't for a nonfiction title, does it contain a bullet list of events in place of actual summary?			
Does the blurb contain any author review-slanted phrases (basically reviews of the work written by the author of it			

himself)?			
Is the back cover blurb of a series book written so that book and the series itself are terrifyingly intimidating and off-putting--not at all welcoming to a new reader?			
Does the back cover blurb give away or deflate a twist, the ending, a surprise inside the pages?			
Does the last sentence of the blurb fizzle instead of sizzle? Is there a hook that has the reader champing at the bit to read the story?			

Blurb Crafting, Revision, and Whittling Worksheet

First Pass

High-Concept Blurb

Fill out as completely as possible for the two components that make up this blurb. Remember, the "who" can be a person, a thing, or simply a concept--your main theme.

Who:
What:

Blurb:

[_ words]

Back Cover Blurb

Basic Story Information: *Fill out as completely as possible, keeping in mind that you may not use all, much or any of this in your final blurb.*

Title of Book:
Genre(s):
Time Period(s):
Main Setting(s):

Basic Character and Plot Information: *Fill out as completely as possible for the major characters in your story (usually no more than two or three main and one villain).*

Main Character Role (specify hero, heroine, villain, etc.):

First and Last Name:

Age and Job:

Description of the character's personality/hobbies/physical

appearance/traumas or hang-ups that factor into his or her story conflicts:

Internal Conflict (i.e., character crisis or what's in jeopardy or at stake):

External Conflict (i.e., plot crisis):

Goals and motivations (i.e., what and why character is compelled to act):

Once you've filled out the form above completely, you can inject your story specifics into this formula (note: fill out one for *each* major character):

Character 1:
Who ______________________ (*name of character*)
wants to ______________________ (*goal to be achieved*)
because ______________________(*motivation for acting*)
but who faces __________ (*conflict standing in the way*).

Character 2:
Who ______________________ (*name of character*)
wants to ______________________ (*goal to be achieved*)
because ______________________(*motivation for acting*)
but who faces __________ (*conflict standing in the way*).

Character 3:
Who ______________________ (*name of character*)
wants to ______________________ (*goal to be achieved*)
because ______________________(*motivation for acting*)
but who faces __________ (*conflict standing in the way*).

Blurb:

[_ words]

Series Blurb

Basic Series Information: *Fill out as completely as possible, keeping in mind that you may not use all, much or any of this in your final blurb.*

Series Title:
Genre(s):
[Who] Series Tie(s): *(circle any or all that apply)*
Recurring or Cast of Characters Series
Premise/Plot Series
Setting Series

Basic Series Arcs:
[What] Conflict or crisis that sets the series in motion:

[Why] What's the worst case resolution scenario to the crisis situation?

Once you've filled out the form above completely, you can inject your series specifics into this formula:

Who _______________________________ *(Series Tie)*
What ________________________ *(Conflict or Crisis)*
Why _______________ *(Worst Case Resolution Scenario)*

Blurb:

[_ words]

First Revision

Series Blurb

Step 1: Drop your first pass at a series blurb here with the word count listed.

[_ words]

Your first Revision *(try to get it down to four lines or less, if you didn't before)*:

[_ words]

High-Concept Blurb

Step 2: Drop your first pass at a high-concept blurb here with the word count listed.

[_ words]

Your first Revision *(try to get it down to two lines, if you didn't before)*:

[_ words]

Back Cover Blurb

Step 3: Drop your first pass at a back cover blurb here with the word count listed.

[_ words]

Your First Revision *(try to get it down to 300 words or less)*:

[_ words]

Second Revision

Series Blurb

Step 4: Drop your revised series blurb here with the word count listed.

[_ words]

Your Second Revision *(try to get it down to three lines or less, if you didn't before)*:

[_ words]

High-Concept Blurb

Step 5: Drop your revised high-concept blurb here with the word count listed.

[_ words]

Your Second Revision *(try to get it down to one line, if you didn't before)*:

[_ words]

Back Cover Blurb

Step 6: Drop your revised back cover blurb here with the word count listed.

[_ words]

Your Second Revision *(try to get it down to 150 words or less)*:

[_ words]

Third Revision

Series Blurb

Step 7: Drop your 2nd revised series blurb here with the word count listed.

[_ words]

Your Third Revision *(try to get it down to two lines, if you didn't before)*:

[_ words]

High-Concept Blurb

Step 8: Drop your 2nd revised high-concept blurb here with the word count listed.

[_ words]

Your Third Revision *(try to get it down to one line, if you didn't before)*:

[_ words]

Back Cover Blurb

Step 9: Drop your 2nd revised back cover blurb here with the word count listed.

[_ words]

Your Third Revision *(try to get it down to 100 words or less)*:

[_ words]

Fourth Revision

Series Blurb

Step 10: Drop your 3rd revised series blurb here with the word count listed.

[_ words]

Your Fourth Revision *(try to get it down to one line, if you didn't before)*:

[_ words]

High-Concept Blurb

Step 11: Drop your 3rd revised high-concept blurb here with the word count listed.

[_ words]

Your Fourth Revision *(try to tighten it a little more, if possible)*:

[_ words]

Back Cover Blurb

Step 12: Drop your 3rd revised back cover blurb here with the word count listed.

[_ words]

Your Fourth Revision *(try to get it down to 75 words or less)*:

[_ words]

WRITING BLURBS THAT SIZZLE--AND SELL!
Bonus Companion Booklet

Frequently I'm asked whether the worksheets, checklists, charts, examples, exercises, and/or other aids from my writing reference titles are available in a usable download format. While the original publisher of the main book did offer free copies of some of these in PDF format on their website, naturally these were only "usable" if they were printed out and written on by hand.

My publisher and I wanted to offer a download of all of these in an editable format (RTF) that allows you to type right into the document and use it over and over as needed.

Writing Blurbs That Sizzle--And Sell! Bonus Companion Booklet contains all the blank worksheets from the main book along with in-depth exercises and examples. Download the free ebook now at https://www.writers-exchange.com/writing-blurbs-that-sizzle-and-sell/. For those who prefer print, a paperback equivalent is available for purchase.

You can find this entire series on Amazon:
http://mybook.to/3dFictionFundamentals

On our website at: http://www.writers-exchange.com/3d-fiction-fundamentals-series/

All Karen's Books at Amazon:
https://www.amazon.com/author/karenwiesner

On our website: http://www.writers-exchange.com/karen-wiesner/

If you enjoyed this author's book, then please place a review up at the site of purchase and any social media sites you frequent!

www.ingramcontent.com/pod-product-compliance
Lightning Source LLC
Chambersburg PA
CBHW070108260726
48658CB00001B/33